100 HATS

TO KNIT & CROCHET

Jean Leinhauser & Rita Weiss

Sterling Publishing Co., Inc.
New York

Library of Congress Cataloging-in-Publication Data

10 9 8 7 6 5 4 3 2 1

Published by Sterling Publishing Co., Inc.
387 Park Avenue South, New York, NY 10016
© 2005 by The Creative Partners, LLC™
Distributed in Canada by Sterling Publishing
c/o Canadian Manda Group, 165 Dufferin Street
Toronto, Ontario, Canada M6K 3H6
Distributed in Australia by Capricorn Link (Australia) Pty. Ltd.
P.O. Box 704, Windsor, NSW 2756, Australia

Sterling ISBN 1-4027-2313-X

For information about custom editions, special sales, premium and
corporate purchases, please contact Sterling Special Sales
Department at 800-805-5489 or specialsales@sterlingpub.com.

INTRODUCTION

Imagine you are strolling down the street and you suddenly notice a new hat shop. Your curiosity draws you inside and you are amazed at what you see.

There are summer garden party hats, newsboy hats, earflap hats, berets and beanies, a tennis visor, even a sombrero! There are hats for kids and teens, for babies, for men , and of course for women. There are hats for every occasion and for just about every person you know.

You are overwhelmed by the variety of hats, the wonderful colors, the beautiful yarns and then you realize – they are all either knitted or crocheted!

The shop owner comes over to you with a big smile and says, "Do you like them? I have patterns for them so you can make them all yourself!"

And that's just what you get here – a hat shop in a book!

We've had a lot of fun putting this book together, and so have the designers, who have come up with so many delightful and wearable creations.

Hats make wonderful gifts. Most of them are easy to make and don't take a lot of time.

You'll enjoy experimenting with the wonderful new yarns available to us today – the imitation furs, the eyelash yarns, the metallics. Don't be afraid to experiment with new colors and textures.

But don't get so busy making hats for family and friends that you forget to make some for yourself! You'll be glad you came into our hat shop – and so are we!

HAT

#1
HIGH ROLLER
6

#2
NEW YORK SKULLY
8

#3
LANDEN'S FAVORITE
BEANIE
10

#4
SHAKER KNIT
12

#5
KID'S FUN BERET
13

#6
LITTLE ROSEBUD
14

#7
WARM WINTER WHITE
15

#8
FLOPPY SUN HAT
16

#9
DASHING DEERSTALKER
18

#10
HEAD WARMER
21

#11
JOCKEY CAP
22

#12
ROMANTIC RUSSIAN
HAT AND MUFF SET
24

#13
FURRY FUN
26

#14
FLOWER CLOCHE
28

#15
RED RAFFIA STUNNER
30

#16
O-LA-LA
32

#17
RED RUFFLES
33

#18
LE BERET
34

#19
PRETTY PIXIE
36

#20
CRAZY PEAKS
38

#21
GARDEN PARTY
42

#22
SALT & PEPPER
45

#23
PILLBOX
46

#24
ELEGANT EARFLAPS
48

#25
ANDEAN ADVENTURER
50

SHOP

#26
SPRING BONNET
53

#27
READY FOR WINTER
54

#28
BLACK AND WHITE
56

#29
LIKE FATHER
58

#30
LIKE SON
58

#31
YAMULKA
62

#32
COZY CLOCHE
64

#33
TAMARA'S FAVORITE BEANIE
66

#34
TENNIS ANYONE
68

#35
GOT ATTITUTDE
70

#36
TWO-TONE CAP
72

#37
ROSES ARE RED
74

#38
HUNTING FOR EASTER EGGS IN THE GRASS
76

#39
IN STYLE
78

#40
STOCKING CAP
80

#41
FRILLY FLOWER
82

#42
BABY BONNET
83

#43
LITTLE BOY'S BASEBALL CAP
84

#44
CLEOPATRA'S CROWN
86

#45
SUGAR DARLING
88

#46
CABLES & CHECKS
90

#47
FOR A PONYTAIL MISS
94

#48
KNITTER'S DELIGHT
96

#49
RAPUNZEL
98

#50
PIPPI
100

#51

BEAUTIFUL IN BLACK
102

#52

FUR TRIMMED BERET
104

#53

ROSY OUTLOOK
106

#54

FUNNY STRIPES
108

#55

FLIRTY FLAPPER
110

#56

PLEASE THINK IT'S MINK
112

#57

STRAWBERRY BONNET
113

#58

BURGUNDY STRIPES
114

#59

PERKY PEAK
116

#60

RAFFIA CLOCHE
118

#61

TEEN'S SKI CAP
120

#62

LITTLE CRUSHER
122

#63

POSH POMPONS
124

#64

PINWHEEL CAP
126

#65

TERRIFIC TAM
129

#66

ON A ROLL
130

#67

FAUX FUR
131

#68

LITTLE GIRL'S FLOWER
CLOCHE
132

#69

PRETTY IN PINK
134

#70

GLITZY BERET
136

#71

CUTIE'S CLOCHE
137

#72

LOTS OF LOOPS
138

#73

FOR THE APPLE
OF YOUR EYE
140

#74

JULIET CAP
142

#75

A HOOD FOR DA HOOD
143

HAT

 #76
BODACIOUS BOBBLES
144

 #77
JUST IN FUN
146

 #78
SMELL THE ROSES
147

 #79
ZIG ZAGS AND CHECKS
148

 #80
HEAD HUGGER
151

 #81
FLOWER CHILD
152

 #82
TRADITIONAL
WATCH CAP
153

 #83
GARTER AND CHECKS
154

 #84
SOMBRERO
156

 #85
BREATH OF FRESH AIR
158

 #86
NEWSBOY CAP
160

 #87
HARD HAT
163

 #88
SHEEPSKIN HAT
164

 #89
TIBETAN HAT
167

 #90
LADY VICTORIA'S
FELTED HAT
170

 #91
CIRCLES AND FUR
172

 #92
CROWNING GLORY
174

 #93
CAROUSEL HAT
178

 #94
RIBBON TRIMMED HAT
181

 #95
VERY RETRO
182

 #96
PANAMA HAT
184

 #97
COZY HAT
186

 #98
SHIRRED BERET
188

 #99
ENTRELAC BRIM HAT
190

 #100
RED GRANADA HAT
194

SHOP

#1

HIGH ROLLER

Designed by Denise Black

SIZE
Fits up to 22" head

MATERIALS
100% Nylon crochet thread size 18, 325 yds white

Note: *Photographed model made with J&P Coats Crochet Nylon, #1 White*

Size F (3.75mm) crochet hook (or size required for gauge)

Stitch marker or small safety pin

GAUGE
Rnds 1 through 4 = 1 3/4" diameter

INSTRUCTIONS

Note: Hat is worked tightly to help keep its shape.

CROWN

Ch 2.

Rnd 1 (right side): 6 sc in 2nd ch from hook: 6 sc; do not join, mark beg of rnds with a st marker or small safety pin.

Rnd 2: (2 sc in next sc) 6 times: 12 sc.

Rnd 3: (2 sc in next sc, sc in next sc) 6 times: 18 sc.

Rnd 4: (2 sc in next sc, sc in next 2 sc) 6 times: 24 sc.

Rnd 5: (2 sc in next sc, sc in next 3 sc) 6 times: 30 sc.

Rnd 6: (2 sc in next sc, sc in next 4 sc) 6 times: 36 sc.

Rnd 7: (2 sc in next sc, sc in next 5 sc) 6 times: 42 sc.

Rnd 8: (2 sc in next sc, sc in next 6 sc) 6 times: 48 sc.

Rnd 9: (2 sc in next sc, sc in next 7 sc) 6 times: 54 sc.

Rnd 10: (2 sc in next sc, sc in next 8 sc) 6 times: 60 sc.

Rnd 11: (2 sc in next sc, sc in next 9 sc) 6 times: 66 sc.

Rnd 12: (2 sc in next sc, sc in next 10 sc) 6 times: 72 sc.

Rnd 13: (2 sc in next sc, sc in next 11 sc) 6 times: 78 sc.

Rnd 14: (2 sc in next sc, sc in next 12 sc) 6 times: 84 sc.

Rnd 15: (2 sc in next sc, sc in next 13 sc) 6 times: 90 sc.

Rnds 16 through 33: Sc in next 90 sc.

BRIM

Rnds are joined from this point on.

Rnd 34: (2 sc in next sc, sc in next 2 sc) 30 times: 120 sc; join in first sc.

Rnds 35 through 37: Ch 1, sc in same sc as joining and in each rem sc; join as before.

Rnd 38: Ch 1, sc in same sc as joining and in next 2 sc, 2 sc in next sc, (sc in next 3 sc, 2 sc in next sc) 29 times: 150 sc; join.

Rnds 39 and 40: Ch 1, sc in same sc as joining and in each rem sc; join.

Rnd 41: Ch 1, sc in same sc as joining and in next 8 sc, 2 sc in next sc, (sc in next 9 sc, 2 sc in next sc) 14 times: 165 sc; join.

Rnds 42 through 51: Ch 1, sc in same sc as joining and in each rem sc; join. At the end of Rnd 51, finish off and weave in ends.

#2 NEW YORK SKULLY

Designed by Nancy Brown

SIZE
Fits up to 23" head

MATERIALS
Rayon ribbon yarn, 200 yds red variegated

Note: Photographed model made with Interlacements New York #105 Reds Plus

Size J (6mm) crochet hook (or size required for gauge)

Size H (5mm) crochet hook

Stitch marker or small safety pin

Fray Check® or fabric glue

GAUGE
3 lps and 4 rnds = 2" (slightly stretched with larger hook)

4 rnds = 2"

INSTRUCTIONS

With larger hook, ch 4, join with a sl st to form a ring.

Rnd 1: (Ch 3, hdc in ring) 4 times: 4 ch-3 lps; do not join or turn, place marker to indicate beg of rnds.

Rnd 2: * Ch 3, (hdc, ch 3, hdc) in next lp: increase made; rep from * around: 8 ch-3 lps.

Rnd 3: Rep Rnd 2: 16 ch-3 lps.

Rnd 4: (Ch 3, hdc in next lp) around, increasing 4 ch-3 lps evenly spaced: 20 ch-3 lps.

Rnd 5: Rep Rnd 4: 24 ch-3 lps.

Rnd 6: Rep Rnd 4 : 28 ch-3 lps.

Rnd 7: (Ch 3, hdc in next lp) around, increasing 5 ch-3 lps evenly spaced: 33 ch-3 lps. Leave marker at end of this rnd.

Work even in pattern as established on 33 ch-3 lps until piece measures approx 3" from marker when slightly stretched.

EDGING

Rnd 1: *(2 sc in next lp, 3 sc in next lp, 3 sc in next lp); rep from * around: 88 sts.

Rnd 2: *(Skip 1 sc, 3 sc in next sc); rep from * around, join with sl st in beg sc. Finish off.

Weave in all ends. Note: Because of the slippery nature of the yarn, use a small amount of Fray Check® or fabric glue on wrong side of cap to secure ends.

ROSE

With smaller hook, ch 4, join with a sl st to form a ring.

Rnd 1: Ch 2, 9 dc in ring, join with sl st in top of beg ch-2.

Rnd 2: Ch 1, sc in same st, sc in each dc around:10 sts.

Rnd 3: Ch 2, skip next st; *(sc in next st, ch 2, skip next st); rep from * around, ending with sl st in beg sc: 5 ch-2 lps.

Rnd 4: *(Sl st, ch 2, 5 dc, ch 2, sl st) in next ch-2 lp; rep from * around: 5 petals made.

Rnd 5: Working behind petals, * sc in next skipped sc on Rnd 2, ch 4; rep from * around, join with sl st in first sc: 5 ch-4 lps.

Rnd 6: *(Sl st, ch 2, 7 dc, ch 2, sl st) in next ch-4 lp; rep from * around: 5 petals.

Rnd 7: Working behind petals, *sc around ch-4 lp of Rnd 5 and next to the center dc on next petal, ch 5; rep from * around: 5 ch-5 lps.

Rnd 8: * (Sl st, ch 2, 9 dc, ch 2, sl st) in next ch-5 lp; rep from * around; finish off, sew rose to cap as shown in photo.

#3

LANDEN'S FAVORITE BEANIE

Designed by Sheila Jones

SIZE

Fits 18¹/₂"
to 21¹/₂" head
(Actual size is determined
in the felting process.)

MATERIALS

Worsted weight 100% wool
yarn,

220 yards variegated blues
and greens

*Note: Use a yarn that felts
easily. Do not use a
Superwash wool.*

*Note: Photographed model
made with Cascade 220
Quatro Wool, #9432.*

20" Size 11 (8mm) circular
knitting needles (or size
required for gauge)

8" Size 11 (8mm) four
double-pointed knitting
needles

1 stitch marker

Dome hat blocker or bowl
with a dome shaped bot-
tom (to use for shaping)

GAUGE

14 sts = 4" in circular
stockinette st (knit each
row on circular needles)
with two strands of yarn
held tog

STITCH GUIDE

Slip, slip, knit (SSK): Sl 2 sts as if to knit, one at a time, to right-hand needle. Insert tip of left-hand needle into fronts of these 2 sts and K them tog: SSK made.

INSTRUCTIONS

Knit with two strands of yarn held tog.

BRIM

Starting at lower edge with a double strand of yarn CO 80 sts. Place marker, join to knit in the round.

Rnd 1: Knit.

Rnd 2: Knit.

Work even in circular stockinette st until hat measures 8" from CO edge.

TOP DECREASES

Change to double-pointed needles when necessary.

Rnd 1: *K6, K2tog; rep from * around: 70 sts.

Rnd 2: Knit.

Rnd 3: *K5, SSK; rep from * around: 60 sts.

Rnd 4: Knit.

Rnd 5: *K4, K2tog; rep from * around: 50 sts.

Rnd 6: Knit.

Rnd 7: *K3, SSK; rep from * around: 40 sts.

Rnd 8: Knit.

Rnd 9: *K2, K2tog; rep from * around: 30 sts.

Rnd 10: *K1, SSK; rep from * around: 20 sts.

Rnd 11: *K2tog; rep from * around: 10 sts.

Rnd 12: *SSK; rep from * around: 5 sts.

Knit even for 2½". Cut yarn leaving a 6" end.

FINISHING

Thread end into a yarn needle and draw through rem sts; tighten and secure end. Weave in all ends.

FELTING

Using the lowest water level setting and hottest water on washing machine, felt to desired size. After the first 10 minutes, check felting process of hat every five minutes for size. You may have to reset your washer to the wash cycle to complete felting process. Do not let it go through spin and rinse cycles. When the felting process is complete, rinse the hat by hand with cold water. Mold to desired shape using hat blocker or bowl, and roll up the edge to form the brim. Let dry.

#4 SHAKER KNIT

Designed by Patons Design Staff

SIZE

Fits up to 21" head

MATERIALS

Worsted weight yarn, 7 oz blue

Note: Photographed model made with Patons® Décor #01622 Rich Country Blue

14" Size 8 (5mm) knitting needles (or size required for gauge)

GAUGE

19 sts = 4" in patt

38 rows = 4" in patt

STITCH GUIDE

K1B: Knit next st one row below, at same time, slipping off unworked st above (see fig below).

INSTRUCTIONS

Starting at bottom of hat, CO 89 sts.

Row 1 (right side): Knit.

Row 2: K1; *K1B, P1; rep from * to last 2 sts, K1B, K1.

Rep Rows 1 and 2 until work measures 10 1/2", ending by working a wrong-side row.

SHAPE TOP

Row 1: K8; *sl 1, K2tog, PSSO, K11; rep from * 4 more times, sl 1, K2tog, PSSO, K8: 77 sts.

Row 2 and all even rows: K1; *K1, P1; rep from * to last 2 sts, K2.

Row 3: K7; *sl 1, K2tog, PSSO, K9; rep from * 4 more times, sl 1, K2tog, PSSO, K7: 65 sts.

Row 5: K6; *sl 1, K2 tog, PSSO, K7; rep from * 4 more times, sl 1, K2tog, PSSO, K6: 53 sts.

Row 7: K5; *sl 1, K2 tog, PSSO, K5; rep from * 4 more times, sl 1, K2tog, PSSO, K5: 41 sts.

Row 9: K4; *sl 1, K2tog, PSSO, K3; rep from * 4 more times, sl 1, K2tog, PSSO, K4: 29 sts.

Row 11: K3; *sl 1, K2 tog, PSSO, K1; rep from * 4 more times, sl 1, K2tog, PSSO, K3: 17 sts.

Cut yarn leaving a long end. Thread into a yarn needle and draw through rem sts, pull up and fasten securely. Sew center back seam, reversing seam in cuff area for turnback.

#5 KID'S FUN BERET

Designed by Jean Leinhauser

SIZE

Fits up to 18" head

MATERIALS

Bulky specialty yarn with eyelash accents, 2 oz pink

Worsted weight yarn, 1 oz blue

Note: Photographed model made with TLC® Macaroon™ #9351 Pink Violet and Red Heart® Classic™ #815 Pale blue

Size K (6.5mm) crochet hook (or size required for bulky yarn gauge)

Size H (5mm) crochet hook (or size required for worsted weight gauge)

GAUGE

4 dc = 2" with bulky yarn and larger hook

4 dc rows = 4" with bulky yarn and larger hook

6 sc = 2" with worsted weight yarn and smaller hook

INSTRUCTIONS

With bulky yarn, ch 4.

Rnd 1: 11 dc in 4th ch from hook: 12 dc, counting beg ch-4 as a dc; join with a sl st in 4th ch of beg ch-4.

Rnd 2: Ch 3, dc in joining; 2 dc in each dc around, join in 3rd ch of beg ch-3: 24 dc, counting beg ch-3 as a dc; join.

Rnd 3: Ch 3, 2 dc in next dc; *dc in next dc, 2 dc in next dc; rep from * around: 36 dc, counting beg ch-3 as a dc; join.

Rnd 4: Ch 3, dc in next dc, 2 dc in next dc; *dc in next 2 dc, 2 dc in next dc; rep from * around: 48 dc; join.

Rnds 5 through 8: Ch 3, dc in each dc around, join.

Rnd 9: Ch 3, 2 dc in next dc; dc in each rem dc around: 49 dc; finish off specialty yarn.

BOTTOM BAND

Rnd 1: With smaller hook, join worsted weight yarn with sc in any dc; sc in each rem dc, join with sl st in beg sc.

Rnd 2: Ch 1, sc in joining; sc in each sc around, join, finish off.

Weave in ends.

#6 LITTLE ROSEBUD

Designed by Rita Weiss

SIZE

Fits 16" head

MATERIALS

Sport weight yarn,
2 oz fuchsia

Note: Photographed model made with Lion Brand Microspun, #146 Fuchsia

14" Size 5 (3.75mm) knitting needles (or size required for gauge)

Eight ³/₄" ribbon roses.

GAUGE

5 sts = 1" in stockinette st (knit one row, purl one row)

INSTRUCTIONS

Starting at bottom of hat, CO 83 sts.

Rows 1 through 9: Knit.

Row 10: Purl.

Row 11(right side): Knit

Row 12: Purl.

Row 13: K6, (P1, K9) 7 times, P1, K6.

Rows 14, 16, 18, 20: Purl.

Rows 15, 17, 19, 21: Knit.

Rows 22 through 29: Knit.

Row 30: Knit to last 2 sts, K2tog: 82 sts

SHAPE TOP

Row 1: K1, (K2tog tbl, K16, K2tog) 4 times, K1: 74 sts.

Rows 2 through 6: Knit.

Row 7: K1, (K2tog tbl, K14, K2tog) 4 times, K1: 66 sts.

Rows 8 through 10: Knit.

Row 11: K1, (K2tog tbl, K12, K2tog) 4 times, K1: 58 sts.

Row 12 and all even rows: Knit.

Row 13: K1, (K2tog tbl, K10, K2tog) 4 times, K1: 50 sts.

Row 15: K1, (K2tog tbl, K8, K2tog) 4 times, K1: 42 sts.

Row 17: K1, (K2tog tbl, K6, K2tog) 4 times, K1: 34 sts.

Row 19: K1, (K2tog tbl, K4, K2tog) 4 times, K1: 26 sts.

Row 21: K1, (K2tog tbl, K2, K2tog) 4 times, K1: 18 sts.

Row 23: K1, (K2tog tbl, K2tog) 4 times, K1: 10 sts.

Cut yarn, leaving a long end. Thread yarn into yarn needle and draw through rem sts and fasten securely. Sew back seam.

FINISHING

Sew the ribbon roses in place over each purl stitch in Row 13.

#7 WARM WINTER WHITE

Designed by Laura Polley

SIZE
Fits 19" to 20" head

MATERIALS
Chunky weight yarn, 5 oz white

Note: Photographed model made with Lion Brand Wool-Ease® Chunky # 301 Tinsel White

14" Size 11 (8mm) knitting needles (or size required for gauge)

GAUGE
13 sts = 4" in pattern

19 rows = 4"

INSTRUCTIONS

Cast on 66 sts.

Row 1 (right side): K1 (selvage st); *P6, K2; rep from * to last st, K1 (selvage st).

Row 2: Knit the knit sts and purl the purl sts.

Row 3: Rep Row 2.

Row 4: Purl.

Row 5: K1, P2; *K2, P6; rep from * to last 7 sts, K2, P4, K1.

Rows 6 and 7: Rep Row 2.

Row 8: Purl.

Rep Rows 1 through 8 once, then rep Rows 1 through 4 once.

SHAPE CROWN

Row 1: K1, P2, P2tog; *(K2, P2tog, P 2, P2tog); rep from * to last 5 sts, P2tog, P2, K1: 50 sts.

Rows 2 and 3: Knit the knit sts and purl the purl sts.

Row 4: Purl.

Row 5: K1; *P4, K2; rep from * to last st, K1.

Rows 6 and 7: Rep Row 2.

Row 8: Purl.

Row 9: K1, P1, K2; * (P2tog) twice, K2; rep from * to last 4 sts, P2tog, P1, K1: 35 sts.

Rows 10 and 11: Rep Row 2.

Row 12: Purl.

Row 13: K1; *P2tog, rep from * to last 2 sts, P1, K1: 19 sts.

Row 14: P1, knit to last st, P1.

Row 15: Rep Row 13: 11 sts.

Row 16: Rep Row 14.

Row 17: Rep Row 13: 7 sts.

Cut yarn, leaving a long end for sewing; thread yarn end into a yarn needle and draw through rem sts twice, pull tightly to secure, weave in end.

Sew back seam, weave in any loose ends.

#8 FLOPPY SUN HAT

Designed by Rona Feldman for Judi & Co

SIZE
Fits 21" to 23" head

MATERIALS
Raffia yarn,
300 yds

Note: Photographed model made with Judi & Co raffia, color Bird of Paradise

Size F (3.75mm) crochet hook or size required for gauge

Stitch marker or small safety pin

Stiffening gel (available at beauty supply stores), disposable foil pan, protective gloves, sponge

GAUGE
9 hdc = 2"

STITCH GUIDE

Reverse sc (rsc): Ch 1; * insert hook in next st to the right (instead of left) of hook and draw up a lp; YO and draw through both lps on hook; rep from *, working to the right instead of the left. This gives a corded edge.

INSTRUCTIONS

Starting at top of crown, ch 4, join with a sl st to form a ring.

Rnd 1: Ch 2 (counts as a hdc), 9 hdc in ring; join with a sl st in 2nd ch of beg ch-2: 10 hdc.

Note: From here through Rnd 14, hat is worked in a spiral; do not join rnds unless specified; mark beg of rnds.

Rnd 2: Ch 2, hdc in joining; 2 hdc in each hdc : 20 hdc.

Rnd 3: 2 hdc in each hdc: 40 hdc.

Rnd 4: * Hdc in next 3 sts, 2 hdc in next st; rep from * around: 50 hdc.

Rnds 5 and 6: Hdc around increasing 10 sts evenly spaced on each Rnd; at end of Rnd 6: 70 hdc.

Rnds 7 through 15: Hdc in each hdc; at end of Rnd 15, join with sl st in beg st of rnd.

BRIM

Rnd 16: Ch 3 (counts as first dc of rnd), dc in BLO around, join.

Rnd 17: Ch 3 (counts as beg dc of rnd), dc in next 2 dc, 2 dc in next dc; *dc in next 3 dc, 2 dc in next dc; rep from * around, ending dc in last 2 dc: 87 sts; join.

Rnd 18: Ch 3, dc in next 3 dc, 2 dc in next dc; *dc in next 4 dc, 2 dc in next dc; rep from * around, dc in last 2 dc, join.

Rnd 19: Ch 3, dc in next 4 dc, 2 dc in next dc; *dc in next 5 dc, 2 dc in next dc; rep from * around, join.

Rnd 20: Ch 3, dc in next 8 sts, 2 dc in next st; *dc in next 9 sts, 2 dc in next st; rep from * around, do not join.

Rnd 21: *Dc in next 14 sts, 2 dc in next st; rep from * around.

Rnd 22: Dc in each dc around, join.

Rnd 23: Working in reverse single crochet, *rsc in next st to right, ch 1, sk next st to right; rep from * around, ending rsc in last st; join, finish off.

Weave in ends.

APPLY STIFFENING GEL

Pour some gel into disposable pan. Dip damp sponge in gel, and cover entire surface of crown with gel. Stuff the crown with plastic trash bags and set on a flat covered surface. Cover the brim evenly with a generous amount of gel. Check periodically during the drying to be sure of the shape. If it is necessary to make changes, lightly spray area with water and re-shape. Let dry completely.

#9

DASHING DEERSTALKER

Designed by Doris Chan

SIZE

Fits 21" to 22" head

MATERIALS

Bulky weight yarn,
5 oz deep blue

Note: Photographed model made with Lion Brand Homespun #368 Montana Sky

Size K (6.5mm) crochet hook (or size required for gauge)

Stitch marker or small safety pin

GAUGE

10 sc = 4"

11 sc rows = 4"

STITCH GUIDE

Front post sc (FPsc): Insert hook from front to back to front around post of specified st, YO and pull up a lp, YO and pull through 2 lps on hook: FPsc made.

Sc decrease (sc dec): (Insert hook in next st, YO and pull up a lp) 2 times, YO and pull through all 3 lps on hook: sc dec made.

INSTRUCTIONS

BODY

Ch 2.

Note: Do not join rnds until specified; place a marker at end of rnds; move marker up as you work.

Rnd 1 (right side): 6 sc in 2nd ch from hook: 6 sc.

Rnd 2: 2 sc in each of next 6 sc: 12 sc.

Rnd 3: (Sc in next sc, 2 sc in next sc) 6 times: 18 sc.

Rnd 4: (Sc in next 2 sc, 2 sc in next sc) 6 times: 24 sc.

Rnd 5: (Sc in next 3 sc, 2 sc in next sc) 6 times: 30 sc.

Rnd 6: (Sc in next 4 sc, 2 sc in next sc) 6 times: 36 sc.

Rnd 7: (Sc in next 5 sc, 2 sc in next sc) 6 times: 42 sc.

Rnd 8: (Sc in next 6 sc, 2 sc in next sc) 6 times: 48 sc.

Rnd 9: (Sc in next 7 sc, 2 sc in next sc) 6 times: 54 sc.

Rnds 10 through 19: Sc in each sc around.

Rnd 20: FPsc in each sc around: 54 FPsc; join with sl st in beg sc; ch 1, turn.

LINING FOR VISOR

Row 1 (wrong side): Sk sl st, sc in front lp of next 6 sc, 2 sc in front lp of next sc, sc in front lp of next 3 sc, 2 sc in front lp of next sc, sc in front lp of next 6 sc: 19 sc; ch 1, turn.

Row 2: Sc dec in next 2 sc, sc in next 15 sc, sc dec in next 2 sc: 17 sc; ch 1, turn.

Row 3: Sc dec in next 2 sc, sc in next 4 sc, 2 sc in next sc, sc in next 3 sc, 2 sc in next sc, sc in next 4 sc, sc dec in next 2 sc: 17 sc; ch 1, turn.

Row 4: Sc dec in next 2 sc, sc in next 13 sc, sc dec in next 2 sc: 15 sc; ch 1, turn.

Row 5: Sc dec in next 2 sc, sc in next 3 sc, 2 sc in next sc, sc in next 3 sc, 2 sc in next sc, sc in next 3 sc, sc dec in next 2 sc: 15 sc; ch 1, turn.

Row 6: Sc dec in next 2 sc, sc in next 11 sc, sc dec in next 2 sc: 13 sc. Finish off and weave in ends.

VISOR

With right side facing, join with sl st in free lp on Rnd 20 where last sc on Row 1 of lining was worked.

Row 1 (right side): Working in free lps of same 17 sc on Rnd 20 where lining was worked, ch 1, sc in same sc as joining, sc in next 5 sc, 2 sc in next sc, sc in next 3 sc, 2 sc in next sc, sc in next 6 sc: 19 sc; ch 1, turn.

Rows 2 through 6: Work same as Rows 2 through 6 of lining.

EARFLAP

(Worked on next 10 sc of Rnd 20)

With wrong side facing, join in both lps of next sc on Rnd 20.

Row 1 (wrong side): Ch 1, sc in same sc as joining, sc in next 9 sc: 10 sc; ch 1, turn.

Rows 2 through 6: Sc in each of next 10 sc; ch 1, turn.

Row 7: Sc dec in next 2 sc, sc in next 6 sc, sc dec in next 2 sc: 8 sc; ch 1, turn.

Row 8: Sc in each of next 8 sc; ch 1, turn.

Row 9: Sc dec in next 2 sc, sc in next 4 sc, sc dec in next 2 sc: 6 sc; ch 1, turn.

Row 10: Sc in each of next 6 sc; ch 1, turn.

Row 11: Sc dec in next 2 sc, sc in next 2 sc, sc dec in next 2 sc: 4 sc; ch 1, turn.

Row 12: Sc in each of next 4 sc; ch 1, turn.

Row 13: (Sc dec in next 2 sc) 2 times: 2 sc; ch 1, turn.

Row 14 (right side): Sc dec in next 2 sc: 1 sc. Finish off and weave in ends.

Make another lining on wrong side and another visor on right side of next 17 sc on Rnd 20.

Make another earflap on wrong side of rem 10 sc on Rnd 20, do not finish off and do not turn.

EDGING

Work one row of sc on right side around entire edge of hat, joining visor to lining and making ties on earflaps at the same time as follows:

Ch 1; Sc in edge of 14 rows of earflap, sl st in sc on Rnd 20 at base of earflap, sl st in next sc on Rnd 20 at base of visor and lining. Holding visor tog with lining, matching sts, sc through both thickness in edge of 6 rows, sc through both thickness in 13 sc on Row 6 of visor and lining, sc through both thicknesses in edge of 6 rows, sl st in sc on Rnd 20 at base of visor and lining, sl st in next sc on Rnd 20 at base of earflap, sc in edge of 14 rows of earflap, sc in sc dec on Row 14 of earflap.

TIE

Ch 30, sl st in 2nd ch from hook, sl st in next 28 chs, sl st in top of sc at base of ch. Rep from * for other half of hat and tie, sl st in beg sc; finish off and weave in ends.

Tie ties with a bow at top of hat to hold earflaps in place or down around ears.

#10 HEAD WARMER

Designed by Jean Leinhauser

SIZE

Fits up to 15" head

MATERIALS

Worsted weight yarn,
2 oz ombre,
1 oz solid color

Note: Photographed model made with TLC® Essentials™ #2953 Brownberry Ombre and #2368 Dark Brown

Size H (5mm) crochet hook (or size required for gauge)

Stitch marker or small safety pin

GAUGE

7 dc = 2"

STITCH GUIDE

Increase (inc): Work 2 sc into the same st.

INSTRUCTIONS

With ombre, ch 2.

Rnd 1: 4 sc in 2nd ch from hook, do not join, mark beg of rows.

Rnd 2: 2 sc in each sc: 8 sc.

Rnd 3: *Sc in first sc, inc in next sc; rep from * around: 12 sc.

Rnd 4: *Sc in first 2 sc, inc in next sc; rep from * around: 16 sc.

Rnd 5: Sc around, inc in every 4th sc: 20 sc.

Rnd 6: Sc around, inc in every 5th sc: 24 sc.

Rnd 7: Sc around, inc in every 6th sc: 28 sc.

Rnd 8: Sc around, inc in every 7th sc: 32 sc.

Rnd 9: Sc around, inc in every 8th sc: 36 sc.

Rnd 10: Sc around, inc in every 9th sc: 40 sc.

Rnd 11: Sc around, inc in every 10th sc: 44sc.

Rnd 12: Sc around, inc in every 11th sc: 48 sc.

Work even in sc until piece measures 4" from Rnd 12. In last st of last row, change to solid-color yarn, finish off ombre.

CUFF

Rnd 1: With solid-color, sc in back lp only of each sc.

Rnds 2 through 7: Working in both lps of each st, sc around.

Finish off, weave in ends. Turn cuff up.

#11

JOCKEY CAP

SIZE
Fits up to 22"

MATERIALS
Worsted weight yarn, 5 oz multi color

Note: Photographed model made with Caron® Jewel Box™, #0029 Amazonite

14" Size 7 (4.5mm) straight needles (or size required for gauge)

Five Size 7 (4.5mm) double-pointed needles

6" x 12" Thin plastic (or cardboard)

GAUGE
4 sts = 1" in stockinette st (knit one row, purl one row)

INSTRUCTIONS

VISOR (make 2)
With straight needles, CO 45 sts.

Row 1 (right side): Knit.

Row 2: Purl.

Row 3: K2tog tbl; knit to last 2 sts, K2tog: 43 sts.

Row 4: Purl.

Rows 5 through 10: Rep Rows 3 and 4. At end of Row 10: 37 sts.

Row 11: K2tog tbl; knit to last 2 sts, K2tog: 35 sts.

Row 12: P2tog; purl to last 2 sts, P2tog tbl: 33 sts.

Rows 13 through 16: Rep Rows 11 and 12 twice. At end of Row 16: 25 sts.

Row 17: Rep Row 11: 23 sts.

Row 18: P2tog; bind off all sts to last 2 sts; P2 tog tbl: 21 sts. Finish off.

Trace one visor piece onto plastic (or cardboard) and cut out. Holding visor pieces with right sides tog, sew, leaving cast-on rows open. Turn right side out. Insert cut plastic (or cardboard). Sew cast-on rows tog.

HEADBAND

With double-pointed needles CO 80 sts. Divide onto 4 needles (20 sts on each needle). Join and work with fifth needle in rnds.

Rnds 1 through 5: Knit.

Rnd 6 (turning row): Purl.

Rnds 7 through 12: Knit. Bind off all sts.

With wrong sides tog, fold headband at turning row. Carefully matching sts, sew tog with overcast st.

BODY

Section One:

Row 1: Hold headband with turning row at top and with straight needles, pick up and knit 1 st in each of the first 10 exposed lps on turning row. Turn. Leave rem sts unworked.

Row 2 (and all even rows): Purl.

Row 3: Inc (Knit in front and back of st); K8, inc: 12 sts.

Row 5: Inc, K10, inc: 14 sts.

Row 7: Knit

Rows 9 through 20: Rep Rows 7 and 8.

Row 21: K2tog tbl, knit to last 2 sts, K2tog: 12 sts.

Row 23 through 30: Rep rows 21 and 22. At end of row 30: 4 sts.

Row 31: K2tog tbl, K2tog: 2 sts.

Row 32: P2tog. Cut yarn, leaving 12" end for sewing.

Thread end into tapestry needle and weave through rem 2 sts, removing needles and drawing yarn tight. Weave in end on wrong side.

Section Two

Row 1: Hold headband with turning row at top and with straight needles, pick up and knit 1 st in each of the next 10 exposed lps on turning row to the left of the first section. Turn. Leave rem sts unworked .

Rows 2 through 32: Rep Rows 2 through 32 of Section One.

Sections Three Through Eight

Work same as Section Two.

FINISHING

With tapestry needle and long ends, sew sections together, carefully matching sts. Sew visor to lower edge of headband.

#12 ROMANTIC RUSSIAN HAT AND MUFF SET

Designed by Patons Design Staff

SIZE

Hat
Fits up to 21" head

Muff
7" wide x 12" long

MATERIALS

Worsted weight yarn,

Hat
1 oz light blue,

Muff
7 oz light blue

Note: Photographed models made with Patons® UpCountry #80953 Ice Blue.

14" Size 10½ (6.5mm) knitting needles (or size required for gauge)

3 stitch markers or small safety pins

GAUGE

13 sts = 4" in stockinette st (knit one row, purl one row)

18 rows = 4"

STITCH GUIDE

Yb: bring yarn to back of work.

Loop Cluster (lpCL): Yb, insert right-hand needle knitwise into next st. Put 2 fingers of your left hand behind your right-hand needle and wind yarn 3 times around the point of the right-hand needle and your fingers in clockwise direction, ending with yarn on needle. Draw the lps through the st, keeping original st on left-hand needle. Remove fingers from the lps and place lps on right-hand needle back onto left-hand needle and knit them tog with the original st. Pull lps firmly through to the right side. (see diagram)

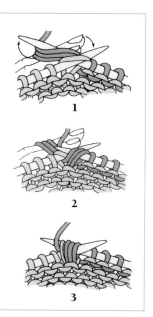

M1: increase one st by picking up horizontal lp lying before next st and knitting into back of lp (see diagram).

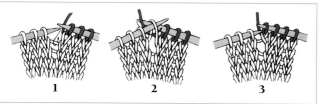

INSTRUCTIONS

MUFF

CO 27 sts.

Row 1 (wrong side): *Pl, lpCL; rep from * to last st, Pl.

Row 2: Knit.

Row 3: Pl; *Pl, lpCL; rep from * to last 2 sts, P2.

Row 4: Knit.

Rep these 4 rows until work measures 14" from CO row, ending by working a wrong-side row. BO.

With right side of work facing, pick up and knit 35 sts along one long side of muff. BO.

Rep on opposite side. Sew CO and BO edges tog.

HAT

CO 7 sts.

Row 1 (right side): Kl, (M1, K1) 6 times: 13 sts.

Row 2 and all even rows: Purl.

Row 3: Kl, (M1, K2) 6 times: 19 sts.

Row 5: Kl, (M1, K3) 6 times: 25 sts.

Row 7: K1, (M1, K4) 6 times: 31sts.

Row 9: K1, (M1, K5) 6 times: 37 sts.

Row 11: K1, (M1, K6) 6 times: 43 sts.

Row 13: K1, (M1, K7) 6 times: 49 sts.

Row 15: K1, (M1, K8) 6 times: 55 sts.

Row 17: K1, (M1, K9) 6 times: 61 sts.

Row 18: K1, (M1, K10) 6 times: 67 sts. Place marker at end of row.

Work even in stockinette st until work measures 3³/₄" from marked row, ending by working a purl row. Place 2nd marker at end of last row.

LOOPY SECTION

Row 1 (right side): *P1, lpCL; rep from * to last st, P1.

Row 2: Knit.

Row 3: Pl; *P1, lpCL; rep from * to last 2 sts, P2.

Row 4: Knit.

Rep Rows 1 through 4 until work measures 4¹/₂" from 2nd marked row, ending by working a wrong-side row and dec 6 sts evenly across last row: 61 sts. Place 3rd marker at end of last row.

Beg with purl row, work in stockinette st for 3³/₄" for lining, ending by working a wrong-side row. BO.

Sew back seam, reversing for turn back. Fold stockinette st lining to right side and sew in position to Loopy section. Turn Loopy section to right side.

#13 FURRY FUN

Designed by Sandy Scoville

SIZE
Fits 20" to 22" head

MATERIALS
Bulky weight yarn, 6 oz variegated tans and browns

Eyelash yarn, 1½ oz variegated tans

Note: Photographed model made with Lion Brand Homespun® #347 Mediterranean, and Fun Fur #205 Sand Stone.

14" Size 9 (5.5mm) knitting needles (or size required for gauge)

GAUGE
16 sts = 4" in stockinette st (knit one row, purl one row)

INSTRUCTIONS

CROWN

Beginning at crown with bulky yarn, cast on 3 sts.

Row 1 (right side): Inc (knit in front and back of st) in each st: 6 sts.

Row 2, and every wrong-side row through Row 18: Purl.

Row 3: Inc in each st as before: 12 sts.

Row 5: Rep Row 3: 24 sts.

Row 9: *K1, inc; rep from * across: 36 sts.

Row 11: K1, *inc, K2; rep from * to last 2 sts; inc, K1: 48 sts.

Row 13: K2, *inc, K3; rep from * to last 2 sts; inc, K1: 60 sts.

Row 15: K2, *inc, K4; rep from * to last 2 sts; inc, K2: 72 sts.

Row 17: K2, *inc, K5; rep from * to last 2 sts; inc, K3: 84 sts.

Row 19 and 20: Knit.

BODY

Join eyelash yarn. Do not cut bulky yarn. Carry unused yarn along side edge.

Rows 21 and 22: With eyelash yarn, knit.

Row 23: Purl.

Row 24: Knit.

Rows 25 through 27: With bulky yarn, knit.

Row 28: Purl.

Row 29: Knit.

Row 30: Purl.

Rows 31 and 32: Knit. At end of Row 32, change to eyelash yarn.

Rows 33 through 44: Rep Rows 21 to 32. At end of Row 44, change to eyelash yarn.

Rows 45 to 48: Rep Rows 21 to 24. At end of Row 48, cut eyelash yarn.

With bulky yarn, BO loosely.

FINISHING

With right sides tog, sew back seam. Weave in ends.

#14 FLOWER CLOCHE

Designed by Nancy Brown

Fits up to 23" head

MATERIALS
Sport weight yarn (for hat), 100 gr (306 yds) pink

Sport weight or ribbon yarn (for floral trim), 45 yds white 30 yds green

Note: Photographed model made with Skacel Polo #06 Pink (for hat) and Silk City Fibers Valencia #001 Ivory (for flowers) and Silk City Fibers #797 Lime (for leaves).

Size H (5mm) crochet hook (or size required for gauge)

Stitch marker or small safety pin

GAUGE (for hat)
8 hdc = 2" with 2 strands of sport weight held together

3 rnds hdc = 1"

INSTRUCTIONS

HAT

With 2 strands of pink sport weight held tog, ch 2.

Rnd 1: 6 hdc in 2nd ch from hook; do not join, mark beg of rnds.

Rnd 2: 2 hdc in each st around: 12 hdc.

Rnd 3: 2 hdc in each st around: 24 hdc.

Rnd 4: *Hdc in next 3 sts, 2 hdc in next st; rep from * around: 30 hdc.

Rnd 5: *Hdc in next 4 sts, 2 hdc in next st; rep from * around: 36 hdc

Rnd 6: *Hdc in next 5 sts, 2 hdc in next st; rep from * around: 42 hdc.

Rnd 7: *Hdc in next 6 sts, 2 hdc in next st; rep from * around: 48 hdc.

Continue to work in hdc and inc 6 sts evenly spaced on each rnd until piece measures about 6½" in diameter ending with a multiple of 4 sts; place marker at end of last rnd.

Work even in hdc until piece measures about 3½" from marker.

Next Rnd: Dc in each st around (cord will be run through this rnd later).

BRIM

Rnd 1: * Hdc in each of next 3 sts, 2 hdc in next st; rep from * around.

Rnds 2 through 7: Hdc in each st around.

Rnd 8: Sl st in each st around; finish off, weave in all ends.

CORD

With two strands, make a ch 36" long, cut yarn and weave in ends.

Thread cord through dc rnd. Adjust to size and secure with a knot.

FLORAL TRIM

Small Flower

With white, ch 2.

Rnd 1 (right side): 5 sc in 2nd ch from hook; do not join.

Rnd 2: (Sl st, ch 1, 5 dc, ch 1, sl st) in each sc around: 5 petals made; finish off, leaving a long end for sewing.

Large Flower

With white, ch 2.

Work Rnds 1 and 2 of Small Flower, finish off.

Rnd 3: Working behind petals of Rnd 2, join white with sc in base of center dc of any petal (work in back of st), ch 3; *sc in base of center dc of next petal, ch 3; rep from * around, join with sl st in beg sc.

Rnd 4: *In next ch-3 sp work (sc, ch 1, 7 dc, ch 1, sc); rep from * around, join in beg sc.

Rnd 5: Ch 3; working behind petals, *sc in first sc of next petal, ch 4; rep from * around, join in beg sc.

Rnd 6: *In next ch-4 sp work (sl st, ch 1, 9 dc, ch 1, sl st; rep from * around, join; finish off, leaving a long end for sewing to hat.

Flower Centers (make 2)

With white, ch 2.

Rnd 1: 3 sc in 2nd ch from hook; do not join.

Rnd 2: Sc in each sc, finish off. Tie ends tog to close. Sew one center in center of each flower.

Leaf (make 3)

With green, ch 6.

Row 1: 6 tr in 5th ch from hook, ch 3, turn.

Row 2: Sk first st, (dc next 2 sts tog) 2 times, dc in next st, leaving last st unworked, ch 1, turn.

Row 3: Sk first st, sc next 2 sts tog, leaving last st unworked; do not turn. For tip of leaf, ch 3, sc in 3rd ch from hook; working down side of leaf, ch 1, sl st in top of st at end of Row 2; ch 2, sl st in top of st at end of Row 1; ch 4, sl st in same ch as 6 tr; work up opposite side in same manner. Finish off, leaving a long yarn end for sewing.

FINISHING

Arrange flowers and leaves on hat as shown in photo, and sew in place.

#15 RED RAFFIA STUNNER

Designed by Rona Feldman for Judi & Co.

SIZE
Fits 20" to 22" head

MATERIALS
Raffia yarn,
200 yds red

Note: Photographed model made with Judi & Co Raffia, China Berry

Size F (3.75mm) crochet hook (or size required for gauge)

Size E (3.5mm) crochet hook

Stitch marker or small safety pin

Stiffening gel (available at beauty supply stores), disposable foil pan, protective gloves, sponge

GAUGE
8 hdc = 2"

INSTRUCTIONS

Starting at top of crown with larger hook, ch 4, join with a sl st to form a ring.

Rnd 1: Ch 2 (counts as a hdc), 9 hdc in ring, join with a sl st in beg ch-2: 10 hdc.

Note: Do not join following rnds unless specified; mark beg of rnds.

Rnds 2 and 3: Ch 2, hdc in base of ch (inc made); 2 hdc in each rem hdc: 40 hdc at end of Rnd 3.

Rnds 4 through 7: Hdc around, working 2 dc in every 4th hdc.

Rnds 8 through 13: Hdc in each st around; at end of Rnd 13, join.

Rnd 14: Ch 3, (counts as first dc) dc in each hdc around, join with sl st in 3rd ch of beg ch-3.

BRIM

Rnd 15: Ch 2, 2 hdc in next st; * hdc in next st, 2 hdc in next st; rep from * around.

Rnds 16 through 18: Ch 2, hdc in each st around, join.

Rnd 19: Ch 2, hdc in next 2 sts, 2 hdc in next st; *hdc in next 3 sts, 2 hdc in next st; rep from * around, join.

Rnd 20: Working in BLO, hdc in each st, join.

Rnd 21: Sl st in each st around, join, finish off. Weave in ends.

CHAIN TIE

With larger hook, make a chain 27" long.

Row 1: Sl st in 2nd ch from hook and in each rem ch; finish off, weave in ends.

Weave tie through Rnd 14, adjust for size, tie and secure

FLOWER TRIM

With smaller hook, ch 4, join with a sl st to form a ring.

Rnd 1: Ch 3 (counts as a dc), 9 dc in ring: 10 dc; join in 3rd ch of beg ch-3.

Rnd 2: Ch 1, sc in joining; sc in each dc around, join in beg sc: 10 sc.

Rnd 3: *Ch 2, sk next sc, sc in next sc; rep from * around, sc in joining sl st of Rnd 2: 5 ch-2 lps.

Rnd 4: In each ch-2 lp work (sl st, ch 2, 4 dc, ch 2, sl st): 5 petals made.

Rnd 5: Working behind petals, ch 1; *sc in BLO of next skipped sc on Rnd 3, ch 4; rep from * around, join in beg sc: 5 ch-4 lps.

Rnd 6: In each ch-4 lp work (sl st, ch 2, 7 dc, ch 2, sl st): 5 petals made.

Finish off, leaving a long yarn end for sewing. Sew flower to hat as shown in photo.

STIFFENING

Cover a flat surface with plastic or aluminum foil. Stuff crown of hat with plastic bags to shape. Place with brim on the flat surface. Wearing protective gloves, use damp sponge to apply gel lightly to crown. Saturate brim with gel, turn up last two rows, use clips or clothes pins to hold in place. To correct shaping, lightly spray with water and re-shape.

Allow to dry complete, at least over night.

#16 O-LA-LA

Designed by Rita Weiss

SIZE
Fits up to 23" head

MATERIALS
Worsted weight mohair blend,
1 1/2 oz blue variegated

Note: Photographed model made with Lion Brand® Imagine #328 Moody Blues

29" Size 7 (4.5mm) circular knitting needle (or size required for gauge)

Size 7 (4.5mm) double-pointed needles

Stitch marker

GAUGE
9 sts = 2" in knitted rnds

INSTRUCTIONS

CO 90 sts on circular needle, join; place marker to indicate beg of rnd.

Rnds 1 through 4: Knit.

Rnd 5: *K9, inc in next st by knitting into front and back of st; rep from * to end of rnd: 99 sts.

Rnds 6 through 12: Knit.

Rnd 13: *K10, inc in next st by knitting into front and back of st; rep from * to end of rnd: 108 sts.

Work even until piece measures 7" from cast-on row.

CROWN

Rnd 1: *K5, K2tog; rep from *to last 3 sts, K3: 93 sts.

Rnds 2 through 4: Knit.

Rnd 5: K4, K2tog rep from* to last 3 sts, K3: 78 sts.

Rnds 6 through 8: Knit.

Note: Change to double-pointed needles

Rnd 9: *K2 tog; rep from * around: 39 sts.

Rnds 10 and 11: Knit.

Cut yarn; thread into a needle and draw through rem sts; finish off securely on wrong side.

#17 RED RUFFLES

Designed by Jean Leinhauser

SIZE
Fits 17" to 18" head

MATERIALS
Worsted weight yarn,
2 oz bright red
2 oz bright blue

Note: Photographed model made with Red Heart® Classic® #902 Jockey Red and #848 Skipper Blue

Size H (5mm) crochet hook (or size required for gauge)

GAUGE
7 dc = 2"

INSTRUCTIONS

With blue, ch 4, join to form a ring.

Rnd 1: Ch 3 (counts as first dc of rnd), 11 dc in ring: 12 dc; join in 3rd ch of beg ch-3.

Rnd 2: Ch 3, dc in joining; 2 dc in each dc around: 24 dc; join.

Rnd 3: Ch 3, 2 dc in next dc; *dc in next dc, 2 dc in next dc; rep from * around: 36 dc; join.

Rnd 4: Ch 3, dc in next dc, 2 dc in next dc; *dc in next 2 dc, 2 dc in next dc; rep from * around: 48 dc; join.

Rnd 5: Ch 3, dc in next 2 dc, 2 dc in next dc; * dc in next 3 dc, 2 dc in next dc; rep from * around: 60 dc; join.

Rnd 6: Ch 3; working in BLO, dc in each dc around, join.

Rnd 7: Ch 3; working in both lps, dc in each dc around, join.

Rnds 8 and 9: Rep Rnd 6.

Rnds 10 and 11: Rep Rnd 7.

Rnds 12 and 13: Rep Rnd 6; at end of Rnd 13, finish off blue.

Rnd 14: Join red with sl st in any dc; ch 1, sc in same st; sc in each dc around, join.

Rnd 15: Ch 1, sc in same st, sc in each sc around, join. Finish off red.

RUFFLES

Hold hat with right side facing and with last row at top.

First Ruffle: Join red with sl st in any unused lp of Rnd 8; ch 3, 2 dc in same lp; 3 dc in each unused lp around; join, finish off.

Second Ruffle: Join red in any unused lp of Rnd 12; ch 3, 2 dc in same lp; 3 dc in each unused lp around; join, finish off.

Weave in all ends.

#18 LE BERET

Designed by Marty Miller

SIZE
Fits up to 21" head

MATERIALS
Worsted weight yarn,
3 1/2 oz white

Note: Photographed model made with Bernat® Denimstyle #3006 Canvas

Size I (5.5mm) crochet hook (or size required for gauge)

GAUGE
3 FPdc = 1"

First 3 rounds = 3 1/2 inches

STITCH GUIDE

Front Post Double Crochet (FPdc): YO, insert hook from front to back to front around post (vertical bar) of specified st, YO, pull lp through; (YO and pull through 2 lps) twice: FPdc made.

Front Post Double Crochet Decrease (FPdc dec): YO, insert hook around the post of the next st in the previous rnd, YO, pull lp through, YO, pull through 2 lps; YO, insert hook around the post of the next st in the previous rnd, YO, pull lp through, YO, pull through 2 lps, YO, pull through all three lps on hook: FPdc dec made.

INSTRUCTIONS

Ch 4, join with a sl st to form a ring.

Rnd 1: Ch 3 (counts as first dc of rnd), 11 dc in ring: 12 dc; join in 3rd ch of beg ch-3.

Rnd 2: Ch 2 (counts as first hdc of rnd), FPdc in same st; *hdc in next st, FPdc in same st; rep from * around: 12 FPdc, 12 hdc; join in 2nd ch of beg ch-2.

Rnd 3: Ch 2, FPdc in same st, FPdc in next st; *hdc in next st, FPdc in same st, FPdc in next st; rep from * around: 24 FPdc, 12 hdc; join as before.

Rnd 4: Ch 2, FPdc in same st, FPdc in next 2 sts; *hdc in next st, FPdc in same st, FPdc in next 2 sts; rep from * around: 36 FPdc, 12 hdc; join.

Rnd 5: Ch 2, FPdc in same st, FPdc in next 3 sts; *hdc in next st, FPdc in same st, FPdc in next 3 sts; rep from * around: 48 FPdc, 12 hdc; join.

Rnds 6 through 8: Continue in same manner, increasing 12 FPdc in each rnd; at end of Rnd 8: 84 FPdc, 12 hdc.

Rnd 9: Ch 2, FPdc in next 7 FPdc; *hdc in next hdc, FPdc in next 7 FPdc; rep from * around: 12 hdc, 84 FPdc; join.

Rnd 10: Rep Rnd 9.

Rnd 11: Ch 2, FPdc dec in next 2 sts, FPdc in next 5 FPdc; *hdc in next hdc, FPdc dec in next 2 sts, FPdc in next 5 FPdc; rep from * around: 72 FPdc, 12 hdc; join.

Rnd 12: Ch 2, FPdc dec in next 2 sts, FPdc in next 4 FPdc; *hdc in next hdc, FPdc dec in next 2 sts. FPdc in next 4 FPdc; rep from * around: 60 FPdc, 12 hdc; join.

Rnds 13 through 15: Continue in same manner, decreasing 12 FPdc in each rnd; at end of Rnd 15: 24 FPdc, 12 hdc; join.

Rnd 16: Ch 2, FPdc in next 2 FPdc;*hdc in next hdc, FPdc in next 2 FPdc; rep from * around: 24 FPdc, 12 hdc; join.

Rnds 17 and 18: Rep Rnd 16.

Rnd 19: Ch 1, sc loosely in each st around; finish off, weave in ends.

#18 PRETTY PIXIE

Designed by Nancy Brown

SIZE

Fits up to 20" head

MATERIALS

Sport weight yarn, 200 yds blue

Novelty yarn, 200 yds blue

Note: Photographed model made with Yeoman Sport #16 Slate and Erdal Luna, Boysenberry

Size J (6mm) crochet hook (or size required for gauge)

GAUGE

1 shell = 1 1/4 " with one strand of each yarn held tog in shell st

2 rows = 2"

Shell: (2 dc, ch 3, 2 dc) in same sp: shell made.

INSTRUCTIONS

With one strand of each yarn held tog, beg at top, ch 5, join with a sl st to form a ring.

Rnd 1: Ch 4 (counts as a dc and ch-1 sp); (dc in ring, ch 1) 8 times, join with sl st in 3rd ch of beg ch-4: 9 ch-1 sps.

Rnd 2: Sl st in next ch-1 sp, ch 6 (counts as a dc and ch-3 sp), dc in same sp; (dc, ch 3, dc in next sp) 8 times, join with sl st in 3rd ch of beg ch-6: 9 ch-3 sps.

Rnd 3: Sl st in next ch-3 sp, ch 3 (counts as a dc), dc in same sp, ch 3, 2 dc in same sp; (shell in next ch-3 sp) 8 times, join in 3rd ch of beg ch-3: 9 shells.

Rnd 4: Sl st in next dc and in ch-3 sp, ch 3, dc in same sp, ch 3, 2 dc in same sp; (2 dc, ch 3, 2 dc in next ch-3 sp) 2 times; *tr in sp between shells, ch 3, dc through bottom lps of tr, (2 dc, ch 3, 2 dc in next ch-3 sp) 3 times; rep from * once more, tr in last sp between shells, ch 3, dc in bottom lps of tr, join: 12 ch-3 sps.

Rnd 5: Sl st in next dc and in ch-3 sp, ch 3, dc in same sp, ch 3, 2 dc in same sp; *work (tr, ch 3, dc) as before in next sp between shells; (2 dc, ch 3, 2 dc in next ch-3 sp) 4 times, rep from * once; (tr, ch 3, dc) as before in next sp between shells; (2 dc, ch 3, 2 dc in next ch-3 sp) 3 times, join: 15 ch-3 sps.

Rnd 6: Sl st in next dc and in ch-3 sp, ch 3, dc in same sp, ch 3, 2 dc in same sp; (2 dc, ch 3, 2 dc in next ch-3 sp) 14 times, join: 15 shells.

Rnds 7 through 11: Rep Rnd 6.

Rnd 12: Sl st in next dc and in ch-3 sp, ch 3, 6 dc in same sp; (7 dc in next ch-3 sp) 14 times, join. Finish off, weave in ends.

TOP CURL

Ch 8.

Row 1: 4 hdc in 2nd ch from hook; 4 dc in each rem ch, finish off, leaving a long yarn end for sewing.

Form into a loose curl, join ends and sew to top of hat.

#20 CRAZY PEAKS

*Designed by JC Briar
(for the advanced knitter)*

SIZES

Child: Fits 18" head

Small Adult: Fits 20" head

Large Adult: Fits 22" head

Note: Instructions are written for Child; changes for Small Adult and Large Adult are in parentheses

MATERIALS

Fingering weight yarn, 1 1/2 (1 1/2, 2) oz variegated

1 1/2 (1 1/2, 2) oz coordinating solid

Note: Photographed model made with Patons® Kroy Socks, #54701 Kool Stripes and #54744 Pink Power

20" Size 3 (3.25mm) circular knitting needle (or size required for gauge)

Size 3 (3.25mm) double-pointed needles

Stitch markers

GAUGE

30 sts = 4" in stockinette stitch (knit one row, purl one row)

NOTES

Each entrelac peak is composed of two units: a solid-colored bottom unit and a variegated top unit. Each solid-colored unit is worked as in conventional entrelac, with stitches picked up from a unit in the previous tier and joined with a neighboring unit. Each variegated unit, in contrast, consists of stitches picked up from a unit in the previous tier and joined with the same unit.

STITCH GUIDE

Lifted Increase (lifted inc): insert tip of right-hand needle knitwise into stitch below stitch on left-hand needle, wrap yarn around right-hand needle, and pull yarn forward to create new stitch on right hand needle.

Slip, slip, knit (SSK): Sl 2 sts as if to knit, one at a time, to right-hand needle. Insert tip of left-hand needle into fronts of these 2 sts and K them tog: SSK made, decreasing 1 st.

INSTRUCTIONS

BODY

With solid yarn and circular needles, cast on 130 (140, 150) sts.

RIBBING

Join into a round. Work K1, P1 rib for 1".

BASE TRIANGLES

Work a single base triangle as follows:

Row 1 (right side): K2. Turn.

Row 2: P2. Turn.

Row 3: K3, picking up next st on needle. Turn.

Row 4: P3. Turn.

Row 5: K4. Turn.

Row 6: P4. Turn.

Row 7: K5. Turn.

Row 8: P5. Turn.

Row 9: K6. Turn.

Row 10: P6. Turn.

Row 11: K7. Turn.

Row 12: P7. Turn.

Row 13: K8. Turn.

Row 14: P8. Turn.

Row 15: K9. Turn.

Row 16: P9. Turn.

Row 17: K10. Turn.

Row 18: P10. Turn.

Row 19: K10. Do not turn.

NEXT BASE TRIANGLE

*Leaving these 10 sts on needle without working them further, knit next 2 sts. Turn. Rep Rows 2 through 19.

Rep from * to work 13 (14, 15) base triangles from right to left around hat. Cut yarn.

RIDGE 1 TOP UNITS

With variegated yarn, work a single left-leaning top unit as follows:

Pick-up row: With right side facing, pick up and knit 10 sts along selvedge of first unit in previous tier. Turn.

Row 1: P10. Turn.

Row 2: K9, SSK (second sl st is next st on base triangle). Turn.

Work Rows 1 and 2 a total of 10 times: unit completed.

Rep with each unit of previous tier to work 13 (14, 15) left-leaning top units from right to left around hat. Cut yarn.

RIDGE 2 BOTTOM UNITS

With wrong side facing, attach solid yarn to last st on right needle tip (at top corner of previous Ridge 1 Top Unit). Work a single right-leaning bottom unit as follows:

Pick-up row: With wrong side facing, pick up and purl 10 sts along selvage of this unit in the previous tier. Turn.

Row 1: K10. Turn.

Row 2: P9, P2tog (second st of P2tog is next variegated st of next unit in previous tier). Turn.

Work Rows 1 and 2 a total of 10 times: unit completed.

Work 13 (14, 15) right-leaning bottom units from left to right around hat. Cut yarn.

RIDGE 2 TOP UNITS

With variegated yarn, work a single right-leaning top unit as follows:

Pick-up row: With wrong side facing, pick up and purl 10 sts along selvedge of unit in previous tier. Turn.

Row 1: K10. Turn.

Row 2: P9, P2tog. Turn.

Work Rows 1 and 2 a total of 10 times: unit completed.

Work 13 (14, 15) right-leaning top units from left to right around hat. Cut yarn.

RIDGE 3 BOTTOM UNITS

With solid yarn, work a single left-leaning bottom unit as follows:

Pick-up row: With right side facing, pick up and knit 10 sts along selvedge of unit in previous tier. Turn.

Row 1: P10. Turn.

Row 2: K9, SSK. Turn.

Work Rows 1 and 2 a total of 10 times: unit completed.

Work 13 (14, 15) left-leaning bottom units from right to left around hat. Break yarn.

RIDGE 3 TOP UNITS

Work as for Ridge 1 top units.

TOP TRIANGLES

With solid yarn, work a single top triangle as follows:

Pick-up row: With wrong side facing, pick up and purl 10 sts along selvedge of unit in previous tier. Turn.

Row 1: K10. Turn.

Row 2: P9, P2tog. Turn.

Row 3: K9. Turn.

Row 4: P8, P2tog. Turn.

Row 5: K8. Turn.

Row 6: P7, P2tog. Turn.

Row 7: K7. Turn.

Row 8: P6, P2tog. Turn.

Row 9: K6. Turn.

Row 10: P5, P2tog. Turn.

Row 11: K5. Turn.

Row 12: P4, P2tog. Turn.

Row 13: K4. Turn.

Row 14: P3, P2tog. Turn.

Row 15: K3. Turn.

Row 16: P2, P2tog. Turn.

Row 17: K2. Turn.

Row 18: P1, P2tog. Turn.

Row 19: K1. Turn.

Row 20: P2tog. Do not turn.

Work 13 (14, 15) top triangles from left to right around hat. Do not cut yarn. At end of Row 20: 130 (140, 150) sts.

CROWN

Place marker to denote start of rounds.

EDGE TRIM

Rnd 1: K5, *lifted inc, K10, rep from * to last 5 sts, end lifted inc, K5: 143 (154, 165) sts.

Rnds 2-6: Purl.

Cut solid yarn. Join variegated yarn.

Rnd 7: *With tip of left-hand needle, reach inside hat and pick up top of lifted-inc stitch created in Rnd 1. Knit picked-up st tog with next st. Rep from * around.

TOP

For Size Child only:

Rnd 8: (K18, K2 tog, K19, K2 tog) three times, K18, K2 tog: 136 sts.

For Size Small Adult only:

Rnd 8: (K75, K2 tog) two times: 152 sts.

For Size Large Adult only:

Rnd 8: (K31, K2 tog) five times: 160 sts.

For All Sizes:

Rnd 9: *K17 (19, 20), place marker, rep from * around.

Rnd 10: *Knit to 2 sts before marker, K2 tog, rep from * around: 128 (144, 152) sts.

Rnd 11: Knit.

Rep Rnds 10 and 11 until 8 sts rem, switching from circular to double-pointed needles as necessary.

I-CORD TASSEL

Knitting all sts onto a spare double-pointed needle, (K2 tog) four times: 4 sts. *Do not turn. Slide sts to right end of needle and bring yarn around back of work. With a spare double-pointed needle, K4. Rep from * until I-cord measures 2" or as desired.

Cut yarn, leaving a 6" tail. With tapestry needle, draw tail through rem 4 sts and into center of I-cord.

FINISHING

Weave in all ends. Block if desired.

#21 GARDEN PARTY

Designed by Ruthie Marks

SIZE
Fits up to 23" head

MATERIALS
Size 3 crochet cotton thread,
300 yds white

13 yds each of lime, teal, plum, rose, yellow and tangerine

Note: Photographed model made with Aunt Lydia's Fashion Crochet Thread, size 3, #201 White; #264 Lime, #65 Warm Teal, #871 Plum, #775 Warm Rose, #423 Maize, and #325 Tangerine

46" of 14-gauge white insulated solid copper electrical wire (available at most hardware stores) or jewelry or milliner's wire

Size E (3.5mm) crochet hook (or size required for gauge) (for hat)

Size D (3.25mm) crochet hook (for flowers)

GAUGE
5 sts = 1" with larger hook

3 rows sc and
2 rows dc = 1 1/2"

STITCH GUIDE

Double Crochet 2 stitches together (dc2tog): (YO, insert hook into next st, YO and pull through, YO and pull through 2 lps) twice; YO and pull through 3 lps: dc2tog made.

Double Crochet 3 stitches together (dc3tog): (YO, insert hook into next st, YO and pull through, YO and pull through 2 lps) 3 times; YO and pull through 4 lps: dc3tog made.

Double Crochet 4 sts tog (dc4tog): (YO, insert hook into next st, YO and pull through, YO and pull through 2 lps) four times; YO and pull through 5 lps: dc4tog made.

Single Crochet 2 (3) stitches together: (insert hook in next st and draw up a lp) 2 (3) times; YO and draw through all 3 (4) lps on hook: sc2(3)tog made.

INSTRUCTIONS

HAT

Starting at top of crown with larger hook, ch 5, join with a sl st to form a ring.

Rnd 1: Ch 3 (counts as a dc), 15 dc in ring, join with a sl st in 3rd ch of beg ch-3: 16 dc.

Rnd 2: Ch 1, sc in same st as joining, 2 sc in each st around: 32 sts; join in beg sc.

Rnd 3: Ch 3, 2 dc in next st, *1 dc in next st, 2 dc in next st, rep from * around: 48 dc; join in 3rd ch of beg ch-3.

Rnd 4: Ch 1, sc in same st as joining and each st around; join in beg sc.

Rnd 5: Ch 3, dc in same st, dc in each of next 2 sts; *2 dc in next st, dc in each of next 2 sts); rep from * around: 64 sts; join.

Rnd 6: Rep Rnd 4.

Rnd 7: Ch 3, dc in each of next 2 sts, 2 dc in next st; *dc in each of next 3 sts, 2 dc in next st; rep from * around: 80 sts; join.

Rnd 8: Rep Rnd 4.

Rnd 9: Ch 3, dc in each of next 3 sts, 2 dc in next st; *dc in each of next 4 sts, 2 dc in next st; rep from * around: 96 sts; join.

Rnd 10: Rep Rnd 4.

Rnd 11: Ch 3, dc in each st around, join.

Rnd 12: Rep Rnd 4.

Rnds 13 through 22: Rep Rnds 11 and 12 five times more.

BRIM

Rnd 1: Ch 3, dc in next st, 2 dc in next st; *dc in each of next 2 sts, 2 dc in next st; rep from * around: 128 sts; join.

Rnd 2: Ch 1, sc in same st as joining and in each st around, join.

Rnd 3: Ch 3, dc in next 2 sts, 2 dc in next st; *dc in each of next 3 sts, 2 dc in next st; rep from * around: 176 sts; join.

Rnd 4: Rep Rnd 2.

Rnd 5: Ch 3, dc in next 3 sts, 2 dc in next st; * dc in each of next 4 sts, 2 dc in next st; rep from * around: 220 sts; join.

Rnd 6: Rep Rnd 2.

Rnd 7: Ch 3, dc in next 4 sts, 2 dc in next st; *dc in each of next 5 sts, 2 dc in next st; rep from * around: 264 sts; join.

Rnd 8: Rep Rnd 2.

Rnd 9: Ch 3, dc in next 5 sts, 2 dc in next st; *dc in each of next 6 sts, 2 dc in next st; rep from * around: 256 sts; join.

Rnd 10: Form wire into a circle. Holding wire on top of Rnd 9, ch 1 and, working over wire, 2 sc in each st around: 512 sc; join, finish off.

HATBAND

Row 1: Leaving a 14" yarn tail, ch 2, sc in first sc, turn.

Row 2: Ch 1, sc in sc, turn.

Row 3: Ch 1, 3 sc in sc, turn: 3 sc.

Row 4: Ch 1, sc across, turn.

Row 5: Ch 1, 2 sc in first sc, sc in next sc, 2 sc in last sc: 5 sc; turn.

Row 6: Ch 1, sc across, turn.

Row 7: Ch 1, 2 sc in first sc, sc to last sc, 2 sc in last sc: 7 sc; turn.

Row 8: Ch 1, sc across, turn.

Rep Row 8 until hatband measures 18" from beg, turn.

Decrease Rows

Row 1: Ch 1, sc2tog, sc in next 3 sc, sc2tog: 5 sc; turn.

Row 2: Ch 1, sc in each sc across, turn.

Row 3: Ch 1, sc2tog, sc in next 2 sc, sc2tog: 3 sc; turn.

Row 4: Ch 1, sc in each sc across, turn.

Row 5: Ch 1, sc3tog: 1 sc; turn.

Row 6: Ch 1, sc, fasten off, leaving a 14" yarn tail.

TIES

Cut 2 pieces of crochet thread each 28" long. At each end of hatband, with tapestry needle, draw one 28" piece of thread halfway through last st on each end of the hat band: this gives 3 strands on each end. Braid the three strands.

Cut two short pieces of thread and knot one around end of each braid; trim braid ends evenly.

FLOWERS

Make 2 each of teal, yellow and tangerine. Make 1 each of lime, plum and rose.

With smaller hook and leaving a 6" yarn tail, ch 6, join with a sl st to form a ring.

Rnd 1: Ch 1, 12 sc in ring, join with sc in back lp of first sc.

Rnd 2: *Ch 9, sc in 2nd ch from hook and next 7 chs, sc in back lp of next sc; rep from * around, ending sc in front lp of beg sc.

Rnd 3: *Ch 6, sc in 2nd ch and next 4 chs, sc in front lp of next sc; rep from * around, ending sl st in beg sc; finish off, leaving a 6" yarn tail.

FLOWER CENTERS (make 9)

Leaving a 6" yarn tail, ch 8, dc3tog in each of next 3 chs, dc4tog in each of next 4 chs, sl st in last ch, finish off, leaving a 6" yarn tail.

Thread tails of one flower center through center of one flower. Tie flower and flower center tails into a knot. Arrange flowers as desired on hat band, thread tails through to wrong side, and secure in place.

Tie band around hat at beg of brim.

#22 SALT & PEPPER

Designed by Sandy Scoville

SIZE
Fits 21" to 23" head

MATERIALS
Bulky weight yarn,
2 1/2 oz black and white mixture

Fur-type yarn,
1 3/4 oz black

Note: Photographed model made with TLC® Macaroon™, #9318 Salt & Pepper (A), and Lion Brand Fun Fur #153 Black (B).

14" Size 10 (6mm) knitting needles (or size required for gauge)

GAUGE
14 sts = 4" in stockinette st (knit one row, purl one row)

INSTRUCTIONS

RIBBING

With A, cast on 71 sts.

Row 1 (right side): K1; * P1, K1, rep from * across.

Row 2: P1; * K1, P1, rep from * across.

Rep Rows 1 and 2 until ribbing measures 3", ending by working a wrong-side row. Change to B.

BODY

Row 1 (right side): With 2 strands of B held tog, knit.

Row 2: Knit.

Row 3: Purl.

Rows 4 through 7: Rep Rows 2 and 3 twice more.

Row 8: Knit. Change to A.

Row 9: With A, knit.

Row 10: Purl.

Continue in stock st with A until hat measures 6" from cast-on row, ending by working a wrong-side row.

CROWN

Row 1 (right side): K2; * K2 tog, K3, rep from * 12 times more; K2 tog, K2: 57 sts.

Row 2: Purl.

Row 3: K1; * K2 tog, K2, rep from * across: 43 sts.

Row 4: Purl.

Row 5: K1; * K2 tog, K1, rep from * across: 29 sts.

Row 6: Purl.

Row 7: K1, (K2 tog) 14 times: 15 sts.

Row 8: Purl.

Row 9: K1, (K2 tog) 7 times: 8 sts.

Row 10: (P2 tog) 4 times.

Do not bind off.

FINISHING

Cut yarn, leaving a 24" end. Thread end into tapestry needle, and draw through rem 4 sts on needle; drop sts from needle and draw tight. Sew back seam, carefully matching rows.

#23 PILLBOX

Designed by Zelda K

SIZE
Fits 21" to 23" head

MATERIALS
Sport weight yarn,
1 3/4 oz charcoal

Eyelash yarn,
1 3/4 oz black

Note: Photographed model made with Patons® Astra #2938 Charcoal Mix and Bernat® Boa #81040 Raven

Size F (3.75mm) crochet hook (or size required for gauge)

Size H (5mm) crochet hook (for eyelash trim)

GAUGE
First two rnds
= 2" diameter

INSTRUCTIONS

With smaller hook and sport weight yarn, ch 3 (counts as beg dc of next rnd).

Rnd 1: 15 dc in 3rd ch from hook, join with a sl st 3rd ch of beg ch: 16 dc.

Rnd 2: Ch 1; hdc in same st as joining, ch 1; *hdc in next st, ch 1; rep from * 14 times more, join with sl st in beg hdc: 16 hdc.

Rnd 3: Sl st in next ch-1 sp, hdc in same sp, ch 2; * hdc in next sp, ch 2; rep from * around, join: 16 hdc.

Rnd 4: Sl st in next ch-2 sp, (hdc in same sp, ch 1) twice; * (hdc, ch 1) twice in next sp; rep from * around, join: 32 hdc.

Rnd 5: Sl st in next ch-1 sp, hdc in same sp, ch 1; (hdc, ch 1) in each of next 2 ch-1 sps, (hdc, ch 1) twice in next sp, *(hdc in next sp, ch 1) in each of next 3 ch-1 sps, (hdc, ch 1) twice in next sp; rep from * around, join: 40 hdc.

Rnd 6: Sl st in first ch-1 sp, hdc in same sp, ch 1; *(hdc in next sp, ch 1) 12 times, (hdc, ch 1) twice in next sp; rep from * twice; join: 43 hdc.

Rnd 7: Sl st in first ch-1 sp; hdc in same sp, ch 1; *(hdc in next sp, ch 1) 13 times, (hdc, ch 1) twice in next sp; rep from * twice; join: 46 hdc.

Rnd 8: Sl st in first ch-1 sp, hdc in same sp, ch 1; *(hdc in next sp, ch 1)10 times, (hdc, ch 1) twice in next sp; rep from * 3 times more, (hdc, ch 1) in last sp; join: 50 hdc.

Rnd 9: Sl st in first ch-1 sp, hdc in same sp, ch 1; *(hdc in next sp, ch 1) 15 times, (hdc, ch 1) twice in next sp; rep from * twice more, (hdc, ch 1) in last sp; join: 53 hdc.

Rnds 10 through 21: Sl st in first ch-1 sp, hdc in same sp, ch 1; *hdc in next sp, ch 1; rep from * around, join.

Note: To sc 2 sps tog, (draw up a lp in next sp) twice, YO and draw through all 3 lps on hook.

Rnd 22: Sl st in first sp, (sc, ch 1) 3 times in same sp, sc next 2 sps tog, ch 1; * (sc in next sp, ch 1) 3 times, sc next 2 sps tog, ch 1, rep from * around without joining until 3 sps remain, sc in next sp, ch 1, sc next 2 sps tog, ch 1, join. Finish off.

FINISHING

Note: To work sc around post, insert hook from front to back to front again around specified st, and complete as sc.

With right side facing and larger hook, join eyelash yarn from front to back around post of any st in Rnd 21.

Rnd 1: *Sc around post of next hdc on Rnd 21, ch 1, rep from * around, end rnd with sc around same post as beginning sc, ch 1.

Rnd 2: Working up, sk Rnd 20, sc around post of hdc in Rnd 19 directly above last sc made and work as for Rnd 1.

Rnds 3 through 6: Sk rnd immediately above rnd just worked and work as for Rnd 1 in next rnd above. Finish off at end of Rnd 6.

Weave in all ends.

CROCHET

#24 ELEGANT EARFLAPS

Designed by Marty Miller

SIZE
Fits up to 23" head

MATERIALS
Worsted weight yarn,
3 1/2 oz denim

*Note: Photographed
model made with
Bernat® Denimstyle
#03117 Stonewash*

Size G (4mm) crochet
hook (or size required
for gauge)

GAUGE
3 FPdc = 1"

First 5 rounds = 4.5"

STITCH GUIDE

Front Post dc (FPdc): YO, insert hook around the post (vertical bar) of specified st from front to back to front; YO, pull lp through, (YO and pull through 2 lps) twice: FPdc made.

Back Post dc (BPdc): YO, insert hook around the post (vertical bar) of specified st from back to front to back, YO and pull lp through; (YO and pull through 2 lps) twice: BPdc made.

INSTRUCTIONS

Ch 4.

Rnd 1: 7 dc in 4th ch from hook: 8 dc, counting beg skipped chs as a dc; join with a sl st in 3rd ch of beg ch-3.

Rnd 2: Ch 2 (counts as first hdc), FPdc around ch-3 of Rnd 1; *hdc in next st, FPdc around same st; rep from * around: 8 hdc, 8 FPdc; join in 2nd ch of beg ch-2.

48

Rnd 3: Ch 2, FPdc around ch-2 of prev rnd, FPdc around next st; *hdc in next hdc, FPdc around same st, FPdc around next st; rep from * around: 8 hdc, 16 FPdc; join as in Rnd 2.

Rnd 4: Ch 2, FPdc around ch-2 of prev rnd, FPdc around next 2 sts; *hdc in next hdc, FPdc around same st, FPdc around next 2 sts; rep from * around: 8 hdc, 24 FPdc; join.

Rnd 5: Ch 2, FPdc around ch-2 of Rnd 4, FPdc around next 3 sts; *hdc in next hdc, FPdc around same st, FPdc around next 3 sts; rep from * around: 8 hdc, 32 FPdc; join.

Rnds 6 through 8: Ch 2, continue in same manner, increasing 8 FPdc in each rnd; at end of Rnd 8: 8 hdc, 56 FPdc.

Rnd 9: Ch 2, sk first ch-2, FPdc around next 7 sts; *hdc in next hdc, FPdc in next 7 FPdc; rep from * around, join.

Rnds 10 through 16: Rep Rnd 9. At end of Rnd 16, do not finish off.

EARFLAPS

Right Flap

Row 1: Ch 2, sk next hdc, FPdc in next 7 FPdc, dc in next hdc: 7 FPdc, 1 hdc, 1 dc; ch 3, turn.

Row 2: Sk next dc; BPdc around each FPdc of previous row, hdc in top of ch-2: 7 BPdc, 1 hdc, 1dc; ch 2 (counts as first hdc of next row), turn.

Row 3: Sk next hdc, FPdc in next 7 sts, dc in next hdc; ch 3, turn.

Rows 4 through 9: Rep Rows 2 and 3 three more times; finish off.

Left Flap

With right side of hat facing you, sk 23 sts on Rnd 16 of hat. Attach yarn in next dc.

Row 1: Ch 3 (counts as first dc), sk next dc, FPdc in next 7 FPdc, hdc in top of next dc: 7 FPdc, 1 dc, 1 hdc; ch 2 (counts as first hdc of next row), turn.

Row 2: Sk first hdc, BPdc in next 7 sts, dc in 3rd ch of beg ch-3: 1 hdc, 7 Bpdc, 1 dc; ch 3, turn.

Row 3: Sk next dc, FPdc in next 7 sts, hdc in top of ch-2: 1 dc, 7 FPdc, 1 hdc; ch 2, turn.

Rows 4 through 9: Rep Rows 2 and 3 three more times; at end of Row 9, do not finish off.

FINISHING

Sl st evenly along the back side of the left ear flap to the first row of the ear flap. Working along the last rnd of the hat, FPdc in the next 7 FPdcs, hdc in next hdc, FPdc in next 7 FPdcs, hdc in next hdc, FPdc in next 7 FPdcs, sl st in top of ch-2 of right earflap, sl st along side edge of earflap to top corner.

Finish off. Weave in ends.

#25 ANDEAN ADVENTURER

SIZE
Fits up to 23" head

MATERIALS
Worsted weight yarn,
3 ozs natural (MC)
3 ozs lt. brown (B)
3 ozs blue (C)
3 ozs plum (D)

Note: Photographed model made with Lion Brand Wool-Ease® #98 Natural Heather (MC) #124 Caramel (B), #116 Delft (C) and #145 Plum (D)

14" Size 7 (4.5mm) knitting needles (or size required for gauge)

Size G (4mm) crochet hook

2 stitch holders

Size 16 tapestry needle

GAUGE
5 sts = 1 inch in stockinette st (knit one row, purl one row)

Note: When working from charts, carry color not in use loosely along the back of the work. Always bring the new color from under the old color to avoid holes.

INSTRUCTIONS

LEFT EARFLAP

With MC cast on 6 sts.

Row 1 (right side): Inc (work in front and back of st), knit to last st, inc: 8 sts.

Row 2 (wrong side): Purl.

Row 3: Rep Row 1: 10 sts.

Row 4: Purl; cut MC and join D.

Row 5: Rep Row 1: 12 sts.

Row 6: Purl; cut D and join C.

Row 7: Rep Row 1: 14 sts.

Row 8: Purl; cut C and join MC.

Row 9: Rep Row 1: 16 sts.

Row 10: Purl.

Rows 11 through 14: Rep Rows 1 and 2. At the end of row 14: 20 sts.

Rows 15 through 28: Follow Chart 1, starting with Row 15, increasing one st at beginning and end of every knit row. At end of Row 28: 34 sts.

Row 29: With right side facing, CO 4 sts; knit to end of row: 38 sts.

Row 30: Purl.

Rows 31 and 33: Knit.

Rows 32 and 34: Purl.

Place sts on stitch holder.

RIGHT EARFLAP

Work Rows 1 through 27 of Left Earflap.

Row 28: With RS facing, work Row 28 of Chart. CO 4 sts at end of row: 38 sts.

Row 29: Knit.

Rows 30 through 34: Rep Rows 30 through 34 of Left Earflap.

Place sts on st holder.

BODY

With right side facing and using Color B, K38 sts of Left Earflap; CO 34 sts; K38 sts of Right Earflap: 110 sts.

Next Row: Purl.

Cut Color B and join MC. Following Chart 2, changing colors as indicated, work all 28 rows. At end of chart, cut C, join B and begin to shape crown.

SHAPE CROWN

Row 1: *K3, K2tog; rep from * to end: 88 sts.

Row 2: Purl.

Row 3: Knit.

Row 4: Purl; cut B and join D.

Row 5: Knit.

Row 6: Purl.

Row 7: *K3, K2tog; rep from * to last 3 sts, K3: 71 sts.

Row 8: Purl; cut D and join MC.

Row 9: *K4, K2tog; rep from * to last 5 sts, K3, K2 tog: 59 sts.

Row 10: Purl.

Row 11: Knit.

Row 12: Purl; cut MC and join C.

Row 13: *K3, K2tog; rep from * to last 4 sts, K2, K2tog: 47 sts.

Row 14: Purl.

Row 15: Knit.

Row 16: Purl; cut C and join MC.

Row 17: *K4, K2tog; rep from * to last 5 sts. K3, K2tog: 39 sts.

Row 18: Purl.

Row 19: *K3, K2tog; rep from * to last 4 sts, K2, K2tog: 31sts.

Row 20: Purl.

Row 21: *K2, K2tog; rep from * to last 3 sts, K1, K2tog: 23 sts.

Row 22: Purl.

Row 23: *K1, K2tog; rep from * to last 2 sts, K2tog: 15 sts.

Row 24: Purl.

Row 25: *K2tog; rep from * to last 3 sts, K3tog: 7 sts.

Cut yarn, leaving a long end. Thread end into yarn needle and draw through the rem sts on the needle and secure. Sew the back seam, making sure to match colors and motifs.

FINISHING

With right side facing, using Color D and crochet hook, beg at lower center left earflap and work 1 row sc around the entire lower edge of cap, spacing sts to keep the work flat. Join to first sc with a sl st. Ch 3.

Next row: *Dc in next sc; ch 1, sk 1 sc; rep from * around lower edge of cap, dc in last sc, ch 1, join to first dc. Finish off.

Weave in all ends.

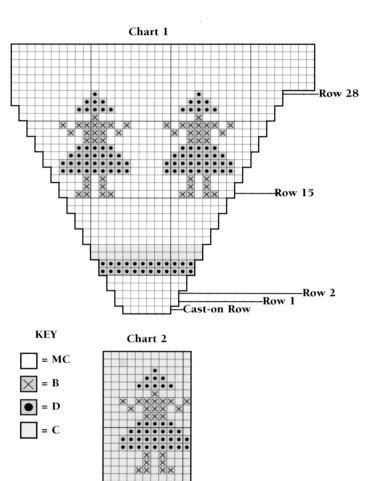

Chart 1

Row 28

Row 15

Row 2

Row 1

Cast-on Row

KEY

☐ = MC

☒ = B

⬤ = D

☐ = C

Chart 2

Row 1

← Repeat →

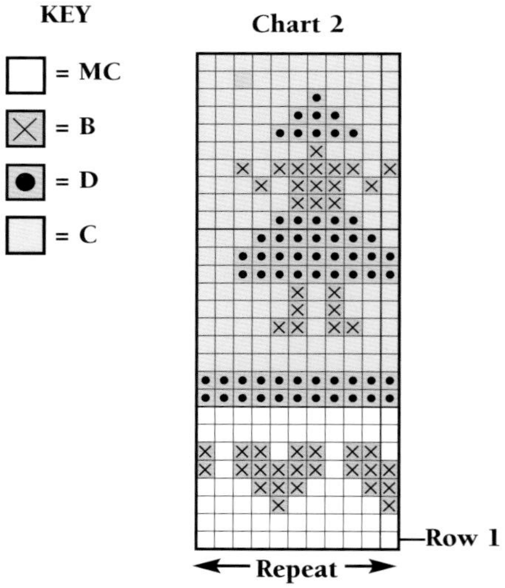

#26 SPRING BONNET

Designed by Jean Leinhauser

SIZE
Fits 15" to 16" head

MATERIALS
Worsted weight yarn,
2 oz ombre

Note: Photographed model made with Bernat® Berella® "4" #09301 Spring Meadow Ombre

Size G (4mm) crochet hook
(or size required for gauge)

GAUGE
8 dc = 2"

INSTRUCTIONS

Ch 4.

Rnd 1: 11 dc in 4th ch from hook, join with sc in 4th ch of beg ch-4: 12 dc, counting beg ch-4 as a st.

Rnd 2: Sc in joining, 2 sc in each dc around: 24 sc; join with sl st in beg sc.

Rnd 3: Ch 3, 2 dc in next sc; *dc in next sc, 2 dc in next sc; rep from around: 36 dc; join with sl st in 3rd ch of beg ch-3.

Rnd 4: Ch 3, dc in next dc, 2 dc in next dc; *dc in next 2 dc, 2 dc in next dc; rep from * around: 48 dc; join.

Rnd 5: Ch 3, dc in next 2 dc, 2 dc in next dc; *dc in next 3 dc, 2 dc in next dc; rep from * around: 60 dc; join.

Rnd 6: Ch 1, 2 sc in joining; working in back lps only, sc in each dc around, join in beg sc: 61 sc.

Rnd 7: Ch 4 (counts as a dc and ch-1 sp), skip next sc, dc in next sc; *ch 1, skip next sc, dc in next sc; rep from * around, ending ch 1, join in 3rd ch of beg ch-4.

Rnd 8: Ch 4, dc in next dc; *ch 1, dc in next dc; rep from * around, join.

Rnds 9 and 10: Rep Rnd 8.

Rnd 11 (ruffle): Ch 3, 2 dc in joining; work 3 dc in each ch-1 sp and in each dc around; join, finish off, weave in ends.

#27 READY FOR WINTER

Designed by Patons Design Staff

SIZE

Fits up to 20" head

MATERIALS

Worsted weight yarn,
3 ¹/₂ oz multicolored
3 ¹/₂ oz aran
3 ¹/₂ oz taupe

Note: Photographed model made with Patons® Décor #16231 Woodbine Ombre, #1602 Aran and #1631 Taupe

For hat: 14" Size 15 (10mm) knitting needles (or size required for gauge)

For scarf: 14" Size 12 (17mm) knitting needles (or size required for gauge)

GAUGE

For hat: 9 sts = 4" with 3 strands of yarn in stockinette st (knit one row, purl one row)
14 rows = 4" with 3 strands of yarn in stockinette st

For scarf: 17 sts = 8" with 3 strands of yarn in stockinette st
12 rows = 4" with 3 strands of yarn in stockinette st

INSTRUCTIONS

HAT

Note: Hat is worked with 3 strands of yarn (one of each color of yarn) held tog throughout.

Earflaps (make 2)

CO 4 sts.

Row 1 (wrong side): Knit.

Row 2: Inc (knit in front and back of st), knit to last st, inc: 6 sts.

Row 3: Knit.

Row 4: Rep Row 2: 8 sts.

Row 5: Knit.

Row 6: Rep Row 3: 10 sts.

Row 7: Knit.

Rep Row 7 until Earflap measures 4", ending by working a right-side row.

Cut yarn at end of last row on First Earflap. Do not cut yarn at end of of Second Earflap, continue with this yarn to Body.

BODY

CO 4 sts.

Row 1 (wrong side): K4, knit 10 sts of Second Earflap; CO 16 sts; knit 10 sts of First Earflap, CO 4 sts: 44 sts.

Rows 2 through 5: Knit.

Row 6: (P5, K1) 7 times, P2.

Row 7: K2, (P1, K5) 7 times.

Rep Rows 6 and 7 until work measures 6" from Row 1 of body, ending by working a wrong-side row.

SHAPE TOP

Row 1: (P3, P2tog, K1) 7 times, P2: 37 sts.

Row 2: K2, (P1, K4) 7 times.

Row 3: (P2, P2tog, K1) 7 times, P2: 30 sts.

Row 4: K2, (P1, K3) 7 times.

Row 5: (P1, P2tog, K1) 7 times, P2: 23 sts.

Row 6: K2, (P1, K2) 7 times.

Row 7: (P2tog, K1) 7 times, P2: 16 sts.

Row 8: K2, (P1, K1) 7 times.

Row 9: P1, (K2tog) 7 times, P1: 9 sts.

Row 10: K1, P7, K1.

Row 11: (K2tog) 4 times, K1: 5 sts.

Cut yarn, leaving a long end. Thread end through yarn needle and draw it through rem sts, pull up and fasten securely. Sew center back seam.

BRAIDS

Cut six 32" lengths of each color. Thread 3 lengths of each color halfway through tip of each Ear Flap. Separate strands into 3 groups, each group containing 2 strands of each color and braid as shown in diagram. Adjust length as desired and knot the end of Braid. Trim ends evenly.

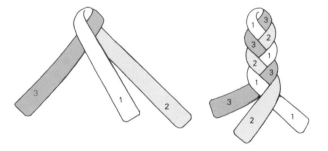

SCARF

With one strand of each color, CO 19 sts.

Row 1 (right side): Knit.

Row 2: K2, purl to last 2 sts, K2.

Rep Rows 1 and 2 until scarf measures 67" from beg, ending by working a right- side row. Knit 2 rows. Bind off.

FRINGE

Cut 20" lengths of yarn and work single knot fringe (see page 200) using 6 strands tog (2 of each color) in each knot, evenly spaced across top and bottom of scarf.

#28 BLACK AND WHITE

Designed by Denise Black

SIZE
Fits up to 23" head

MATERIALS
Worsted weight cotton yarn,
5 oz black and white variegated

Note: Photographed model made with Lion Brand Cotton, #201 Salt and Pepper

Size F (3.75mm) crochet hook, or size required for gauge

GAUGE
Rnds 1 through 3
= 2¹/₂" diameter

INSTRUCTIONS

CROWN

Ch 3.

Rnd 1 (right side): 11 hdc in 3rd ch from hook (2 skipped chs count as hdc): 12 hdc; join in 2nd ch of beg 2 skipped chs.

Rnd 2: Ch 2 (counts as first hdc on this and following rnds), hdc in same ch as joining, 2 hdc in each rem hdc: 24 hdc; join in first hdc.

Rnd 3: Ch 2, 2 hdc in next hdc; *hdc in next hdc, 2 hdc in next hdc; rep from * around: 36 hdc; join as before.

Rnd 4: Ch 2, hdc in next hdc, 2 hdc in next hdc; *hdc in next 2 hdc, 2 hdc in next hdc; rep from * around: 48 hdc; join.

Rnd 5: Ch 2, hdc in next 2 hdc, 2 hdc in next hdc; *hdc in next 3 hdc, 2 hdc in next hdc; rep from * around: 60 hdc; join.

Rnd 6: Ch 2, hdc in next 3 hdc, 2 hdc in next hdc; *hdc in next 4 hdc, 2 hdc in next hdc; rep from * around: 72 hdc; join.

Rnd 7: Ch 2, hdc in next 4 hdc, 2 hdc in next hdc; *hdc in next 5 hdc, 2 hdc in next hdc; rep from * around: 84 hdc; join.

Rnd 8: Ch 2, hdc in BLO of each hdc; join.

Rnds 9 through 18: Ch 2, hdc in each hdc; join.

BRIM

Rnd 19: Ch 1, sc in same ch as joining, 2 sc in next hdc; *sc in next hdc, 2 sc in next hdc; rep from * around: 126 sc; join in first sc.

Rnds 20 through 23: Ch 1, sc in same sc as joining and in each rem sc; join as before.

Rnd 24: Ch 1, sc in same sc as joining and in next 4 sc, 2 sc in next sc; *sc in next 5 sc, 2 sc in next sc; rep from * around: 147 sc; join.

Rnds 25 and 26: Ch 1, sc in same sc as joining and in each rem sc; join. At end of Rnd 26, finish off and weave in ends.

FINISHING

With right side facing, join yarn with sl st in front lp of any hdc on Rnd 8, sl st in front lp of each hdc on Rnd 8; join in first sl st. Finish off and weave in ends.

#29 & #30
LIKE FATHER, LIKE SON

Designed by Patons Design Staff

SIZE

Son's version fits child 4 to 6 years

Father's version fits up to 21" head

MATERIALS

Son's version
Worsted weight yarn,
3 1/2 oz natural (MC)
3 1/2 oz dark grey (A)
3 1/2 oz black (B)

Father's version
Worsted weight yarn,
3 1/2 oz natural (MC)
3 1/2 oz dark grey (A)
3 1/2 oz black (B)

Note: Both photographed models made with Patons® Classic Merino Wool, #229 Natural Mix (MC), #225 Dark Grey Mix (A) and #226 Black (B)

14" Size 7 (4.5mm) knitting needles (or size required for gauge)

14" Size 5 (3.75mm) knitting needles

29" Size 5 (3.75mm) circular knitting needle (for son's version)

2 Stitch holders

GAUGE

20 sts = 4" with larger needles in stockinette st (knit one row, purl one row)

26 rows = 4"

STITCH GUIDE

M1: make one st by picking up horizontal lp lying before next st and knitting into back of lp.

M1P: make one st by picking up horizontal lp lying before next st and purling into back of lp.

INSTRUCTIONS

SON'S VERSION

Earflap (make 2)

With MC and larger needles CO 13 sts.

Row 1 (right side): Knit.

Row 2: P1, M1P, purl to last st, M1P, P1: 15 sts.

Row 3: K1, M1, knit to last st, M1, K1: 17 sts.

Row 4: Rep Row 2: 19 sts.

Row 5: K1, M1, K1; attach A and knit Row 1 of Chart 1 across next 15 sts; K1, M1, K1: 21 sts.

Row 6: P1, M1P, P2; purl Row 2 of Chart 1 across next 15 sts, P2, M1P, P1: 23 sts.

Row 7: K4, knit next row of chart across next 15 sts, K4.

Row 8: P4, purl next row of chart across next 15 sts, P4.

Rep Rows 7 and 8, working Chart 1 to end of chart. Cut A.

With MC, work 3 rows even in stockinette st, ending by working a wrong-side row. Cut yarn and place rem sts on st holder.

Body of Hat

With MC and larger needles, CO 6 sts.

Row 1: K6, K23 sts of first Earflap from holder; CO 36 sts; K23 sts of second Earflap from holder, CO 6 sts: 94 sts.

Row 2: Purl. Join B.

Chart 1

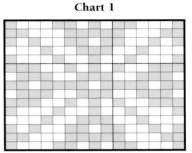

Start Here

Chart 2

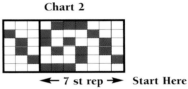

← 7 st rep → Start Here

Chart 3

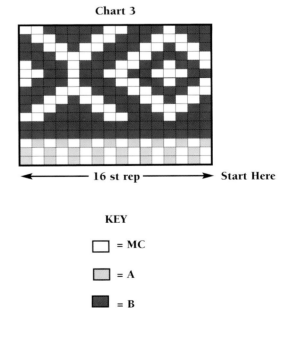

← 16 st rep → Start Here

KEY

☐ = MC

▨ = A

■ = B

Rows 3 through 8: Work Chart 2 to end of chart noting the 7-st rep will be worked 13 times.

Row 9: *With MC, K9, K2tog; rep from * 7 times more, K6 : 86 sts.

Row 10: Purl.

Row 11: *K12, K2tog; rep from * 5 times more, K2: 80 sts.

Row 12: Purl. Join A.

Rows 13 through 28: Work Chart 3 to end of chart noting the 16-st rep will be worked 5 times. Cut MC.

Row 29 (right side): With B, K1, K2 tog, knit to last 3 sts, K2 tog, K1: 78 sts.

Row 30: Purl.

Row 31: K2, sl 1, Kl, PSSO; *K13, K2tog, K2, sl 1, Kl, PSSO; rep from * twice more, K13, K2tog, K2: 70 sts.

Row 32: Purl.

Row 33: K2, sl 1, Kl, PSSO; *K11, K2tog, K2, sl 1, Kl, PSSO; rep from * twice more, K11, K2tog, K2: 62 sts.

Row 34: Purl.

Row 35: K2, sl 1, Kl, PSSO; *K9, K2tog, K2, sl 1, Kl, PSSO; rep from * twice more, K9, K2tog, K2: 54 sts.

Row 36: Purl.

Row 37: K2, sl 1, Kl, PSSO; *K7, K2tog, K2, sl 1, Kl, PSSO; rep from * twice more, K7, K2tog, K2: 46 sts.

Row 38: Purl.

Row 39: K2, sl 1, Kl, PSSO; *K5, K2tog, K2, sl 1, Kl, PSSO; rep from * twice more, K5, K2tog, K2: 38 sts.

Row 40: Purl.

Row 41: K2, sl 1, Kl, PSSO; *K3, K2tog, K2, sl 1, Kl, PSSO; rep from * twice more, K3, K2tog, K2: 30 sts.

Row 42: Purl.

Row 43: K2, sl 1, Kl, PSSO; *Kl, K2tog, K2, sl 1, Kl, PSSO; rep from * twice more, Kl, K2tog, K2: 22 sts.

Row 44: P2;*P2tog, P2; rep from * to end of row: 17 sts.

Row 45: Kl, (K2tog) 8 times: 9 sts.

Rows 46, 48 and 50: Purl.

Rows 47 and 49: Knit.

Cut yarn, leaving a long end. Thread end into a yarn needle and draw through rem sts and fasten securely.

Edging

With MC and circular needle, pick up and knit 6 sts along center back cast-on sts, 53 sts around Earflap, 32 sts across center front cast-on sts, 53 sts around 2nd Earflap and 6 sts along rem center back cast-on sts: 150 sts. Do not join. Knit two rows.

BO, leaving long yarn end; sew center back seam.

FATHER'S HAT

Starting at bottom of hat with MC and smaller needles, CO 108 sts.

Work 4 rows of garter st (knit every row).

Row 1(right side): Knit

Row 2: Purl. Join B and change to larger needles.

Rows 3 through 8: Work Chart 2 to end of chart noting the 7-st rep will be worked 15 times.

Row 9: *With MC, K11, K2tog; rep from * 7 times more, K4 : 100 sts.

Row 10: Purl.

Row 11: *K23, K2tog; rep from * 3 times more: 96 sts.

Row 12: Purl. Join A.

Rows 13 through 28: Work Chart 3 to end of chart noting the 16-st rep will be worked 6 times. Cut MC.

Row 29 (right side): With B, K1, K2tog, K to last 3 sts, K2 tog, K1: 94 sts.

Row 30: Purl.

Row 31: K2, sl l, Kl, PSSO; *K17, K2tog, K2, sl l, Kl, PSSO; rep from * twice more, K17, K2tog, K2: 86 sts.

Row 32: Purl.

Row 33: K2, sl l, Kl, PSSO; *K15, K2tog, K2, sl l, Kl, PSSO; rep from * twice more, K15, K2tog, K2: 78 sts.

Row 34: Purl.

Row 35: K2, sl l, Kl, PSSO; *K13, K2tog, K2, sl 1, Kl, PSSO; rep from * twice more, K13, K2tog, K2: 70 sts.

Row 36: Purl.

Row 37: K2, sl l, Kl, PSSO; *K11, K2tog, K2, sl 1, Kl, PSSO; rep from * twice more, K11, K2tog, K2: 62 sts.

Row 38: Purl.

Row 39: K2, sl l, Kl, PSSO; *K9, K2tog, K2, sl 1, Kl, PSSO; rep from * twice more, K9, K2tog, K2: 54 sts.

Row 40: Purl.

Row 41: K2, sl l, Kl, PSSO; *K7, K2tog, K2, sl 1, Kl, PSSO; rep from * twice more, K7, K2tog, K2: 46 sts.

Row 42: Purl.

Row 43: K2, sl l, Kl, PSSO; *K5, K2tog, K2, sl 1, Kl, PSSO; rep from * twice more, K5, K2tog, K2: 38 sts.

Row 44: Purl.

Row 45: K2, sl l, Kl, PSSO; *K3, K2tog, K2, sl 1, Kl, PSSO; rep from * twice more, K3, K2tog, K2: 30 sts.

Row 46: Purl.

Row 47: K2, sl l, Kl, PSSO; *Kl, K2tog, K2, sl l, Kl, PSSO; rep from * twice more, Kl, K2tog, K2: 22 sts.

Row 48: P2;*P2tog, P2; rep from * to end of row: 17 sts.

Row 49: Kl, (K2tog) 8 times: 9 sts.

Rows 50, 52 and 54: Purl.

Rows 51 and 53: Knit.

Cut yarn leaving a long end. Thread end into a yarn needle and draw through rem sts, draw up and fasten securely. Sew center back seam.

#31 YAMULKA

Designed by Jean Leinhauser

SIZE
Adult

MATERIALS
DK weight yarn,
1 oz gold
1 oz aqua
1 oz white

Note: Photographed model made with Patons® Grace #202 Sungold, #203 Peacock and #231 Snow

Size D (3.25mm) crochet hook (or size required for gauge)

GAUGE
10 dc = 2"

STITCH GUIDE

Front Post Triple Crochet (FPtr): YO twice, insert hook from front to back to front around post (vertical bar) of specified st, YO and draw up a lp; (YO and draw through first 2 lps on hook) 3 times: FPtr made.

Reverse sc (rev sc): Ch 1;*insert hook in next st to the right (instead of left) of hook and draw up a lp; YO and draw through both lps on hook; rep from *, working to the right instead of the left. This gives a corded edge.

INSTRUCTIONS

With gold, ch 4.

Rnd 1: 11 dc in 4th ch from hook, join with a sc in 3rd ch of beg ch-4: 12 dc, counting beg ch as a dc.

Rnd 2: *Ch 3, skip next dc, sc in next dc; rep from * around, join with sl st in joining sc: 6 ch-3 lps; finish off gold.

Rnd 3: Join aqua with sl st in any ch-3 lp; ch 3 (counts as a dc), 3 dc in same lp, ch 1; *4 dc in next ch-3 lp, ch 1; rep from * around, join in 3rd ch of beg ch-3; finish off aqua.

Rnd 4: Join white in any ch-1 sp; ch 3, dc in next 2 dc, FPtr around skipped dc below on Rnd 1, dc in next 2 dc on Rnd 3; *dc in next ch-1 sp and in next 2 dc, FPtr around skipped dc below on Rnd 1, dc in next 2 dc on Rnd 3; rep from * around, join in 3rd ch of beg ch-3.

Rnd 5: Ch 3, dc in next 2 dc, 2 FPtr around next FPtr (inc made); *dc in next 5 dc, 2 FPtr around next FPtr; rep from * around to last 2 dc, dc in last 2 dc; join in 3rd ch of beg ch-3. Finish off white.

Rnd 6: Join gold with sc between any 2 FPtr, ch 4, skip next 3 dc, sc in next dc; ch 4, skip next 3 dc; *sc between next 2 FPtr, ch 4, skip next 3 dc; sc in next dc, ch 4, skip next 3 dc; rep from * around, join in beg sc.

Rnd 7: Sl st into next ch-4 lp, ch 4 (counts as a tr), 4 tr in same lp; * ch 2, 5 tr in next ch-4 lp; rep from * around, ending ch 2, join in 4th ch of beg ch-4; finish off gold.

Rnd 8: Join aqua with sc in first tr of any 5-tr group, sc in next 4 tr; *in next ch-2 sp work (sc, FPtr in sc below in Rnd 6, sc); sc in next 5 tr; rep from * around, ending last rep, in last ch-2 sp work (sc, FPtr in sc below in Rnd 5, sc); join with sc in beg sc.

Rnd 9: Sc in each sc around, skipping the FPtr sts; join with sc in beg sc.

Rnd 10: Sc in each sc, join; finish off aqua.

Rnd 11: Join white in any sc, ch 2 (counts as a hdc); hdc in each st around, join.

Rnds 12 and 13: Hdc in each st around, join. At end of Rnd 13, finish off white.

Rnd 14: Join gold with sc in any hdc; sc in each st around, join.

Rnd 15: Sc in each st around, join, finish off gold.

Rnd 16: Join aqua with sc in any sc; sc in each st around, join.

Rnd 17: Sc in each st around, join.

Rnd 18: Ch 1, work in reverse sc in each st around, join.

Weave in all ends. Lightly steam edge if needed to keep from curling.

#32 COZY CLOCHE

Designed by Patons Design Staff

SIZE
Fits 20" to 22" head

MATERIALS
Bulky weight yarn, 3 1/2 oz variegated

Note: Photographed model made with Patons Shetland Chunky #03607 Harvest Variegated

Size J (6mm) crochet hook (or size required for gauge)

GAUGE
12 sc = 4"

14 sc rows = 4"

STITCH GUIDE
Reverse sc (rev sc): Working from left to right, ch 1; *insert hook in next st to the right, YO and draw up a lp, YO and draw through 2 lps on hook: rev sc made; rep from *.

INSTRUCTIONS

Ch 2.

Rnd 1: 8 sc in 2nd ch from hook: 8 sc; join with sl st in first sc.

Rnd 2: Ch 1, 2 sc in same sc as joining, 2 sc in each sc around: 16 sc; join as before.

Rnd 3: Ch 1, 2 sc in same sc as joining; *sc in each of next 3 sc, 2 sc in next sc; rep from * 2 times more, sc in each of next 3 sc: 20 sc; join.

Rnd 4: Ch 1, 2 sc in same sc as joining; *sc in each of next 3 sc, 2 sc in next sc; rep from * 3 times more, sc in each of next 3 sc: 25 sc; join.

Rnd 5: Ch 1, 2 sc in same sc as joining; *sc in each of next 4 sc, 2 sc in next sc; rep from * 3 times more, sc in each of next 4 sc: 30 sc; join.

Rnd 6: Ch 1, 2 sc in same sc as joining; *sc in each of next 4 sc, 2 sc in next sc; rep from * 4 times more, sc in each of next 4 sc: 36 sc; join.

Rnd 7: Ch 1, 2 sc in same sc as joining; *sc in each of next 5 sc, 2 sc in next sc; rep from * 4 times more, sc in each of next 5 sc: 42 sc; join.

Rnd 8: Ch 1, sc in same sc as joining, sc in each of next 2 sc; *2 sc in next sc, sc in each of next 6 sc; rep from * 4 times more, 2 sc in next sc, sc in each of next 3 sc: 48 sc; join.

Rnd 9: Ch 1, sc in same sc as joining, sc in each sc around; join.

Rnd 10: Ch 1, sc in same sc as joining, sc in each of next 10 sc; *2 sc in next sc, sc in each of next 11 sc; rep from * 2 times more, 2 sc in next sc: 52 sc; join.

Rnd 11: Rep Rnd 9.

Rnd 12: Ch 1, sc in same sc as joining, sc in each of next 5 sc; *2 sc in next sc, sc in each of next 12 sc; rep from * 2 times more, 2 sc in next sc, sc in each of next 6 sc: 56 sc; join.

Rnd 13: Ch 1, 2 sc in same sc as joining; *sc in each of next 10 sc, 2 sc in next sc; rep from * 3 times more, sc in each of next 11 sc: 61 sc; join.

Rnds 14 through 16: Rep Rnd 9 three times more.

Rnd 17: Ch 1, sc in same sc as joining, sc in each of next 5 sc; *2 sc in next sc, sc in each of next 11 sc; rep from * 3 times more, 2 sc in next sc, sc in each of next 6 sc: 66 sc; join.

Rnds 18 through 20: Rep Rnd 9 three times more.

Rnd 21: Ch 1, 2 sc in same sc as joining; *sc in each of next 12 sc, 2 sc in next sc; rep from * 3 times more, sc in each of next 13 sc: 71 sc; join.

Rnds 22 and 23: Rep Rnd 9 two times more.

Rnd 24: Ch 1, sc in same sc as joining, sc in each of next 6 sc; *2 sc in next sc, sc in each of next 13 sc; rep from * 3 times more, 2 sc in next sc, sc in each of next 7 sc: 76 sc; join.

Rnds 25 and 26: Rep Rnd 9 two times more.

Rnd 27: Ch 1, 2 sc in same sc as joining; *sc in each of next 14 sc, 2 sc in next sc; rep from * 3 times more, sc in each of next 15 sc: 81 sc; join.

Rnd 28: Rep Rnd 9.

Rnd 29: Ch 1, sc in same sc as joining, sc in each of next 7 sc; *2 sc in next sc, sc in each of next 15 sc; rep from * 3 times more, 2 sc in next sc, sc in each of next 8 sc: 86 sc; join.

Rnds 30 and 31: Rep Rnd 9 two times more.

Rnd 32: Ch 1, rev sc in each sc around; join. Finish off and weave in ends.

#33
TAMARA'S FAVORITE BEANIE

Designed by Sheila Jones

SIZE
Fits 20 1/2" to 23 1/2" head

MATERIALS
Worsted weight yarn, 110 yds black (A)

Short Lash component yarn, 110 yds multi-color (B)

Note: Photographed model made with Cascade 220 Wool #8555 Black and Trendsetter Flora #22 Passion Flower.

16" Size 10 (6mm) circular knitting needle (or size required for gauge)

8" Size 10 (6mm) double-pointed knitting needles

One marker

GAUGE
14 sts = 4" in circular stockinette st (knit every row on circular needle) with Color A and Color B held together.

STITCH GUIDE

Slip, slip, knit (SSK): Sl 2 sts as if to knit, one at a time, to right-hand needle. Insert tip of left-hand needle into fronts of these 2 sts and K them tog: SSK made.

INSTRUCTIONS

Note: Knit with strand each of Color A and Color B together throughout.

Starting at lower edge, CO 70 sts.

Rnd 1: Place marker, join, knit across.

Rnds 2 through 40: Knit. At end of Rnd 40, piece should measure 7".

TOP DECREASES

Note: Change to double-pointed needles when necessary.

Rnd 1: *K5, K2tog; rep from* across: 60 sts.

Rnds 2 and 3: Knit.

Rnd 4: *K4, SSK; rep from * across: 50 sts.

Rnd 5: Knit.

Rnd 6: * K3, K2tog; rep from * across: 40 sts.

Rnd 7: Knit.

Rnd 8: *K2, SSK; rep from *across: 30 sts.

Rnd 9: Knit.

Rnd 10: *K1, K2tog; rep from * across: 20 sts.

Rnd 11: *SSK: rep from * across: 10 sts.

Rnd 12: *K2tog; from * across: 5 sts

FINISHING

Cut yarns, leaving a 10" end; thread ends into yarn needle and slip through rem sts; draw up tightly, finish off and weave in ends.

#34 TENNIS ANYONE

SIZE

Fits up to 23" head

MATERIALS

DK weight yarn,
3 1/2 oz white

Note: Photographed model made with Patons® Grace #231, White

12" square cardboard, plastic canvas or template plastic

3/4" wide x 6" long white sew-on Velcro® strip

Size E (3.5mm) crochet hook (or size required for gauge)

GAUGE

5 sc = 1"

INSTRUCTIONS

VISOR (make 2)

Starting at outside edge, ch 85.

Row 1: Sc in 2nd ch from hook and in each rem ch: 84 sc, ch 2, turn.

Row 2: *Sc in next 5 sts, dec (to dec, draw up a lp in each of next 2 sts, YO and draw through all 3 lps on hook); rep from * 11 times more: 72 sc; ch 1, turn.

Row 3: Sc in first st, dec as before over next 2 sc; sc to last 3 sc, dec over next 2 sc, sc in last sc: 70 sc; ch 1, turn.

Rows 4 and 5: Rep Row 3: 66 sc at end of Row 5.

Row 6: *Sc in next 4 sc, dec over next 2 sts; rep from * 10 times more: 55 sc; ch 1, turn.

Rows 7 through 11: Rep Row 3: 45 sc at end of Row 11.

Row 12: *Sc in next 3 sts, dec; rep from * 8 times more: 36 sc; ch 1, turn.

Row 13: *Sc in next 4 sts, dec; rep from * 5 times more: 30 sc; ch 1, turn.

Row 14: Rep Row 3: 28 sc

Row 15: Sl st across first 4 sc, sc to last 4 sc, finish off, leaving last 4 sts unworked: 20 sc.

Place one crocheted piece on square of cardboard or plastic, and draw around it. Cut out, cutting about ⅛" inside of outline.

Place the two crocheted pieces together.

Working through both pieces and matching sts and rows, join along outer edge, leaving Row 15 open; do not cut yarn. Insert plastic or cardboard piece between the two crocheted pieces, trim to fit if needed. Complete joining with sc. Finish off.

HEADBAND

Front

Ch 75.

Row 1 (right side): Sc in 2nd ch from hook and in each rem sc: 74 sc; ch 1, turn.

Rows 2 through 5: Sc in each sc, ch 1, turn.

Row 6: Sl st across first 6 sts, sc to last 6 sts; finish off, leaving last 6 sts unworked.

Back

Hold piece upside down with right side facing and beg ch at top.

Row 1: Working in unused lps of beg ch, sc in each ch across: 74 sc; ch 1, turn.

Rep Rows 2 through 5 of Front.

With right side out, fold piece in half lengthwise and join open edges with sc, matching sts.

Center joined edge on top of visor, and sew tog, leaving 6 sl st ends to extend free on either side.

BACK STRAPS (make 2)

Ch 25.

Row 1: Sc in 2nd ch from hook and in each rem ch: 24 sc.

Rows 2 through 4: Sc in each sc, ch 1, turn.

Row 5: Sc in each sc, finish off.

FINISHING

Sew one strap to each side edge of headband. Following package directions, sew 3" piece of Velcro® to right side of one strap and wrong side of other strap. Adjust to size and overlap straps as needed.

#35 GOT ATTITUDE

Designed by Doris Chan

SIZE
Fits 21" to 22" head

MATERIALS
Super bulky weight yarn, 3 oz multi-color

Bulky weight wool/acrylic blend yarn, 1 oz grass green

Note: Photographed model made with Lion Brand Lion Bouclé #205 Sorbet and Lion Brand Kool Wool #130 Grass

Size M (9mm) crochet hook (or size required for gauge)

Stitch marker or small safety pin

9" round plate

GAUGE
7 sc = 4" with super bulky yarn:

8 rows = 4"

STITCH GUIDE

Back post single crochet (BPsc): Insert hook from back to front to back around post of specified st, YO and pull up a lp, YO and pull through 2 lps on hook: BPsc made.

Back Post single crochet decrease (BPsc dec): (Insert hook from back to front to back around post of next specified st, YO and pull up a lp) 2 times, YO and pull through all 3 lps on hook: BPsc dec made.

Front Post single crochet (FPsc): Insert hook from front to back to front around post of specified st, YO and pull up a lp, YO and pull through 2 lps on hook: FPsc made.

Sc decrease (sc dec): (Insert hook in next st, YO and pull up a lp) 2 times, YO and pull through all 3 lps on hook: sc dec made.

INSTRUCTIONS

CROWN

With super bulky yarn, ch 2.

Rnd 1 (right side): 6 sc in 2nd ch from hook: 6 sc; do not join, place marker at end of rnds and move marker up as you work.

Rnd 2: 2 sc in each of next 6 sc: 12 sc.

Rnd 3: (Sc in next sc, 2 sc in next sc) 6 times: 18 sc.

Rnd 4: (Sc in next 2 sc, 2 sc in next sc) 6 times: 24 sc.

Rnd 5: (Sc in next 3 sc, 2 sc in next sc) 6 times: 30 sc.

Rnd 6: (Sc in next 4 sc, 2 sc in next sc) 6 times: 36 sc.

Rnd 7: (Sc in next 5 sc, 2 sc in next sc) 6 times: 42 sc.

Rnd 8: (Sc in next 6 sc, 2 sc in next sc) 6 times: 48 sc.

Rnd 9: BPsc in each sc around: 48 BPsc.

Rnds 10 through 12: Sc in each sc around: 48 sc.

Rnd 13: (BPsc in each of next 6 sc, BPsc dec in next 2 sc) 6 times: 42 BPsc.

Rnd 14: (Sc in each of next 5 sc, sc dec in next 2 sc) 6 times, changing to wool blend yarn in last sc: 36 sc. Finish off super bulky yarn and weave in ends.

Rnd 15: With wool blend yarn, sc in each sc around: 36 sc.

Rnd 16: Sc in next 12 sc, place marker; sc in next 24 sc, join with sl st in beg sc. Finish off and weave in ends.

LINING FOR VISOR

Row 1: With right side facing, join wool blend yarn with sl st around front post of marked sc (12th sc) on Rnd 16, ch 1, FPsc in same sc, FPsc in next 14 sc: 15 FPsc; ch 1, turn.

Row 2: Sc in front lp of next 5 sc, 2 sc in front lp of next sc, sc in front lp of next 3 sc, 2 sc in front lp of next sc, sc in front lp of next 5 sc: 17 sc; ch 1, turn.

Row 3: Sc dec in next 2 sc, sc in next 13 sc, sc dec in next 2 sc: 15 sc; ch 1, turn.

Row 4: Sc dec in next 2 sc, sc in next 3 sc, 2 sc in next sc, sc in next 3 sc, 2 sc in next sc, sc in next 3 sc, sc dec in next 2 sc: 15 sc; ch 1, turn.

Row 5: Sc dec in next 2 sc, sc in next 11 sc, sc dec in next 2 sc: 13 sc. Finish off and weave in ends.

VISOR

With right side facing, join wool blend with sl st in free lp of first sc on Row 1 of lining.

Row 1: Working in free lps of same 15 sc on Row 1 of lining, ch 1, sc in same sc as joining, sc in next 4 sc, 2 sc in next sc, sc in next 3 sc, 2 sc in next sc, sc in next 5 sc: 17 sc; ch 1, turn.

Rows 2 through 4: Rep Rows 3 through 5 of lining once.

EDGING

With right side facing, join wool blend with sl st in joining sl st on Rnd 16 of crown, sl st in next 10 sc on Rnd 16, sc in edge of Row 1 of lining. Holding visor and lining tog, matching sts, sc through both thicknesses in edge of 4 rows, sc through both thicknesses in 13 sc on Row 5 of lining and Row 4 of visor, sc through both thicknesses in edge of 4 rows, sc in edge of Row 1 of lining, sl st in next 10 sc on Rnd 16, sl st in joining sl st; finish off and weave in ends.

Dampen hat and block. Slip hat over 9"-diameter round plate. Smooth top around form and allow to dry completely.

#36 TWO-TONE CAP

Designed by Zelda K

SIZE

Fits up to 20" head

MATERIALS

Worsted weight yarn, 2¹/₂ oz tan-and-brown mix (MC) 1¹/₂ oz beige-and-cream mix (CC)

Note: Photographed model made with Caron® Jewel Box #0005 Tigereye (MC) and #0002 Moonstone (CC)

Size I (5.5mm) and Size J (6mm) crochet hooks (or sizes required for gauge)

GAUGE

14 sc = 4" with smaller hook

12 sc = 4" with larger hook

STITCH GUIDE

Sc2tog decrease (sc2tog dec): (Insert hook in next st and draw up a lp) twice, YO and draw through all 3 lps on hook: sc2 tog dec made.

Reverse sc (rev sc): Ch 1; *insert hook in next st to the right (instead of left) of hook and draw up a lp; YO and draw through both lps on hook; rep from *, working to the right instead of the left. This gives a corded edge.

INSTRUCTIONS

Note: Hat is made from the crown (top) down, in spiral sections that join to make a circle.

CROWN

Section 1

With larger hook and MC, ch 15.

Row 1: Sc in 2nd ch from hook and in each rem ch: 14 sc; turn.

Row 2: Sl st in first sc, ch 1, sc in each sc across, ch 1, turn: 13 sc.

Row 3: Sc in each sc to last st, skip last st, turn: 12 sc.

Row 4: Sl st in first sc, ch 1, sc across; ch 1, turn.

Row 5: Sc in each sc to last st, skip last st: one st decreased; turn.

Rows 6 through 14: Rep Rows 4 and 5, decreasing one st each row; at end of Row 14, change to CC, ch 1, turn; mark Row 14 as wrong side.

Row 15 (also serves as Row 1 of next section): Sc in end of each row of Section 1 (you are working along the side of just-completed section), turn: 14 sc.

Sections 2 through 8

Rep Rows 2 through 15 of Section 1, omitting Row 15 at end of Section 8. Finish off, leaving enough yarn to sew Section 8 to Section 1 on wrong side. Sew Section 8 to Section 1: crown formed.

SIDES

With smaller hook, Join MC at beg of any Section. Unless otherwise noted, do not join rnds, mark beg of each rnd.

Rnd 1: Sc in end of each row along outer edges of each section: 112 sc.

Rnd 2: *Sc in next 12 sc, sc2tog; rep from * 7 times more: 104 sc.

Rnd 3: *Sc in next 11 sc, sc2tog; rep from * 7 times more: 96 sc.

Rnd 4: *Sc in next 10 sc, sc2tog; rep from * 7 times more: 88 sc.

Rnd 5: *Sc in next 9 sc, sc2tog; rep from * 7 times more: 80 sc.

Rnd 6: *Sc in next 8 sc, sc2tog, rep from * 7 times more: 72 sc.

Rnd 7: *Sc in next 7 sc, sc2tog, rep from * 7 times more: 64 sc.

Rnds 8 through 10: Sc in each sc, finish off.

VISOR

With right side facing, determine where you want center front to be (in the middle of a section or between two sections). At bottom edge, count 14 sts to each side of the center for a total of 28 sts. With smaller hook, join CC in first of these 28 sts.

Row 1: Sc in each of 28 sc, sl st in next st, turn.

Row 2: Sk sl st and first sc, sc in each of next 26 sc, sl st in next st, turn.

Row 3: Sk sl st and first sc, sc in each of next 24 sc, sl st in next st, turn.

Row 4: Sk sl st and first sc, sc in each of next 22 sc, sl st in next st, turn.

Row 5: Sk sl st and first sc, sc in each of next 20 sc. Finish off.

EDGING

With right side facing and continuing with smaller hook, join CC in any sc along back edge of hat.

Rnd 1: Sc in each sc to edge of visor and along edge of visor to last row of visor (front edge); across the 20 sc of last row of visor work (5 sc, sc2tog, 6 sc, sc2tog, 5 sc); sc along opposite side of visor and in each sc to end of rnd, join, ch 1, do not turn.

Rnd 2: Reverse sc in each sc, join. Finish off, weave in ends.

#37 ROSES ARE RED

Designed by Jean Leinhauser

SIZE
Fits up to 18" head

MATERIALS
Worsted weight yarn,
2 oz black,
1 oz red,
20 yds dark red

Note: Photographed model made with Red Heart® Classic™ #12 Black, #902 Jockey Red and # 760 New Berry

Size H (5mm) crochet hook (or size required for gauge)

GAUGE
7 dc = 2"

INSTRUCTIONS

HAT

With black, ch 4, join with a sl st to form a ring.

Rnd 1: Ch 1, 12 sc in ring; join with sl st in beg sc.

Rnd 2: Ch 3 (counts as a dc), dc in joining; 2 dc in each sc around: 24 dc; join in 3rd ch of beg ch-3.

Rnd 3: Ch 3, 2 dc in next dc; *dc in next dc, 2 dc in next dc; rep from * around: 36 dc; join.

Rnd 4: Ch 3, dc in next dc, 2 dc in next dc; *dc in next 2 dc, 2 dc in next dc; rep from * around: 48 dc; join.

Rnd 5: Ch 3, dc in next 2 dc, 2 dc in next dc; *dc in next 3 dc, 2 dc in next dc; rep from * around: 60 dc; join.

Rnd 6: Ch 3, dc in each dc around, join.

Rnds 7 through 11: Rep Rnd 6.

Rnd 12: Ch 1, sc in each dc around, join; finish off, weave in ends.

ROSE

With red, ch 5, join with a sl st to form a ring.

Rnd 1: Ch 1, 8 sc in ring, join with sc in beg sc.

Rnd 2: *Ch 3, sc in BLO of next sc; rep from * around, ending ch 3, join with sl st in beg sc: 8 ch-3 sps made.

Rnd 3: Sl st into first ch-3 sp, ch 1, in same sp work (sc, hdc, dc, hdc, sc); *in next ch-3 sp work (sc, hdc, dc, hdc, sc); rep from * around: 8 petals made; join with sl st in beg sc.

Rnd 4: Ch 6 (counts as a dc and ch-3 sp); dc around next sc on Rnd 2 (insert hook from back to front to back); working behind petals, *ch 3, dc around next sc on Rnd 2 (insert hook from front to back to front); rep from * around, join in 3rd ch of beg ch-6: 8 ch-3 sps.

Rnd 5: Sl st into next ch-3 sp; working behind petals of Rnd 3, in same sp work (sc, hdc, 3 dc, hdc, sc); * in next ch-3 sp work (sc, hdc, 3 dc, hdc, sc): 8 petals made; rep from * around, join in beg sc.

Rnd 6: Ch 7 (counts as a dc and ch-4 sp), dc around next sc on Rnd 4; *ch 4, dc around next dc on Rnd 4; rep from * around, join in 3rd ch of beg ch-7: 8 ch-4 sps.

Rnd 7: Sl st into next ch-4 sp; in same sp work (sc, hdc, dc, 2 tr, dc, hdc, sc); * in next ch-4 sp work (sc, hdc, dc, 2 tr, dc, hdc, sc); rep from * around, join in beg sc: 8 petals made. Finish off, leaving a long end for sewing.

FLOWER CENTER

Join dark red with sl st in FLO of any sc in Rnd 1; *ch 3, sc in FLO of next sc of Rnd 1; rep from * around, join; finish off.

FINISHING

Sew rose to hat as shown in photo.
Weave in all ends.

CROCHET

#38

HUNTING FOR EASTER EGGS IN THE GRASS

Designed by Ruthie Marks

SIZE
Fits 18" to 22" head

MATERIALS
Worsted weight yarn, 3 1/2 oz white

Fine sport weight yarn,
2 oz green
1 1/2 oz gold

Note: Photographed model made with Lion Brand Cotton-Ease, #100 Vanilla (A) and Red Heart® Lustersheen, #615 Tea Leaf (B), #604 Gold (C)

Size F (3.75mm) crochet hook (or size required for gauge)

167 Perler beads in assorted colors

Stitch marker

GAUGE
8 sc = 2" with worsted yarn

7 sc rows (worked in back lps only) = 2"

INSTRUCTIONS

Note: Do not join rnds, but place marker at end of each rnd.

BASE

With A, ch 4; join with sl st to form a ring.

Note: Work in BLO throughout.

Rnd 1: Ch 1, 2 sc in same ch as joining and in each of next 3 chs: 8 sc.

Rnd 2: 2 sc in each sc around: 16 sc.

Rnd 3: Rep Rnd 2: 32 sc.

Rnd 4: Sc in each sc around.

Rnd 5: *Sc in first sc, 2 sc in next sc, rep from * around: 48 sc.

Rnd 6: Rep Rnd 4.

Rnd 7: Rep Rnd 5: 72 sc.

Rnd 8: Rep Rnd 4.

Rnd 9: *Sc in next 5 sc, 2 sc in next sc, rep from * around: 84 sc.

Rnds 10 through 26: Rep Rnd 4 seventeen times more.

Rnd 27: Rep Rnd 5: 126 sc.

Rnds 28 through 35: Rep Rnd 4 eight times more, sl st in next 4 sc. Finish off and weave in ends.

SECOND LAYER

Rnds 1 through 26: Thread beads randomly onto B. With right side facing, join B with sl st in first unworked front lp on Rnd 1, ch 1, sc in same sp, *sc in front lp of next 10 sc, slide a bead up next to hook and work sc with bead, rep from * around to end of Rnd 26; join C in next sc. Finish off B and weave in ends.

Rnds 27 through 34: With C, sc in front lp of each rem sc. Finish off and weave in ends.

CROCHET
#39 IN STYLE

Designed by Nancy Brown

SIZE
Fits 20" to 22" head

MATERIALS
Worsted weight wool yarn, 100 yds blue/green/violet variegated

Note: Photographed model made with Interlacements Oregon Worsted #203 Submarine

Size 7 (4.5mm) crochet hook (or size required for gauge)

GAUGE
6 dc = 2"

3 dc rows = 2"

STITCH GUIDE

V-St: (Dc, ch 1, dc) in specified st.

5-Dc shell: 5 dc in specified st.

7-Dc shell: 7 dc in specified st.

Picot: Ch 3, sc in 3rd ch from hook.

INSTRUCTIONS

Ch 4, join with sl st to form a ring.

Rnd 1: Sl st in ring, ch 3 (counts as first dc), 7 dc in ring: 8 dc; join with sl st in first dc.

Rnd 2: Ch 3 (counts as first dc), dc in same st as joining, 2 dc in each dc around: 16 dc; join with sl st in first dc.

Rnd 3: Rep Rnd 2: 32 dc.

Rnd 4: Ch 3 (counts as first dc), 2 dc in next dc; *dc in next dc, 2 dc in next dc; rep from * around: 48 dc; join with sl st in first dc.

Rnd 5: Ch 4, dc in same st as joining (counts as first V-St); *sk next dc, V-St in next dc; rep from * around: 24 V-sts; join with sl st in 3rd ch of beg ch-4.

Rnd 6: *Sc in next ch-1 sp, 5-dc shell in next ch-1 sp; rep from * around: 12, 5-dc shells; join with sc in beg sc.

Rnd 7: (Ch 5, sc in middle dc of next shell) 2 times; *(ch 5, sc in next sc, ch 5, sc in middle dc of next shell) 2 times, ch 5, sc in middle dc of next shell; rep from * 2 times more, ch 5, sc in next sc, ch 5, sc in middle dc of next shell, ch 5, join with sl st in beg sc: 20 ch-5 sps.

Rnd 8: Sl st in next 2 chs, sc in same ch-5 sp; *ch 5, sc in next ch-5 sp; rep from * around, ch 5, join with sl st in beg sc: 20 ch-5 sps.

Rnd 9: Rep Rnd 8.

Rnd 10: Sl st in next 3 chs, ch 3 (counts as first dc), 6 dc in same ch as last sl st (beg 7-dc shell made); *sc in next ch-5 sp, 7-dc shell in middle ch of next ch-5 sp; rep from * 8 times more, sc in next ch-5 sp, join with sl st in beg ch-3: 10, 7-dc shells.

Rnd 11: Sl st in next 2 dc, sc in next dc; *7-dc shell in next sc, sc in middle dc of next shell; rep from * 8 times more, 7-dc shell in next sc, join with sc in beg sc: 10, 7-dc shells.

Rnd 12: Ch 3 (counts as first dc), work 6 dc in same dc: beg 7-dc shell made; *sc in middle dc of next shell, 7-dc shell in next sc; rep from *9 times more, sc in middle dc of last 7-dc shell, join with sl st in beg ch-3: 10, 7-dc shells.

Rnd 13: Sl st in next 2 dc, sc in next dc, ch 5, sc in next sc, *ch 5, sc in middle of next shell, ch 5, sc in next sc; rep from * 8 times more, ch 5, join with sl st in beg sc: 20 ch-5 sps.

Rnd 14: Sl st in next 2 chs, sc in same ch-5 sp; *ch 5, sc in next ch-5 sp; rep from * around, ch 5, join with sl st in beg sc: 20 ch-5 sps.

Rnd 15: Sl st in next 2 chs, sc in same ch-5 sp; *(4 dc, picot, 3 dc) in middle ch of next ch-5 sp, sc in next ch-5 sp; rep from * 8 times more, (4 dc, picot, 3 dc) in middle ch of next ch-5 sp, join with sl st in beg sc: 10, 7-dc shells with picots. Finish off and weave in ends.

#40 STOCKING CAP

Designed by Rita Weiss

SIZE
Fits up to 18" head

MATERIALS
Worsted weight yarn,
1/2 oz green
1/2 oz yellow
1/2 oz variegated
3/4 oz red

Note: Photographed model made with Red Heart® Kids™, #2652 Lime, #2230 Yellow, #2930 Crayon, #2390 Red

14" Size 8 (5mm) knitting needles (or size required for gauge)

14" Size 6 (4.25mm) knitting needles

GAUGE
9 sts = 4" with larger needles in stockinette st (knit one row, purl one row)

STITCH GUIDE
Slip, slip, knit (SSK): Sl 2 sts as if to knit, one at a time, to right-hand needle. Insert tip of left-hand needle into fronts of these 2 sts and K them tog: SSK made.

COLOR SEQUENCE
4 rows green

2 rows red

4 rows variegated

2 rows red

4 rows yellow

2 rows red.

Note: Do not cut red. Carry red yarn loosely along the side.

INSTRUCTIONS
With smaller needles and red, and starting at bottom of hat, CO 78 sts.

Rows 1 through 5: *K1, P1; rep from * across. Change to larger needles. Attach green.

Row 6 (right side): Knit.

Row 7: Purl.

Rows 8 and 9: Rep Rows 6 and 7. At end of Row 9, cut green.

Row 10: With red, knit across row.

Row 11: Knit. Attach variegated.

Rows 12 through 15: Rep Rows 6 through 9. At end of Row 15, cut variegated.

Row 16: With red, K 11, (SSK, K2tog, K22) twice; ssk, K2tog, K11: 72 sts

Row 17: Rep Row 10. Attach yellow.

Rows 18 through 21: Rep Rows 6 through 9. At end of Row 21, cut yellow.

Row 22: With red, Knit.

Row 23: K8, (SSK, K2tog, K16) twice, SSK, K2tog, K8: 54 sts. Attach green.

Rows 24 through 27: Rep Rows 6 and 7. At end of Row 27, cut green.

Rows 28 and 29: With red, rep Rows 10 and 11. At end of Row 29, attach variegated.

Rows 30 through 33: Rep Rows 6 and 7. At end of Row 33, cut variegated.

Row 34: With red, K7 (SSK, K2tog, K14) twice; SSK, K2tog, K7: 48 sts.

Row 35: Rep Row 10. Attach yellow,

Rows 36 through 39: Rep Rows 6 through 9. At end of Row 39, cut Yellow.

Row 40: With red, rep Row 10.

Row 41: K6, (SSK, K2tog, K12) twice, SSK, K2tog, K6: 42 sts. Attach green.

Rows 42 through 45: Rep Rows 6 through 9. At end of Row 45, cut green.

Rows 46 and 47: With red, rep Row 10. At end of Row 47, attach variegated.

Rows 48 through 51: Rep Rows 6 through 9. At end of Row 51, cut variegated.

Row 52: With red, K5, (SSK, K2tog, K10) twice, SSK, K2tog, K5: 36 sts.

Row 53: Rep Row 10. Attach yellow.

Rows 54 through 57: Rep Rows 6 through 9. At end of Row 57, cut yellow.

Row 58: With red, K4, (SSK, K2tog, K8) twice, SSK, K2tog, K4: 30 sts.

Row 59: Rep Row 10. Attach green.

Rows 60 through 63: Rep Rows 6 through 9. At end of Row 63, cut green.

Rows 64 and 65: Rep Row 10. At end of Row 65, attach variegated.

Rows 66 through 69: Rep Rows 6 through 9. At end of Row 69, cut variegated.

Row 70: With red, K1 (SSK, K2tog, K2) twice, SSK, K2tog, K1: 12 sts.

Row 71: Rep Row 10. Attach yellow.

Rows 72 through 75: Rep Rows 6 through 9. At end of Row 75, cut yellow,

Row 76: With red, (SSK, K2tog) 3 times: 6 sts

Row 77: Rep Row 10. Attach green.

Rows 78 through 81: Rep Rows 6 through 9. At end of Row 81, cut green.

Rows 82 and 83: With red, rep Row 10.

Cut yarn, leaving long end. Thread yarn into yarn needle and draw through rem sts. Fasten securely and finish off. Sew sides, weave in all ends.

POMPON

With variegated yarn and following pompon instructions on page 200, make a 2" pompon and sew to top of hat.

#41 FRILLY FLOWER

Designed by Jean Leinhauser

SIZE
Fits 14" to 18" head

MATERIALS
Worsted weight yarn,
2 oz blue,
5 yds yellow

Note: Photographed model made with Red Heart® Classic™ #815 Pale Blue and #230 Yellow

Size I (5.5mm) crochet hook (or size required for gauge)

GAUGE
6 dc = 2"

INSTRUCTIONS

With blue, ch 4, join with a sl st to form a ring.

Rnd 1: Ch 3 (counts as first dc of rnd), 11 dc in ring; join with sl st in 3rd ch of beg ch-3: 12 dc.

Rnd 2: Ch 3, dc in joining; 2 dc in each rem dc around: 24 dc; join as before.

Rnd 3: Ch 3, dc in joining; * dc in next dc, 2 dc in next dc; rep from * around, ending dc in last dc: 36 dc; join.

Rnd 4: Ch 3, dc in joining and in next 2 dc; *2 dc in next dc, dc in next 2 dc; rep from * around: 48 dc; join.

Rnd 5: Ch 1, 2 sc in joining, *sc in next 3 dc, 2 sc in next dc; rep from * around, ending sc in next 2 dc, 2 dc in last dc: 61 sts; join.

Rnd 6: Ch 3, skip next sc, dc in next sc, dc in skipped sc; * skip next sc, dc in next sc, dc in skipped sc; rep from * around, join in 3rd ch of beg ch-3.

Rnd 7: Ch 1, sc in joining and in each dc around, join.

Rnd 8: Ch 3, dc in each sc around, join.

Rnds 9 through 12: Rep Rnds 7 and 8 two times more.

Rnds 13 and 14: Ch 1, sc in each sc around, join.

Rnd 15: Ch 1, (sc, ch 4, sc) in joining; * (sc, ch 4, sc) in each sc around; join in beg sc, finish off, weave in ends.

FRILLY FLOWER APPLIQUE

With yellow, ch 4.

Rnd 1: 14 dc in 4th ch from hook; join in 3rd ch of beg ch 4: 15 dc, counting beg ch-4 as a st; finish off yellow, weave in ends.

Rnd 2: Join blue with sc in any dc; *ch 11, sc in next dc; rep from * around, join with sc in beg sc: 14 ch-11 lps.

Rnd 3: *12 dc in next ch-11 lp, sc in next sc; rep from * around; finish off, leaving a long yarn end for sewing.

Sew flower to top of hat.

#42 BABY BONNET

Designed by Rita Weiss

SIZE

Fits 9 to 12 month old baby

MATERIALS

Baby weight yarn, 1 1/2 oz white

14" Size 7 (4.5mm) knitting needles (or size required for gauge)

GAUGE

6 sts = 1" in pattern

PATTERN

Row 1: Knit.

Row 2: Purl.

Row 3: K2; *YRN, P1, P3tog, P1, YO, K1; rep from * to end.

Row 4: Purl.

INSTRUCTIONS

EDGING

Cast on 81 sts.

Rows 1 and 2: Knit.

Row 3: K1; *YO, K2tog; rep from * to end of row. This row forms picot edge.

Row 4: Purl.

Rows 5 and 6: Knit.

Fold hem at picot edge and knit together one st from needle and one lp from cast-on edge, carefully matching sts and lps; continue across.

Next Row: Knit to last 2 sts, K2tog: 80 sts. This row creates ridge on right side of the work.

BODY

Work in patt until work measures 4" from picot edge, ending by working a Row 4.

CROWN

Row 1: *K6, K2tog; rep from * across: 70 sts.

Rows 2 through 4: Knit.

Row 5: *K5, K2tog; rep from * across: 60 sts.

Rows 6 through 8: Knit.

Row 9: *K4, K2tog; rep from * across: 50 sts.

Rows 10 through 12: Knit.

Row 13: *K3, K2tog; rep from * across: 40 sts.

Rows 14 through 16: Knit.

Row 17: *K2, K2tog; rep from * across: 30 sts.

Rows 18 through 20: Knit.

Row 21: *K1, K2tog; rep from * across: 20 sts.

Rows 22 through 24: Knit.

Row 25: *K2tog; rep from * across: 10 sts.

Cut yarn, leaving sufficient yarn to sew back seam; thread yarn into a tapestry needle and draw through rem sts, drawing up tightly. Sew back seam.

#43
LITTLE BOY'S BASEBALL CAP

Designed by Jean Leinhauser

SIZE
Fits up to 16" head

MATERIALS
Worsted weight yarn,
2 oz white
1 oz red

Note: Photographed model made with Red Heart® Classic™ #1 White and #902 Jockey Red

Size I (5.5mm) crochet hook (or size required for gauge)

GAUGE
6 dc = 2"

STITCH GUIDE

Front Post Double Crochet (FPdc): YO, insert hook from front to back to front around post (vertical bar) of specified st, (YO and draw through 2 lps) twice: FPdc made

Sc decrease (sc dec): (Insert hook in next st, YO and pull up a lp) 2 times, YO and pull through all 3 lps on hook: sc dec made.

INSTRUCTIONS

With white, ch 4, join with a sl st to form a ring.

Rnd 1: Ch 1, work 12 sc in ring, join with sl st in beg sc.

Rnd 2: Ch 3, dc in joining; work 2 dc in each sc around, join with sl st in 3rd ch of beg ch-3: 24 sc.

Rnd 3: Ch 3 (do not count beg Ch-3 as dc for remainder of cap), work FPdc around Ch-3 of Rnd 2, 2 dc in next dc; *FPdc around next dc, 2 dc in next dc; rep from * around, join to top of first FPdc: 36 sts (24 dc, 12 FPdc).

Rnd 4: Ch 3, FPdc around first FPdc, dc in next dc, 2 dc in next dc; *FPdc around next FPdc, dc in next dc, 2 dc in next dc; rep from * around, join as before: 48 dc.

Rnd 5: Ch 3; *FPdc around next FPdc, dc in next 2 dc, 2 dc in next dc; rep from * around, join: 60 dc.

Rnds 6 through 10: Ch 3; * FPdc around next FPdc, dc in next 4 dc; rep from * around, join.

Rnd 11: Ch 1, sc in joining and in next dc; draw up a lp in each of next 2 dc, YO and draw through all 3 lps on hook: sc decrease made; sc in next dc; *sc in next FPdc and next dc; sc dec over next 2 dc, dc in next dc; rep from * around: 48 sc. Finish off white.

BILL

Row 1 (right side): Hold hat with right side facing and last row at top; join red with sc in any sc; sc in next 13 sc: 14 sc; ch 1, turn.

Row 2: Sc in each sc, ch 1, turn.

Row 3: Sc in first sc, sc dec over next 2 sc, sc in 8 sc, sc dec over next 2 sc, sc in last sc: 12 sc; ch 1, turn.

Row 4: Sc in each sc, ch 1, turn.

Row 5: Sc in first sc, sc dec over next 2 sc, sc in next 6 sc, sc dec over next 2 sc, sc in last sc: 10 sc; ch 1, turn.

Row 6: Sc in first sc, sc dec over next 2 sc, sc in next 4 sc, sc dec over next 2 sc, sc in last sc: 8 sc; ch 1, turn.

Row 7: Sc in first sc, sc dec over next 2 sc, sc in next 2 sc, dec over next 2 sc, sc in last sc: 6 sc; do not ch or turn.

Row 8: Sc in each row up side of bill to last row of white; sc in each white sc to first st of bill on opposite side, sc down side of bill and across front, join, finish off, weave in ends.

#44 CLEOPATRA'S CROWN

Designed by Doris Chan

SIZE

Fits 21" to 22" head

MATERIALS

Super bulky weight yarn,
2¹/₂ oz multi-color

Worsted weight yarn,
1¹/₂ oz black

Note: Photographed model made with Lion Brand Lion Bouclé #207 Gelato and Lion Brand Wool-Ease® #153 Black

Size M (9mm) crochet hook (or size required for gauge)

Size K (6.5mm) crochet hook (used to attach hair)

Size 13 (0.85mm) steel crochet hook (for attaching beads)

Pony beads, 6 X 9mm size, 126 total (3 colors, 42 of each)

Stitch marker or scrap of contrasting yarn

GAUGE

8 sc = 4" with super bulky weight yarn and larger hook

8 rows = 4"

STITCH GUIDE

Back post single crochet (BPsc):
Insert hook from back to front to back around post of specified st, YO and pull up a lp, YO and pull through 2 lps on hook: BPsc made.

INSTRUCTIONS

Note: Place marker or scrap of contrasting yarn at end of rnds. Move marker up as you work.

CROWN

With super bulky yarn and larger hook, ch 2.

Rnd 1 (right side): 6 sc in 2nd ch from hook: 6 sc.

Rnd 2: 2 sc in each of next 6 sc: 12 sc.

Rnd 3: (Sc in next sc, 2 sc in next sc) 6 times: 18 sc.

Rnd 4: (Sc in next 2 sc, 2 sc in next sc) 6 times: 24 sc.

Rnd 5: (Sc in next 3 sc, 2 sc in next sc) 6 times: 30 sc.

Rnd 6: (Sc in next 4 sc, 2 sc in next sc) 6 times: 36 sc.

Rnd 7: (Sc in next 5 sc, 2 sc in next sc) 6 times: 42 sc.

Rnd 8: BPsc in each sc around: 42 BPsc.

Rnds 9 through 13: Sc in each sc around: 42 sc. At end of Rnd 13, join with sl st in beg sc. Finish off and weave in ends.

HAIR

Bangs: With worsted weight yarn, cut 36 strands 8" long. Hold together 3 strands. Using K hook, draw one end of strands through center front sc on Rnd 13. Hold all ends even and apply 3 beads to end of yarn (see Applying Beads). Slide beads up yarn to hat edge. Tie overhand knot to secure. Repeat for remaining 8" lengths, drawing 3 strands through sc sts on each side of center front sc on Rnd 13 to make 12 bangs total.

Long hair: With worsted weight yarn, cut 90 strands 30" long. Hold together 3 strands. Fold strands in half. Using K hook, pull fold through any remaining sc on Rnd 13. Pull ends through fold. Hold all ends even. Pull fold up against edge of hat to make snug fringe. Repeat with remaining 30" lengths, drawing 3 strands through remaining sc sts on Rnd 13 to make 30 fringes total. Take 3 strands from first fringe (leave 3 strands unworked) and hold together with 3 strands from next fringe. Tie overhand knot 1" down from top edge. Repeat for remaining fringes, leaving last 3 strands unworked. Take first 3 unworked strands and hold together with 3 strands from next fringe. Tie overhand knot 1" down from previous knot. Hold remaining 3 strands from next fringe together with 3 strands from following fringe. Tie overhand knot as before. Repeat for remaining fringes, working last 3 unworked strands into last knot. Apply 3 beads to each fringe end (see Applying Beads). Slide beads up to knot. Tie overhand knot to secure.

Trim bangs 2" from hat edge and long hair 8" from hat edge.

APPLYING BEADS

Slip beads on steel hook. Fold all ends of fringe around loop of hook. Slide beads onto fringe and up into position. Knot as directed.

FINISHING

To draw in hat bottom, work rnd of sl st as follows: With right side facing, using super bulky yarn and larger hook (keeping hair out of the way), join with sl st in last sc on Rnd 13, sl st in each sc around, join with sl st in beg sl st. Finish off and weave in ends.

Lightly steam hair to remove kinks in yarn.

#45 SUGAR DARLING

Designed by Doris Chan

SIZE

Fits 21" to 22" head

MATERIALS

Super bulky weight yarn,
2 1/2 oz multi-color

Worsted weight yarn,
1 1/2 oz off-white

Note: Photographed model made with Lion Brand Lion Bouclé #208 Parfait and Lion Brand Wool-Ease® #099 Fisherman

Size M (9mm) crochet hook (or size required for gauge)

Size K (6.5mm) crochet hook (used to attach hair)

Size 13 (0.85mm) steel crochet hook (or similar fine hook for attaching beads)

Pony beads, 6 X 9mm size (42 of one color)

Stitch marker or small safety pin

GAUGE

8 sc = 4" with super bulky weight yarn and larger hook

8 rows = 4"

Back post single crochet (BPsc): Insert hook from back to front to back around post of specified st, YO and pull up a lp, YO and pull through 2 lps on hook: BPsc made.

INSTRUCTIONS

Note: Place marker at end of rnds. Move marker up as you work.

HAT

With super bulky yarn and larger hook, ch 2.

Rnd 1 (right side): 6 sc in 2nd ch from hook: 6 sc.

Rnd 2: 2 sc in each of next 6 sc: 12 sc.

Rnd 3: (Sc in next sc, 2 sc in next sc) 6 times: 18 sc.

Rnd 4: (Sc in next 2 sc, 2 sc in next sc) 6 times: 24 sc.

Rnd 5: (Sc in next 3 sc, 2 sc in next sc) 6 times: 30 sc.

Rnd 6: (Sc in next 4 sc, 2 sc in next sc) 6 times: 36 sc.

Rnd 7: (Sc in next 5 sc, 2 sc in next sc) 6 times: 42 sc.

Rnd 8: BPsc in each sc around: 42 BPsc.

Rnds 9 through 13: Sc in each sc around: 42 sc. At end of Rnd 13, join with sl st in beg sc. Finish off and weave in ends.

HAIR

Bangs: With worsted weight yarn, cut 36 strands 8" long. Hold together 3 strands. Using K hook, draw one end of strands through center front sc on Rnd 13. Hold all ends even and apply one bead to end of yarn (see Applying Beads). Slide bead up

yarn to hat edge. Tie overhand knot to secure. Rep for remaining 8" lengths, drawing 3 strands through sc sts on each side of center front sc on Rnd 13 to make 12 bangs total.

Braids: With worsted weight yarn, cut 90 strands 36" long. Hold together 3 strands. Fold strands in half. Using K hook, pull fold through any remaining sc on Rnd 13. Pull ends through fold. Hold all ends even. Pull fold up against edge of hat to make snug fringe. Repeat with remaining 36" lengths, drawing 3 strands through remaining sc sts on Rnd 13 to make 30 fringes total. Divide each braid fringe into 3 sections of 2 strands each and braid to within 4 inches of ends. Apply one bead to end of strands (see Applying Beads). Tie overhand knot to secure.

Trim bangs 2" from hat edge and braids 13" from hat edge.

APPLYING BEADS

Slip bead on steel hook. Fold all ends of fringe around loop of hook. Slide bead onto fringe and up into position. Knot as directed.

FINISHING

To draw in hat bottom, work rnd of sl st as follows: With right side facing, using super bulky yarn and larger hook (keeping hair out of the way), join with sl st in last sc on Rnd 13, sl st in each sc around, join with sl st in beg sl st. Finish off and weave in ends.

Lightly steam hair to remove kinks in yarn.

#46 CABLES & CHECKS

Designed by Patons Design Staff

Small fits child 6-12 months

Large fits child 18 months to 2 years

Note: Instructions are written for small size; changes for large size are in parentheses.

DK weight yarn,
1 oz dark blue (MC)
3/4 oz medium blue(A)
3/4 oz fuchsia (B)

Note: Photographed model made with Patons® Astra, #2763 Copen Blue (MC), #2774 Medium Blue (A) and #8728 Fuchsia (B)

14" Size 6 (4mm) knitting needles (or size required for gauge)

14" Size 5 (3.75mm) knitting needles

Cable needle

4 yarn bobbins

22 sts = 4" with larger needles in stockinette st (knit one row, purl one row)

30 rows = 4"

C6B: slip next 3 sts onto a cable needle and leave at back of work, K3, then K3 from cable needle.

Cr5B: slip next 2 sts onto a cable needle and leave at back of work, K3, then P2 from cable needle.

Cr5F: slip next 3 sts onto a cable needle and leave at front of work, P2, then K3 from cable needle.

MK: P2tog without slipping sts off needle, then K2tog same sts.

PANEL PATTERN (worked over 18 sts)

Row 1 (right side): P6, C6B, P6.

Row 2 and all even rows: Knit all knit sts and purl all purl sts as they appear.

Row 3: P4, Cr5B, Cr5F, P4.

Row 5: P2, Cr5B, P4, Cr5F, P2.

Row 7: P2, K3, P8, K3, P2.

Row 9: P2, Cr5F, P4, Cr5B, P2.

Row 11: P4, Cr5F, Cr5B, P4.

Row 12: Rep Row 2.

These 12 rows form panel.

INSTRUCTIONS

Note: When working separate sections of colors, wind small balls of the colors to be used, (or wind yarn bobbins) one for each area of color in the design. Start new colors as indicated in instructions. To change colors, twist the two colors around each other where they meet, on wrong side, to avoid a hole.

RIBBING

Starting at bottom of hat with MC and smaller needles CO 98 (106) sts.

Row 1 (right side): K2, *P2, K2; rep from * to end of row.

Row 2: P2; *K2, P2; rep from * to end of row.

Rep Rows 1 and 2 until work measures 3" ending by working Row 2 and inc 6 (10) sts evenly across last row: 104 (116) sts.

BODY

Change to larger needles and proceed in patt as follows:

Row 1 (right side): With MC, P1. Work Row 1 of panel patt. Attach A, and with A, K33 (39). Attach second MC, and with MC, work Row 1 of panel patt. With MC knit to end of row.

Row 2: With MC, P2, (MK) 16 (19) times. Work Row 2 of panel patt. With A, P33 (39). With MC, work Row 2 of panel patt, K1.

Row 3: With MC, P1. Work Row 3 of panel patt. With A, P3,(K3, P3) 5 (6) times. With MC, work Row 3 of panel patt. Attach B and with B, knit to end of row.

Row 4: With B, P1, (MK) 16 (19) times, P1. With MC, work Row 4 of panel patt. With A, (K3, P3) 5 (6) times, K3. With MC, work Row 4 of panel patt, K1.

Row 5: With MC, P1. Work Row 5 of panel patt. With A, P3,(K3, P3) 5 (6) times. With MC, work Row 5 of panel patt. With MC knit to end of row.

Row 6: With MC, P2, (MK) 16 (19) times. Work Row 6 of panel patt. With A, P33 (39). With MC, work Row 6 of panel patt, K1.

Row 7: With MC, P1. Work Row 7 of panel patt. With A, K3, (P3, K3) 5 (6) times. With MC, work Row 7 of panel patt. With B, knit to end of row.

Row 8: With B, P1, (MK) 16 (19) times, P1. With MC, work Row 8 of panel patt. With A, (P3, K3) 5 (6) times, P3. With MC, work Row 8 of panel patt, K1.

Row 9: With MC, P1. Work Row 9 of panel patt. With A, K3, (P3, K3) 5 (6) times. With MC, work Row 9 of panel patt. With MC knit to end of row.

Row 10: With MC, P2, (MK) 16 (19) times. Work Row 10 of panel patt. With A, P33 (39). With MC, work Row 10 of panel patt, K1.

Row 11: With MC, P1. Work Row 11 of panel patt. With A, P3,(K3, P3) 5 (6) times. With MC, work Row 11 of panel patt. With B, knit to end of row.

Row 12: With B, P1, (MK) 16 (19) times, P1. With MC, work Row 12 of panel patt. With A, (K3, P3) 5 (6) times, K3. With MC, work Row 12 of panel patt, K1.

Row 13: With MC, P1. Work Row 1 of panel patt. With A, P3,(K3, P3) 5 (6) times. With MC, work Row 1 of panel patt. With MC knit to end of row.

Row 14: With MC, P2, (MK) 16 (19) times. Work Row 2 of panel patt. With A, P33 (39). With MC, work Row 2 of panel patt, K1.

Row 15: With MC, P1. Work Row 3 of panel patt. With A, K3, (P3, K3) 5 (6) times. With MC, work Row 3 of panel patt. With B, knit to end of row.

Row 16: With B, P1, (MK) 16 (19) times, P1. With MC, work Row 4 of panel patt. With A, (P3, K3) 5 (6) times, P3. With MC, work Row 4 of panel patt, K1.

Row 17: With MC, P1. Work Row 5 of panel patt. With A, K3, (P3, K3) 5 (6) times. With MC, work Row 5 of panel patt. With MC knit to end of row.

Row 18: With MC, P2, (MK) 16 (19) times. Work Row 6 of panel patt. With A, P33 (39). With MC, work Row 6 of panel patt, K1.

Row 19: With MC, P1. Work Row 7 of panel patt. With A, P3, (K3, P3) 5 (6) times. With MC, work Row 7 of panel patt. With B, knit to end of row.

Row 20: With B, P1, (MK) 16 (19) times, P1. With MC, work Row 8 of panel patt. With A, (K3, P3) 5 (6) times, K3. With MC, work Row 8 of panel patt, K1.

Row 21: With MC, P1. Work Row 9 of panel patt. With A, P3, (K3, P3) 5 (6) times. With MC, work Row 9 of panel patt. With MC knit to end of row.

Row 22: With MC, P2, (MK) 16 (19) times. Work Row 10 of panel patt. With A, P33 (39). With MC, work Row 10 of panel patt, K1.

Row 23: With MC, P1. Work Row 11 of panel patt. With A, K3,(P3,K3) 5 (6) times. With MC, work Row 11 of panel patt. With B, knit to end of row.

Row 24: With B, P1, (MK) 16 (19) times, P1. With MC, work Row 12 of panel patt. With A, (P3. K3) 5 (6) times. P3. With MC, work Row 12 of panel patt, K1.

Row 25: With MC, P1. Work Row 1 of panel patt. With A, K3,(P3,K3) 5 (6) times. With MC, work Row 1 of panel patt. Knit to end of row.

Row 26: With MC, P2, (MK) 16 (19) times. Work Row 2 of panel patt. With A, P33 (39). With MC, work Row 2 of panel patt, K1.

Rows 27 through 34: Rep Rows 3 through 10.

Rows 35 through 42: Rep Rows 11 through 18.

Row 43: With MC, P1, (K2tog) 9 times. With A, P3, (K3, P3) 5 (6) times. With MC, (K2tog) 9 times. With B, knit to end of row: 86 (98) sts.

Row 44: With B, P2, (P2tog) 16 (19) times. With MC, P9. With A, (P2tog) 16 (19) times. P1. With MC, P10: 54 (60) sts.

Cut yarn, leaving a long end. Thread end into yarn needle and draw through rem sts and fasten securely. Sew center back seam, reversing seam for cuff turn back.

POMPON

With MC and following pompon instructions on page 200, make a 3" pompon and sew to top of hat.

#47 FOR A PONYTAIL MISS

Designed by Sandy Scoville

SIZE
Fits 21" to 23" head

MATERIALS
Worsted weight yarn,
2 1/2 oz blue
12 yds tan
12 yds celery
12 yds red

Note: Photographed model made with Red Heart® Plush™ #9823 French Blue, #9627 Light Sage, and #9907 Red; and TLC® Amoré, #3220 Wheat

14" Size 9 (5.5mm) knitting needles (or size required for gauge)

GAUGE
15 sts = 4" in stockinette st (knit one row, purl one row) with two strands of yarn held tog.

INSTRUCTIONS

Knit with two strands of yarn held tog.

BOTTOM RIBBING

With two strands of blue, cast on 75 sts.

Row 1 (right side): K1; *P1, K1; rep from * across.

Row 2: P1; *K1, P1; rep from * across.

Rep Rows 1 and 2 until ribbing measures 1¼".
End by working a wrong-side row.

BODY

Row 1 (right side): Knit.

Row 2: Purl.

Join tan. Do not cut blue. Carry unused strands along side edge.

Row 3: With tan, K2, sl 1 as to knit, *K4, sl 1 as to knit; rep from * to last 2 sts; K2.

Row 4: P2, sl 1 as to purl, *P4, sl 1 as to purl; rep from * to last 2 sts; P2.

Row 5: With blue, Knit.

Row 6: Purl.

Rows 7 and 8: Rep Rows 5 and 6.

Rows 9 and 10: Join celery. Do not cut blue or tan. With celery, rep Rows 3 and 4.

Rows 11 through 14: With blue, rep Rows 5 and 6 twice.

Rows 15 and 16: Join red. Do not cut other colors. With red, rep Rows 3 and 4. Cut red.

Row 17: With blue, K4, K2tog; (K3, K2tog) 13 times, K4: 61 sts.

Row 18: Purl.

Row 19: Knit.

Row 20: Purl.

Row 21: With celery, K2, sl 1 as to knit, *K3, sl 1 as to knit; rep from * to last 2 sts; K2. Cut celery.

Row 22: P2, sl 1 as to purl, *P3, sl 1 as to purl, rep from * to last 2 sts; P2.

Row 23: With blue, K2tog; (K2, K2tog) 14 times; K3: 46 sts.

Row 24: Purl.

Row 25: Knit.

Row 26: Purl.

Row 27: With tan, K1, *sl 1 as to knit, K2; rep from * around.

Row 28: *P2, sl 1 as to purl; rep from * to last st, P1. Cut tan.

Rows 29 to 32: With blue, rep Rows 5 and 6 twice.

Row 33: K1, (YO, K2tog) 22 times; YO, K1: 47 sts.

Row 34: Purl.

Rows 35 and 36: Rep Rows 5 and 6.

TOP RIBBING

Row 1: K1; *P1, K1; rep from * across.

Row 2: P1, *K1, P1; rep from * across.

Rep Rows 1 and 2 until top ribbing measures 1½".

BO in ribbing.

FINISHING

With right sides tog, sew back seam, reversing seam for top ribbing for fold over.

#48 KNITTER'S DELIGHT

SIZE
Fits 20" (21") head

Note: The instructions are written for small size; changes for large are in parentheses.

MATERIALS
Worsted weight yarn,
1¹/₂ oz rose (Color A)
¹/₂ oz beige (Color B)
¹/₂ oz oatmeal
(Color C)

Note: Photographed model made with Patons® Canadiana, #013 Cranberry (A), #304 Beige (B), and #105. Oatmeal (C)

14" Size 11 (8mm) knitting needles (or size required for gauge)

14" Size 9 (5.5mm) knitting needles

3 st markers or small safety pins

GAUGE
20 sts = 4" in pattern stitch with larger needles

SPECIAL NOTES

Slip all slipped sts as to purl.

Carry colors not in use loosely up side of work.

SPECIAL ABBREVIATIONS

YF: yarn forward, as to purl

YB: yarn in back, as to knit

INSTRUCTIONS

CUFF

With smaller needles, cast on 81 (85) sts with Color A. Knit eight rows.

BODY

Row 1 (right side): With larger size needles and Color B, K 1; *YF, sl 1, YB, K 1; rep from * across.

Row 2: With Color C, sl 1; *P 1, YB, sl 1, YF; rep from * across.

Row 3: With Color A, rep Row 1.

Row 4: With Color B, rep Row 2.

Row 5: With Color C, rep Row 1.

Row 6: With Color A, rep Row 2.

Rep Rows 1 through 6 for pattern.

Continue working in pattern until piece measures about 5" (6") from cast-on row, ending by working a wrong-side row.

SHAPE TOP

Join, or continue with, Color A. Cut other colors; work only with Color A from now on.

Row 1: K 5, K 2 tog, knit across: 80 (84) sts.

Row 2: *P 20 (21), place a marker on needle; rep from * two times more; P 20 (21).

Row 3: K 2 tog; *knit to 2 sts before marker, K 2 tog; sl marker, K 2 tog; rep from * 2 times more; knit to last 2 sts, K 2 tog: 72 (76) sts.

Row 4: Purl

Rep Rows 3 and 4 until 24 (28) sts rem, ending by working a purl row.

Next Row: *K 2 tog; rep from * across: 12 (14) sts.

Next Row: *P 2 tog; rep from * across: 6 (7) sts.

Cut yarn, leaving a 26" end; thread yarn into a tapestry needle and draw through rem sts, drawing up tightly.

Fold hat with right sides tog; carefully matching rows, sew back seam to beg of cuff. Turn work right side out and sew seam at cuff. Finish off. Weave in yarn ends.

#49 RAPUNZEL

Designed by Doris Chan

SIZE
Fits child's head size 18"
to 19"

MATERIALS
Bulky weight bouclé
yarn,
2$^{1}/_{2}$ oz for hat

Worsted weight yarn,
3 oz for hair

*Note: Photographed
model made with Lion
Brand Bouclé #201
Sprinkles and Lion Brand
Wool-Ease® #158
Buttercup*

Size N (9mm) crochet
hook (or size required
for gauge)

Size K (6.5mm) crochet
hook (for attaching
hair)

Stitch marker or small
safety pin

GAUGE
8 sc = 4" with larger
hook and bouclé yarn,

8 sc rows = 4"

STITCH GUIDE

Front Post single crochet (FPsc): Insert hook from front to back to front around post (vertical bar) of specified sc, YO and draw lp through; YO and draw through both lps on hook: FPsc made.

INSTRUCTIONS

HAT

Starting at top with bouclé yarn and larger hook, ch 2.

Rnd 1 (right side): 6 sc in 2nd ch from hook; do not join, place marker to indicate beg of rnds; move marker as you complete a rnd, through Rnd 5.

Rnd 2: 2 sc in each sc: 12 sc.

Rnd 3: (Sc in next sc, 2 sc in next sc) 6 times: 18 sc.

Rnd 4: (Sc in next 2 sc, 2 sc in next sc) 6 times: 24 sc.

Rnd 5: (Sc in next 3 sc, 2 sc in next sc) 6 times: 30 sc.

Rnd 6: (Sc in next 4 sc, 2 sc in next sc) 6 times: 36 sc; join with a sl st in beg sc, ch 1, turn, remove marker. Piece should measure 6" in diameter.

Rnd 7: Ch 1, FPsc in each sc around, join in beg sc; ch 1, turn.

Rnds 8 through 10: Sc in each sc around, join in beg sc; ch 1, turn.

Rnd 11: Sc in each sc around, join, finish off; weave in ends.

HAIR

Hair strands are knotted in the last rnd of sc as you would make fringe (see Fringe Instructions on page 200).

Cut 76 strands of worsted weight yarn, each 44" long, and two 10" long strands for tying braids. If yarn is kinky, steam lightly.

Hold hat with last row at top and with right side facing you. In center back sc, with smaller hook, tie a knot using 4 strands of yarn. Using two strands of yarn in each knot, tie a knot in each of the next 17 sc. In center front sc, tie a knot with 4 strands; in rem 17 sc, tie a knot with 2 strands.

Divide fringe on each side into 3 sections of 6, 6, and 7 strands and braid loosely, taking half the strands from the center back and front knots. Center braid 1" toward back of hat. Tie ends of braid with 10" strand to secure.

FINISHING

Trim ends of braids. Adding hair stretches out the bottom of hat; a rnd of sl st allows some adjustment for fit.

With right side facing, working in same direction as it was crocheted, with bouclé and larger hook, join yarn with sl st in same sc as finished off. Keeping hair out of the way, sl st in each sc (same sc as used for hair), join, finish off.

CROCHET
#50 PIPPI

Designed by Doris Chan

SIZE

Fits child's head size 18" to 19"

MATERIALS

Bulky weight boucle yarn, 2¹/₂ oz for hat

Worsted weight yarn, 3 oz for hair

Note: Photographed model made with Lion Brand Bouclé, #203 Jelly Bean and Lion Brand Wool-Ease® #102 Ranch Red)

Size N (9mm) crochet hook or size required for gauge

Size K (6.5mm) crochet hook (for attaching hair)

Stitch marker or small safety pin

GAUGE

8 sc = 4" with larger hook and bouclé yarn,

8 sc rows = 4"

STITCH GUIDE

Front Post single crochet (FPsc):
Insert hook from front to back to front around post (vertical bar) of specified sc, YO and draw lp through; YO and draw through both lps on hook: FPsc made.

INSTRUCTIONS

HAT

Starting at top with bouclé yarn and larger hook, ch 2.

Rnd 1 (right side): 6 sc in 2nd ch from hook; do not join, place marker to indicate beg of rnds through Rnd 5.

Rnd 2: 2 sc in each sc: 12 sc

Rnd 3: (Sc in next sc, 2 sc in next sc) 6 times: 18 sc

Rnd 4: (Sc in next 2 sc, 2 sc in next sc) 6 times: 24 sc

Rnd 5: (Sc in next 3 sc, 2 sc in next sc) 6 times: 30 sc

Rnd 6: (Sc in next 4 sc, 2 sc in next sc) 6 times: 36 sc; join with a sl st in beg sc, ch 1, turn, remove marker. Piece should measure 6" in diameter.

Rnd 7: Ch 1, FPsc in each sc around, join with sl st in beg sc, ch 1, turn.

Rnds 8 through 10: Sc in each sc around, join; ch 1, turn.

Rnd 11: Sc in each sc around, join; finish off, weave in ends.

HAIR (1¼" bangs, 9" braids)

Hair strands are knotted in the last rnd of sc as you would make fringe (see Fringe Instructions on page 200.)

Cut 16 strands of worsted weight yarn 8" long for bangs; cut 56 strands 30" long for braids; cut 2 strands 10" long for tying braids. If yarn is kinky, steam lightly.

Hold hat with last row at top and right side facing you.

For bangs, hold tog two 8" pieces of yarn and fold in half; using smaller crochet hook, draw lp through any sc of last row, then draw strands through lp and tighten knot. Rep in next 7 sc: 8 bang fringes made.

In rem 28 sc, hold tog 2 strands of 30" length, make fringe for braids in same manner.

Divide braid fringes, half (14) on each side of hat.

Divide each half into 3 sections of 5, 4 and 5 strands and braid loosely, centering braid slightly to back of hat. Wrap one 10" yarn strand tightly around braid end several times, knot to secure, tuck ends into braid. Make other braid same way.

FINISHING

Trim bangs to desired length, trim ends of braids evenly.

Adding hair stretches out the bottom of hat. A rnd of sl st allows some adjustment for fit.

With right side of hat facing, working in the same direction as it was crocheted, with boucle and larger hook join with sl st in same sc as finished off. Keeping hair out of the way, sl st in each sc (same sc as used for hair), join, finish off.

#51 BEAUTIFUL IN BLACK

Designed by Nancy Brown for Judi & Co

SIZE

Fits up to 22" head

MATERIALS

Raffia yarn,
200 yds black

Note: Photographed model made with Judi & Co Raffia, color black

Size H (5mm) crochet hook (or size required for gauge)

2 stitch markers or small safety pins

GAUGE

7 hdc = 2"

INSTRUCTIONS

Ch 4, join with a sl st to form a ring.

Rnd 1: 8 hdc in ring; do not join, mark beg of rnds.

Rnd 2: 2 hdc in each st around: 16 hdc.

Rnd 3: 2 hdc in each st around: 32 hdc.

Rnd 4: Work around in hdc, increasing 6 hdc evenly spaced on each rnd.

Rep Rnd 4 until piece measures 6" in diameter ending with a multiple of 4 sts; mark last rnd.

Next Rnd: Dc in each hdc.

BRIM

Rnd 1: *Hdc in each of next 3 sts, 2 hdc in next st; rep from * around.

Rnds 2 through 5: Hdc in each hdc. Finish off, weave in ends.

TIE

With 2 strands of yarn held together, make a ch about 30" long; finish off, weave in ends.

Weave tie through dc rnd, adjust for size, knot and finish off

CABBAGE ROSE TRIM

Ch 4, join with a sl st to form a ring.

Rnd 1: Ch 1, 10 sc in ring, join in beg ch-1.

Rnd 2: Ch 2, sk next sc; *sl st in next sc, ch 2, sk next sc; rep from * around, join in beg sc: 5 ch-2 lps.

Rnd 3: *(Sl st, ch 2, 4 dc, ch 2, sl st) in next ch-2 sp; rep from * around, join: 5 petals made.

Rnd 4: Working behind petals, *sl st in next skipped sc on Rnd 2, ch 3; rep from * around, join: 5 ch-3 lps.

Rnd 5: (Sl st, ch 2, 7 dc, ch 2, sl st) in each ch-3 sp, join: 5 petals made.

Rnd 6: Working behind petals, *sc around next ch lp of Rnd 4, next to center dc on next petal, ch 4; rep from * around: ending join with sl st: 5 ch-4 lps.

Rnd 7: *(Sl st, ch 2, 10 dc, ch 2, sl st) in next ch-4 lp; rep from * around; join, finish off, leaving a 6" yarn end for sewing.

FINISHING

Sew rose to hat over tie knot.

#52 FUR TRIMMED BERET

Designed by Nancy Brown

SIZE

Fits up to 23" head

MATERIALS

Sport weight yarn, 400 yds

Eyelash yarn, 50 grams

Note: Photographed model made with Silk City Fibers Kashmir #926 Foxglove and Patons® Cha Cha |#2006 Jazz

Size H (5mm) crochet hook (or size required for gauge)

Size G (4mm) crochet hook

Stitch marker

GAUGE

8 hdc = 2" with larger hook and 2 strands of sport weight yarn

6 hdc rows = 2"

STITCH GUIDE

To decrease in hdc, (YO, draw up a lp in next st) twice, YO and draw through 4 lps on hook: hdc 2 tog made.

INSTRUCTIONS

With 2 strands of sport weight yarn and larger hook, ch 2.

Rnd 1: 8 hdc in 2nd ch from hook; do not join, mark beg of rnds.

Rnd 2: 2 hdc in each st around: 16 hdc.

Rnd 3: * Hdc in next st, 2 hdc in next st; rep from * around: 24 hdc.

Rnd 4: * Hdc in each of next 2 sts, 2 hdc in next st; rep from * around: 32 hdc.

Rnd 5: * Hdc in each of next 3 sts, 2 hdc in next st; rep from * around: 40 hdc.

Rnds 6 through 14: Continue in this manner, adding 8 more sts each on each rnd; at end of Rnd 14: 112 hdc.

Rnds 15 and 16: Hdc in each hdc.

Rnd 17 (decrease rnd): * Hdc in each of next 12 sts, hdc 2 tog; rep from * around: 104 hdc.

Rnd 18: * Hdc in each of next 11 sts, hdc 2 tog; rep from * around: 96 hdc.

Rnds 19 and 20: Continue in this manner, decreasing 8 sts each rnd; at end of Rnd 20: 80 hdc.

Rnd 21: Working in BLO, hdc in each st around: 80 hdc.

Rnds 22 and 23: Working in both lps, hdc in each st around. At end of Rnd 23, join with sl st in next st; ch 1, do not turn.

Rnd 24: Working in BLO, * sk 1 st to the right, 1 reverse sc in next st to right, ch 1; rep from * around, finish off, weave in ends.

TRIM

Top Rnd: Hold piece with right side facing. With one strand of eyelash yarn and smaller hook, join yarn with sc in FLO of first st at end of Rnd 21. *Ch 1, working from left to right, sk 1 st, sc in next st; rep from * around, join in beg sc; finish off.

Bottom Rnd: Rep Top Rnd, working in Rnd 23.

Weave in ends.

FLOWER

With two strands of sport weight and larger hook, ch 2.

Rnd 1: 5 sc in 2nd ch from hook, join in beg sc; finish off.

Rnd 2: With larger hook, join eyelash yarn in FLO of any sc, ch 5, sl st in same st; * sl st in FLO of next st, ch 5, sl st in same st; rep from * around: 5 ch-5 lps.

Rnd 3: Working in BLO, sl st in next sc, ch 9, sl st in same st; * sl st in BLO of next st, ch 9, sl st in same st; rep from * around: 5 ch-9 lps. Finish off, leaving a long yarn end for sewing.

Sew flower to beret trim at left side.

#53 ROSY OUTLOOK

Designed by Nancy Brown

SIZE
Fits up to 22" head

MATERIALS
DK weight yarn, 100g (240 yds) dark rose, 50g (120 yds) medium rose

Note: Photographed model made with Bryspun Kid-n-Ewe.

Size H (5mm) crochet hook (or size required for gauge)

stitch marker or small safety pin

GAUGE
8 hdc = 2"

6 hdc rows = 2"

STITCH GUIDE

Reverse sc (rev sc): Ch 1; *insert hook in next st to the right (instead of left) of hook and draw up a lp; YO and draw through both lps on hook; rep from *, working to the right instead of the left. This gives a corded edge.

INSTRUCTIONS

HAT

With dark rose, ch 2.

Rnd 1: 8 hdc in 2nd ch from hook; do not join, mark beg of rnds and move marker as you work.

Rnd 2: 2 hdc in each st around: 16 hdc.

Rnd 3: 2 hdc in each st around: 32 sts.

Rnd 4: Work around in hdc, increasing 6 hdc evenly spaced on each rnd.

Rep Rnd 4 until piece measures about 6" in diameter, ending with a multiple of 4 sts; mark last rnd.

After last rnd, leave marker in work.

Work even in hdc until piece measures about 2½" from marker; change to medium rose in last st, sl st in next st, ch 1, turn. Do not cut dark rose; carry until it is used again.

CONTRAST BAND

Rnd 1: *Sc in next st, dc in next st; rep from * around, join with sl st in beg sc; ch 3, turn.

Rnd 2: *Sc in next dc, dc in next sc; rep from * around, join with sl st in 3rd ch of beg ch-3; ch 1, turn.

Rnd 3: Rep Rnd 1.

Rnd 4: Rep Rnd 2.

Rnd 5: Rep Rnd 1,

Finish off medium rose; pick up dark rose and work 1 hdc in each st around, do not join or turn. Piece should measure about 4" from marker.

Next Rnd: Dc in each hdc around.

BRIM

Rnd 1: *Hdc in each of next 3 dc, 2 hdc in next dc; rep from * around.

Rnd 2: *Hdc in each of next 4 hdc, 2 hdc in next hdc; rep from * around.

Rnds 3 and 4: Hdc in each st around. At end of Rnd 4, ch 1.

Rnd 5: Working in reverse single crochet, *sk 1 st to right, sc in next st to right, ch 1; rep from * around, finish off.

TIE

With 2 strands of dark rose, ch about 30". Fasten off. Thread tie through dc rnd just before brim. Adjust for fit, and knot tie; trim ends to desired length.

ROSE

With medium rose, ch 4, join with a sl st to form a ring.

Rnd 1: Ch 3, 9 dc in ring, join with sl st in 3rd ch of beg ch-3.

Rnd 2: Ch 1, sc in same st, sc in each dc around, ending with sc in first st: 10 sc.

Rnd 3: Ch 2, sk next st; *sc in next st, ch 2, sk next st; rep from * around, ending with sl st in first sc: 5 ch-2 lps.

Rnd 4: *In next ch-2 lp work (sl st, ch 2, 5 dc, ch 2, sl st); rep * around: 5 petals made.

Rnd 5: Working behind petals, *sc in next skipped sc on Rnd 2, ch 4; rep from * around, join in first sc: 5 ch-4 lps.

Rnd 6: *In next ch-4 lp work (sl st, ch 2, 7 dc, ch 2, sl st) in next ch-4 lp; rep from * around: 5 petals.

Rnd 7: Working behind petals, *sc around ch-4 lp of Rnd 5 next to the center dc on next petal, ch 5; rep from * around, join in first sc: 5 ch-5 lps.

Rnd 8: *Work (sl st, ch2, 9dc, ch2, sl st) in next ch-5 lp; rep from * around, join in beg sl st: 5 petals. Finish off, leaving a long yarn end for sewing.

FINISHING

Weave in all ends. Sew rose to hat as shown in photo.

#54 FUNNY STRIPES

Designed by Patons Design Staff

SIZE

12 months, 18 months, 2 years

Note: Instructions are written for size 12 months; changes for larger sizes are in parentheses

MATERIALS

DK weight yarn,
1 3/4 oz pink (MC)
1 3/4 oz lilac (A)
1 3/4 oz blue (B)

Note: Photographed model made with Patons®Astra #2210 Pink (MC), #2216 Lilac(A) and #8742 Ultra Blue (B)

14" Size 5 (3.75mm) knitting needles

14" Size 6 (4mm) knitting needles (or size required for gauge)

GAUGE

22 sts = 4" with larger needles in stockinette st (knit one row, purl one row)

INSTRUCTIONS

With MC and smaller needles, cast on 83 (87, 91) sts.

Row 1(right side): K1; *P1, K1; rep from * to end of row.

Row 2: P1; *K1, P1; rep from * to end of row.

Rep Rows 1 and 2 until piece measures 2", ending by working a Row 2; on final row, inc 4 (0, 1) sts: 87 (87, 92) sts.

BODY

Change to larger needles; cut MC and join B.

Row 1 (right side): With B, knit.

Row 2: Purl.

Rows 3 through 6: Rep Rows 1 and 2 twice. At end of Row 6, cut B and join MC.

Rows 7 through 12: With MC, rep Rows 1 and 2 three times. At end of Row 12, cut MC and join A.

Rows 13 through 18: With A, rep Rows 1 and 2 three times. At end of Row 18, cut A, and join MC.

Rows 19 through 24: With MC, rep Rows 1 and 2 three times. At end of Row 24, cut MC, and join B.

Rep Rows 1 through 24 until work measures 6 1/2" (7", 7 1/2") from cast-on row, ending by working a wrong-side row.

SHAPE TOP

Continue in stripe pattern as established.

Row 1: K1; *K2tog, K15 (15, 16); rep from * to last st, K1: 82 (82, 87) sts.

Row 2: P1; *P14 (14, 15), P2tog; rep from * to last st, P1: 77 (77, 82) sts.

Row 3: K1; *K2tog, K13 (13, 14); rep from * to last st, K1: 72 (72, 77) sts.

Row 4: P1; *P12 (12, 13), P2tog; rep from * to last st, K1: 67 (67, 72) sts.

Row 5: K1; *K2tog, K11 (11, 12); rep from * to last st, K1: 62 (62, 67) sts.

Row 6: P1; *P10 (10, 11), P2tog; rep from * to last st, P1: 57 (57, 62) sts.

Row 7: K1; *K2tog, K9 (9, 10); rep from * to last st, K1: 52 (52, 57) sts.

Row 8: P1; *P8 (8, 9), P2tog; rep from * to last st: 47 (47, 52) sts.

Row 9: K1; *K2tog, K7 (7, 8); rep from * to last st, K1: 42 (42, 47) sts.

Row 10: P1; *P6 (6, 7), P2tog; rep from * to last st, P1: 37 (37, 42) sts.

Row 11: K1; *K2tog, K5 (5, 6); rep from * to last st, K1: 32 (32, 37) sts.

Row 12: P1; *P4 (4, 5), P2tog; rep from * to last st: 27 (27, 32) sts.

Row 13: K1; *K2tog, K3 (3, 4); rep from * to last st, K1: 22 (22, 27) sts.

Row 14: P1; *P2 (2, 3), P2tog; rep from * to last st, P1: 17 (17, 22) sts.

Row 15: K1; *K2tog, K1 (1, 2); rep from * to last st, K1: 12 (12, 17) sts.

Cut yarn leaving a long end. Thread yarn into a yarn needle and draw through rem sts. Fasten off securely.

Sew back seam, reversing seam for turn back.

TIES AND EARFLAPS (make 2)

Ties

With larger needles and MC cast on 6 (8, 8) sts.

Row 1 (right side): K2, (Pl, K1) 2 (3, 3) times.

Row 2: K2, (Pl, K1) 2 (3, 3) times.

Rep Rows 1 and 2 for 10 (10, 11)", ending by working a wrong- side row.

Earflap shaping

Row 1: Inc 1 st in first st; work K1, P1 ribbing to last 2 sts, inc 1 st in next st, K1: 8 (10, 10) sts.

Row 2: P1, work K 1, P1 ribbing to last st, P1

Rep last 2 rows until there are 20 (22, 22) sts; work even in ribbing for 8 rows; bind off in ribbing.

Place markers on last row of ribbing of hat, at each side 2" from center back seam. Sew earflaps to inside of hat along last row of ribbing, beg at markers.

POMPON

Following instructions on page 200, make a 3" diameter pompon, using 4 lengths of MC, 1 length of A, and 1 length of B. Sew pompon to top of Hat.

#55 FLIRTY FLAPPER

Designed by Marty Miller

SIZE
Fits up to 20" head

MATERIALS
Worsted weight yarn,
3 1/2 oz lavender
1 1/2 oz lime

Novelty fur-type yarn
1/4 oz variegated

Note: Photographed model made with Patons® Katrina #10315 Iris, #10712 Limon and Patons® Cha Cha #02002 Vegas

Size H (5mm) crochet hook (or size required for gauge)

GAUGE
4 sc = 1" in worsted weight yarn

Rnds 1 through 4 = 2 1/2" diameter

STITCH GUIDE

Front Post Puff Stitch (FPPS): YO, insert hook from front to back to front around post of specified sc, YO and pull up a lp; (YO, insert hook from front to back to front around post of same st, YO and pull up a lp) 3 times; YO and pull through all 9 lps on hook: FPPS made.

INSTRUCTIONS

HAT

With lavender, ch 2.

Rnd 1: 6 sc in 2nd ch from hook: 6 sc; join with sl st in first sc.

Rnd 2: Ch 1, 2 sc in same sc as joining, 2 sc in each sc around: 12 sc; join as before.

Rnd 3: Ch 1, 2 sc in same sc as joining, sc in next sc; *2 sc in next sc, sc in next sc; rep from * around: 18 sc; join.

Rnd 4: Ch 1, 2 sc in same sc as joining, sc in next 2 sc; *2 sc in next sc, sc in next 2 sc; rep from * around: 24 sc; join.

Rnd 5: Ch 1, 2 sc in same sc as joining, sc in next 3 sc; *2 sc in next sc, sc in next 3 sc; rep from * around: 30 sc; join.

Rnds 6 through 15: Continue in pattern as established, inc 6 sc evenly spaced in each rnd: 90 sc at end of Rnd 15; join.

Rnds 16 through 24: Ch 1, sc in same sc as joining, sc in each sc around; join.

Rnd 25: Ch 1, sc in same sc as joining, sc in each sc around; join lime with sl st in first sc, finish off lavender.

Rnd 26: With lime, ch 1, sc in same sc as joining, sc in each sc around; join.

Rnd 27: Ch 4 (counts as first dc and ch-1 sp), skip 1 sc; *FPPS in next sc, ch 1, skip 1 sc, dc in next sc, ch 1, skip 1 sc; rep from * around: 23 dc, 22 FPPS; join with sl st in 3rd ch of beg ch-4.

Rnd 28: Ch 1, sc in same ch as joining, sc in each st around, including ch 1: 90 sc; join with sl st in first sc.

Rnd 29: Rep Rnd 27.

Rnd 30: Rep Rnd 28; join lavender with sl st in first sc, finish off lime.

Rnd 31: With lavender, ch 3 (counts as first dc), dc in same sc as joining, dc in next 14 sc; *2 dc in next sc, dc in next 14 sc; rep from * around: 96 dc; join with sl st in first dc.

Rnd 32: Ch 3 (counts as first dc), dc in same st as joining, dc in next 15 dc; *2 dc in next dc, dc in next 15 dc; rep from * around: 102 dc; join as before.

Rnd 33: Ch 3 (counts as first dc), dc in same st as joining, dc in next 16 dc; *2 dc in next dc, dc in next 16 dc; rep from * around: 108 dc; join.

Rnd 34: *Ch 3, sc in 3rd ch from hook, ch 1, skip 2 dc, sl st in next dc; rep from * around, end with sl st in joining sl st. Finish off and weave in ends.

FLOWER

With one strand each of lime and variegated, ch 2.

Rnd 1: 6 sc in 2nd ch from hook: 6 sc; join with sl st in first sc.

Rnd 2: Ch 1, 2 sc in same sc as joining, 2 sc in each sc around: 12 sc; join as before.

Rnd 3: Ch 1, sc in same sc as joining, ch 2, skip 1 sc; *sc in next sc, ch 2, skip 1 sc; rep from * around: 6 sc and 6 ch-2 sp; join.

Rnd 4: (Sc, hdc, dc, tr, dc hdc, sc) in first ch-2 sp: petal made; work petal in each ch-2 sp around: 6 petals; join. Finish off and weave in ends.

Fold bottom edge of hat up on one side as desired. Pin or sew flower to folded side of hat as shown in photograph.

#56 PLEASE THINK IT'S MINK

Designed by Jean Leinhauser

SIZE

Fits up to 22" head

MATERIALS

Super bulky weight chenille yarn, 3oz

Note: Photographed model made with Lion Brand Chenille Thick & Quick® #126 Soft Brown

Size K (6.5mm) crochet hook (or size required for gauge)

GAUGE

4 dc = 2"

INSTRUCTIONS

Ch 4.

Rnd 1: 5 dc in 4th ch from hook: 6 dc, counting beg skipped chs as a dc; join in top of beg ch.

Rnd 2: Ch 3, dc in joining; 2 dc in each rem st around: 12 dc.

Rnd 3: Ch 3, 2 dc in next dc; *dc in next dc, 2 dc in next dc; rep from * around, join: 18 dc.

Rnd 4: Ch 3, dc in next dc, 2 dc in next dc; *dc in next 2 dc, 2 dc in next dc; rep from * around, join: 24 dc.

Rnd 5: Ch 3, dc in next 2 dc, 2 dc in next dc; *dc in next 3 dc, 2 dc in next dc; rep from * around: 30 dc; join.

Rnds 6 through 9: Ch 3, dc in each dc around, join.

Rnds 10 and 11: Ch 1, sc in each dc around, join.

At end of Rnd 11, finish off, weave in ends.

#57 STRAWBERRY BONNET

Designed by Sandy Scoville

SIZE
Fits 18" head

MATERIALS
Bulky weight eyelash-type yarn,
2¹/₂ oz variegated pinks

Note: Photographed model made with Crystal Palace Splash® #9219 Strawberry Soda

14" Size 9 (5.5mm) straight knitting needles (or size required for gauge)

1¹/₂ yds ⁵/₈" pink satin ribbon

sewing needle

pink thread to match ribbon color

GAUGE
16 sts = 4" in stockinette st (knit one row, purl one row)

INSTRUCTIONS

Cast on 64 sts.

Row 1 (wrong side): Beginning at front edge, purl.

Row 2 (right side): Knit.

Rep Rows 1 and 2 until piece measures 5¹/₂", ending by working a wrong-side row.

BACK CROWN SHAPING

Row 1 (right side): K2 tog tbl; knit to last 2 sts; K2 tog: 62 sts.

Row 2: Purl.

Rows 3 through 8: Rep rows 1 and 2 three times more. At end of Row 8: 56 sts.

Row 9: Knit.

Row 10: Purl.

Rows 11 and 12: Rep Rows 9 and 10. Bind off loosely, leaving an 18" end.

FINISHING

Step 1: Fold piece in half lengthwise with right sides tog; hold with folded bound-off edge at top; with long yarn end and tapestry needle, sew back seam. Turn right side out.

Step 2: Fold cast-on edge back one inch on outside to form border; tack in place at sides.

Step 3: Cut ribbon into two 18" lengths and two 6" lengths. Tie short lengths into bows. Tack one long length and one bow to side edges at border.

#58 BURGUNDY STRIPES

Designed by Nancy Brown

SIZE
Fits up to 23" head

MATERIALS
Worsted weight yarn,
200 yds black
200 yds burgundy

Note: Photographed model made with Yeoman Yarns Sport #3 Black and #29 Garnet

Size H (5mm) crochet hook (or size required for gauge)

Stitch marker or small safety pin

GAUGE
7 hdc = 3"

3 hdc rows = 1"

INSTRUCTIONS

Note: Hat is worked with two strands of yarn held together throughout.

With 2 strands of black, ch 4, join with a sl st to form a ring.

Rnd 1: Ch 2 (counts as first hdc of rnd throughout), 7 hdc in ring: 8 hdc; join with sl st in beg ch-2.

Rnd 2: Ch 2, hdc in joining; 2 hdc in each hdc around: 16 hdc; join in beg ch-2; drop black, join burgundy (note: do not cut yarn not in use; carry loosely up inside hat until it is used again).

Rnd 3: With 2 strands of burgundy, ch 2, hdc in joining; 2 hdc in each hdc around: 32 hdc; join in beg ch-2; drop burgundy, pick up black.

Rnd 4: With black, work in dc, inc 6 hdc evenly spaced around: 38 hdc; join.

Rnd 5: Rep Rnd 4; at end of rnd, drop black, pick up burgundy.

Continue repeating Rnd 4, alternating one rnd of burgundy with two rnds of black, until piece measures 6¹/₂" in diameter; place marker in this row.

Now work even in hdc, continuing stripe pattern, until piece measures about 4¹/₂" from marker; finish off burgundy, continue with black only.

BRIM

Rnd 1: *Hdc in next 5 sts, 2 hdc in next st; rep from * around, ending hdc in last 2 sts, join.

Rnds 2 through 5: Hdc in each st around, join. At end of Rnd 5, finish off, weave in ends.

FLOWERS (make 2)

For petals, with two strands of burgundy, ch 2.

Rnd 1 (right side): 7 sc in 2nd ch from hook; do not join.

Rnd 2: (Sl st, ch 1, 7 dc, ch 1, sl st) in each sc around: 7 petals made. Finish off.

For center, with two strands of burgundy, ch 2.

Rnd 1: 3 sc in 2nd ch from hook.

Rnd 2: Sc in each sc around, finish off; tie yarn ends tog to close center.

FINISHING

Sew Petal units to hat, one above the other, as shown in photo; sew one center unit in middle of each petal unit. Weave in all ends.

#50 PERKY PEAK

Designed by Patons Design Staff

SIZE

Small fits child 3-6 months

Large fits child 12-18 months

Note: Instructions are written for small size; changes for large size are in parentheses.

MATERIALS

DK weight yarn, 3 1/2 oz ombre 1 1/2 oz yellow

Note: Photographed model made with Patons® Astra #88761 Kool Aid Ombre and #2943 Maize Yellow

14" Size 5 (3.75mm) knitting needles (or size required for gauge)

Stitch holder

GAUGE

24 sts = 4" in stockinette st (knit one row, purl one row)

32 rows = 4"

INSTRUCTIONS

EARFLAPS (make 2)

CO 9 sts.

Row 1 (wrong side): Knit.

Row 2: K1, inc in next st (knit in front and back of st), knit to last 2 sts, inc in next st, K1: 11 sts.

Row 3 and all uneven rows: Knit.

Row 4: Rep Row 2: 13 sts.

Row 6: Rep Row 2: 15 sts.

Row 8: Rep Row 2: 17 sts.

Row 10: Rep Row 2: 19 sts.

For larger size hat only

Row 12: Rep Row 2: 21 sts.

For both sizes

Continue working in garter st (knit every row) until earflap measures 2$\frac{1}{2}$" (2$\frac{3}{4}$"), ending by working a wrong-side row. Cut yarn at end of last row on First Earflap and put sts on st holder. Do not cut yarn at end of Second Earflap, continue with this yarn to Body.

BODY

With right side of Second Earflap facing, CO 10 (11) sts. Knit across these sts and 19 (21)sts of Second Earflap. CO 26 (28) sts. Knit across 19 (21) sts of First Earflap. CO 10 (11) sts: 84 (92) sts.

Work even in garter st across all sts until work measures 3$\frac{1}{4}$" (3$\frac{1}{2}$") from last cast-on row, ending by working a wrong-side row.

SHAPE TOP

Row 1: K2 (3); *K2tog, K5 (4); rep from * to last 5 sts, K2tog, K3: 72 (77) sts.

Rows 2 through 6: Knit.

Row 7: K2 (3); *K2tog, K4 (3); rep from * to last 4 sts, K2tog, K2: 60 (62) sts.

Rows 8 through 12: Knit,

Row 13: K2 (3); *K2 tog, K3 (2); rep from * to last 3 sts, K2tog, K1: 48 (47 sts).

Rows 14 through 24: Knit

Row 25: K0 (2); *K2tog, K1; rep from * to last 3 sts, K2tog, K1: 32 sts.

Rows 26 through 36: Knit.

Row 37: K1; *K2tog; rep from * to last 3 sts, K2tog, K1: 17 sts.

Rows 38 through 40: Knit.

Row 41: K1;*K2tog; rep from * to end of row: 9 sts.

Cut yarn, leaving a long end. Thread yarn into yarn needle and draw through rem sts and fasten securely. Sew center back seam.

POMPONS

With yellow and following pompon instructions on page 200, make two 2" pompons and sew to bottom of ear flaps.

#60 RAFFIA CLOCHE

Designed by Rona Feldman for Judi & Co

SIZE
Fits up to 21" head

MATERIALS
Raffia yarn,
100 yds black
100 yds white

Note: Photographed model made with Judi & Co. raffia

Size F (3.75mm) crochet hook (or size required for gauge)

GAUGE
5 (dc, ch-1) units = 2"

STITCH GUIDE

Reverse sc (rev sc): Ch 1; * insert hook in next st to the right (instead of left) of hook and draw up a lp; YO and draw through both lps on hook; rep from *, working to the right instead of the left. This gives a corded edge.

INSTRUCTIONS

With black, ch 4, join with a sl st to form a ring.

Rnd 1: Ch 1, 9 sc in ring, join with sl st in beg sc.

Rnd 2: Ch 1, 2 sc each st: 18 sc; join with sl st in beg sc.

Rnd 3: Ch 3; * (dc, ch 1) twice in next sc, sk next sc; rep from * around, join with sl st in third ch of beg ch-3; drop black, do not cut; join white.

Note: Colors change every row; carry color not in use loosely up inside.

Rnd 4: With white, ch 3; (dc, ch 1) in each ch-1 sp around, join as before; drop white, pick up black.

Rnd 5: With black, ch 3; * (dc, ch 1) in next 2 ch-1 sps, (dc, ch1) twice in next ch-1 sp; rep from * around, join; drop black, pick up white.

Rnd 6: With white, ch 3; * (dc, ch 1) in next 3 ch-1 sps; (dc, ch 1) twice in next ch-1 sp; rep from * around, join.

Continuing to alternate one rnd of black with one rnd of white:

Rnd 7: Ch 3, (dc, ch 1) in each ch-1 sp around, join.

Rnds 8 through 11: Rep Rnd 7.

Rnd 12: Continuing with black, ch 1, work rev sc in each dc, skipping ch-1 sps; join, finish off, weave in ends.

CROCHETED FLOWER

With white, ch 4, join with a sl st to form a ring

Rnd 1: Ch 3 (counts as a dc), 9 dc in ring, join with sl st in 3rd ch of beg ch-3: 10 dc.

Rnd 2: Ch 1, sc in same st, sc in each dc around, join with sl st to first sc: 10 sc.

Rnd 3: *Ch 2, skip next st, sc in next sc; rep from * around, sc in joining sl st of Rnd 2: 5 ch-2 lps.

Rnd 4: (Sl st, ch 2, 4 dc, ch 2, sl st) in each ch-2 sp around: 5 petals made; drop white, join black.

Rnd 5: With black and working behind petals, ch 1, * sc in back lp of next skipped sc on Rnd 3, ch 4; rep from * around, join with sl st in first sc: 5 ch-4 lps.

Rnd 6: Continuing with black, (sl st, ch 2, 7 dc, ch 2, sl st) in each ch-5 lp around: 5 petals made; join; finish off.

Rnd 7: Working behind petals of Rnd 6, join white with a sl st at bottom back of center dc of any petal on Rnd 6; *ch 5, sl st at bottom back of center dc of next petal on Rnd 6; rep from * 3 times more, ch 5, join with sl st in beg sl st.

Rnd 8: In each ch-5 sp work (sl st, ch 2, 7 dc, ch 2, sl st): petal made; join with sl st in beg sl st. Finish off white.

Rnd 9: Working behind petals of Rnd 8, join black with a sl st as before in back of center dc of any petal on Rnd 8; *ch 6, sl st at bottom back of center dc of next petal on Rnd 8; rep from * 3 times more, ch 6, join with sl st in beg sl st.

Rnd 10: In each ch-6 sp work (sl st, ch 2, 9 dc, ch 2, sl st): petal made; join with sl st in beg sl st; finish off, leaving a 6" yarn end for sewing.

Weave in all ends, sew flower to side of cloche as shown in photo.

#61 TEEN'S SKI CAP

Designed by Jenny King

SIZE
Fits 18" to 20" head

MATERIALS
DK weight yarn, 50 g (190 yds) mauve; 25 g (100 yds) each of red, hot pink, aqua and yellow

Size H (5mm) crochet hook (or size required for gauge)

2 stitch markers or small safety pins

GAUGE
10 dc = 2"

STITCH GUIDE

Front Post dc (FPdc): YO, insert hook around the post (vertical bar) of specified st from front to back to front; YO, pull lp through, (YO and pull through 2 lps) twice: FPdc made.

dc2tog: (YO, insert hook in next st and draw up a lp; YO and draw through first 2 lps on hook) twice; YO and draw through all 3 lps on hook: dc2tog made

INSTRUCTIONS

With mauve, ch 4.

Rnd 1: 11 dc in 4th ch from hook, join with a sl st to form a ring: 12 dc, counting beg ch-4 as a st.

Rnd 2: Ch 3, dc in base of ch; 2 dc in each dc around, join with sl st in 3rd ch of beg ch-4: 24 dc.

Rnd 3: Ch 3, dc in base of ch, dc in next dc; *2 dc in next dc, dc in next dc; rep from * around, join: 36 dc.

Rnd 4: Ch 3, dc in base of ch, dc in next 2 dc; *2 dc in next dc, dc in next 2 dc; rep from * around, join: 48 dc.

Rnd 5: Ch 3, dc in base of ch, dc in next 3 dc; *2 dc in next dc, dc in next 3 dc; rep from * around: 60 dc.

Rnd 6: Ch 3, dc in each dc around, join.

Rnd 7: Ch 3, dc in base of ch, dc in next 4 dc; *2 dc in next dc, dc in next 4 dc; rep from * around: 72 dc

Next section (Rows 8 through 23, below) is worked alternating sc sts with FPdc sts. Stripe pattern begins now in following color sequence:

*1 row red, 1 row mauve,

1 row pink, 1 row mauve,

1 row aqua, 1 row mauve,

1 row yellow, 1 row mauve.

Rep color sequence from * twice. Do not cut yarns; carry colors not in use loosely up side.

Rows 8 through 23: Following color sequence, sc in first st, FPdc around next st; *sc in next st, FPdc around next st; rep from * around, join.

Rows 24 through 27: Continue in pattern, work 1 row red, 1 row pink, 1 row aqua, and 1 row yellow; finish off.

EARFLAPS

First Flap: Hold piece with last row at top and place markers in the first and 29th sts to mark ear flap placement.

Row 1: Join mauve with sc in first marked st; (FPdc around next st, sc in next st) 7 times, ch 1, turn: 15 sts.

Row 2: Sc in first st, ch 1, dc across; ch 1, turn.

Row 3: Sc in first st; *FPdc around next st, sc in next st; rep from * across, ch 1, turn.

Row 4: Skip first st, sc in next st, ch 1; dc2tog, dc to last 4 sts, dc2tog twice, ch 1, turn: 11 sts.

Row 5: Rep Row 3.

Rows 6 and 7: Rep Rows 4 and 5: 7 sts at end of Row 7.

Row 8: Skip first st; sc in next st, ch 1; 5dctog (YO and draw up a lp in next st, YO and draw through first 2 lps on hook) 5 times, YO and draw through all rem lps, ch 35 for tie; finish off.

Second Flap: Join mauve with sc in the next marked st and work as for First Flap.

EDGING

With right side facing, join mauve with sc at last st of one of the ties, sc in each of the 35 chs, sc along side of earflap; across hat edge, work in (sc, FPdc) across to maintain pattern; sc around next earflap, sc in each ch of last tie, working 3 sc in last ch; work up opposite side of tie, and continue in this manner around to beg; finish off, weave in ends.

#62 LITTLE CRUSHER

Designed by Rona Feldman for Judi & Co

SIZE
Fits 16" to 18" head

MATERIALS
Raffia yarn,
100 yds hot pink
100 yds pink

Note: Photographed model made with Judi & Co. Raffia, hot pink and pink

Size F (3.75mm) crochet hook (or size required for gauge)

Size E (3.5mm) crochet hook for flower trim

Stitch marker or small safety pin

GAUGE
7 sc = 2"

INSTRUCTIONS

With larger hook and hot pink, ch 3, join with a sl st to form a ring.

Rnd 1: Ch 1, 8 sc in ring; join with sl st in beg sc.

Rnd 2: Ch 1, 2 sc in each sc: 16 sc; from here on, do not join unless otherwise specified; mark beg of rnds and move marker up as you work.

Rnd 3: *Sc in next sc, 2 sc in next sc; rep from * to last st, change to pink in last st: 24 sc.

Rnd 4: *Sc in next 2 sc, 2 sc in next sc; rep from * around: 32 sc.

Rnd 5: Sc in each sc around.

Rnd 6: *Sc in next 3 sc, 2 sc in next sc; rep from * around: 40 sc.

Rnd 7: Sc in each sc around.

Rnd 8: *Sc in next 4 sc, 2 sc in next sc; rep from * around: 48 sc.

Rnds 9 through 14: Sc in each sc around.

Rnd 15: Sc in each sc around, changing to hot pink in last st.

Rnds 16 through 20: Continuing with hot pink, sc in each sc.

Rnd 21: Ch 3 (counts as a dc), dc in each sc around, join with sl st in 3rd ch of beg ch.

Rnd 22: Ch 1; *sc in next 2 dc, 2 sc in next dc; rep from * around: 64 sc; do not join.

Rnd 23: Sc in each sc around.

Rnd 24: *Sc in next 3 sc, 2 sc in next sc; rep from * around: 80 sc; join in beg sc.

Rnd 25: Ch 1; *sl st in next sc, sc in next sc, hdc in next sc, 2 dc in next sc, dc in next sc, hdc in next sc, sc in next sc, sl st in next sc; rep from * around, join with sl st in beg sl st. Finish off, weave in ends.

FLOWER

With smaller hook and hot pink, ch 6, join with sl st to form a ring.

Rnd 1: 14 sc in ring, join with sl st in beg sc.

Rnd 2: Working in FLO, (sc, ch 6, sc) in each sc around, join.

Rnd 3: Working in BLO, (sc, ch 8, sc) in each sc around; join, finish off. Lightly steam flower to separate lps; sew to top of hat.

#63 POSH POMPONS

Designed by Jenny King

SIZE
Fits up to 23" head

MATERIALS
DK weight yarn,
100 gms (294 yds) navy (MC)
50 gms (147 yds) turquoise (C1)
50 gms (147yds) white (C2)

Note: Photographed model made with Sirdar Silky Look

4 stitch markers or small safety pins

Size G (4mm) crochet hook or size required for gauge

GAUGE
10 sts = 2" in pattern (sc in next st, FPdc around next st)

STITCH GUIDE

Front Post dc (FPdc): YO, insert hook around the post (vertical bar) of specified st from front to back to front; YO, pull lp through, (YO and pull through 2 lps) twice: FPdc made.

Front Post sc (FPsc): Insert hook from front to back to front around post (vertical bar) of specified st, YO and draw up a lp, YO and draw through both lps on hook: FPsc made.

INSTRUCTIONS

With MC, ch 4,

Rnd 1: 11 dc in 4th ch from hook, join with a sl st to form a ring: 12 dc, counting beg 3 skipped chs as a dc.

Rnd 2: Ch 3, dc in base of ch, 2 dc in each st around, join with a sl st in third ch of beg ch-3: 24 dc.

Rnd 3: Ch 3, dc in base of ch, dc in next st; * 2 dc in next st, dc in the next st; rep from * around: 36 dc; join as before.

Rnd 4: Ch 3, dc in base of ch, dc in each of next 2 sts; * 2 dc in next st, dc in each of next 2 sts; rep from * around: 48 dc; join.

Rnd 5: Ch 3, dc in base of ch, dc in each of next 3 sts; * 2 dc in next st, dc in each of next 3 sts; rep from * around to last st, change to Color 1 (C1) in last st: 60 dc; join.

Note: Do not cut colors not in use; carry them loosely up side of work.

Rnd 6: Sc in the first st, FPdc around next st; *sc in next st, FPdc around next st; rep from * around, join in beg sc.

Rnd 7: Ch 1, sc in first st, FPdc around next st; * sc in next st, FPdc around next st; rep from * around, join Main Color (MC) in last st: 60 sts; join.

Rnd 8: With MC, ch 3, dc in base of ch, dc in each of next 4 sts; * 2 dc in next st, dc in each of next 4 sts; rep from * around: 72 sts; join in 3rd ch of beg ch-3.

Rnd 9: Ch 3, dc in base of ch, dc in each of next 5 sts; * 2 dc in next st, dc in each of next 5 sts; rep from * around, changing to Color 2 (C2) in last st: 84 dc; join.

Rnds 10 and 11: With C2, rep Rnd 6.

Rnds 12 through 33: Rep Rnd 6 in the following color sequence:

*1 row MC, 1 row C1, 1 row MC, 1 row C2; rep from * ending by working a C1 row. Finish off at end of last row.

EARFLAPS

Place 4 markers in st 1, st 14, st 33 and st 66 to indicate earflaps. Flaps are worked over 19 sts each, and separated by 33 sts at front of hat and by 13 sts at back of hat.

RIGHT EARFLAP

Hold hat with right side facing you, and join MC in first of the 19 flap sts at the second marker.

Row 1: Ch 2, sc in same st; *FPdc around next st, sc in next st; rep from * to the next marker: 19 sts; turn.

Row 2: Ch1 , *sc in first st, dc in next st; rep from * across, ending sc in last st, turn.

Row 3: Ch 1, sc in first st; * FPdc around next st, sc in next st; rep from * across, turn.

Row 4: Ch 1, skip first st, sc in next st, ch 1;

dc2tog [to work dc2tog: (YO, draw up a lp in next st, YO and draw through first 2 lps on hook) twice, YO and draw through all rem lps: decrease made]; dc in each st to last 4 sts, dc2tog twice: 15 sts, turn.

Row 5: Ch 1, sc in first st; *FPdc around next st; sc in next st; rep from * across, turn.

Rows 6 through 9: Rep Rows 4 and 5, two times more: 7 sts rem.

Row 10: Ch 1, sc in first st, ch 2; work dc5tog decrease over next 5 sts [to work dc5tog decrease: (YO, draw up lp in next st, YO and draw through first 2 lps on hook) 5 times; YO and draw through all rem lps on hook]; ch 40 for neck tie, finish off, leaving a 6" yarn tail for joining pompon.

LEFT EARFLAP

Skip 33 sts at front to last maker, join MC and work as for Right Earflap. Finish off.

EDGING

Working in one continuous rnd, join MC at end of one of the neck ties, ch 1; sc in each of the 40 chs, sc evenly along side of the ear flap, alternate sc and FPsc along the edge to keep in pattern, sc evenly around other ear flap, sc in each ch of the next tie, working 3 sc in the last ch; sc in unused lps of other side of tie, continue in this manner around, ending sc in unused lps of last neck tie, 2 sc in last ch, join in beg sc, finish off. Weave in all ends.

POMPONS

Following Pompon instructions on page 200, make three 4" diameter pompons with MC; sew one to top of hat and one at bottom of each neck chain.

#64 PINWHEEL CAP

Designed by Patons Design Staff

SIZE

Fits up to 20" head

MATERIALS

DK weight yarn,
1 3/4 oz dark purple
(MC)
1 oz ultramarine (A)
1 oz bright green (B)

*Note: Photographed
model made with
Patons® Astra #02740
Purple, #08742 Ultra
Blue and #2911
Spring Green*

Size F (3.75mm) cro-
chet hook (or size
required for gauge)

3 stitch markers or
small safety pins

GAUGE

9 sc = 2"

STITCH GUIDE

Single crochet 2 sts tog (sc2tog): Draw up a lp in each of next 2 sts, YO and draw through all 3 lps on hook: sc2tog decrease made.

INSTRUCTIONS

With MC, ch 23.

First Section

Row 1 (right side): Sc in 2nd ch from hook and in each rem ch: 22 sc; turn.

Row 2: Sl st in first 2 sc, sc in each rem sc: 20 sc; ch 1, turn.

Row 3: Sc in each of first 18 sc, sl st in next sc; leaving next sc unworked, ch 1, turn: 18 sc.

Row 4: Sl st in first 2 sc, sc in each rem sc: 16 sc; ch 1, turn

Row 5: Sc in each of first 15 sc, sl st in next sc, ch 1, turn.

Row 6: Rep Row 4: 13 sc.

Row 7: Sc in first 11 sc, sl st in next sc, ch 1, turn: 11 sc.

Row 8: Sk first sl st, sl st in first sc, sc in each rem sc: 10 sc; ch 1, turn.

Row 9: Sc in first 8 sc, sl st in next sc: 8 sc; ch 1, turn.

Row 10: Rep Row 8: 7 sc.

Row 11: Sc in each of first 5 sc, sl st in next sc: 5 sc; ch 1, turn.

Row 12: Sk first sl st, sl st in first sc, sc in next 4 sc, joining B in last st: 4 sc; ch 1, turn.

Second Section

Row 1: With B, sc in first 4 sc, then work 18 sc evenly along rem edge of First Section: 22 sc.

Rows 2 through 12: Work as for First Section, ending by joining MC in last st; ch 1, turn.

Third Section

With MC, work as given for Second Section, ending by joining A in last st; ch 1, turn.

Fourth Section

With A, work as for Second Section, ending by joining B in last st; ch 1, turn.

Fifth Section

With B, work as for Second Section, ending with joining MC in last st; ch 1, turn.

Sixth Section

With MC, work as for Second Section, ending by joining A in last st; ch 1, turn.

Seventh Section

With A, work as for Second Section, ending by joining B in last st; ch 1, turn.

Eighth Section

With B, work as for Second Section 2; at end of Rnd 12, finish off, leaving a long yarn end for sewing.

With wrong sides tog, place edges of First Sections and Eighth Section together and sew to join. Weave in all ends.

LOWER BAND

Hold cap with right side facing and long edge at top. Join MC with sl st in any st.

Rnd 1: Ch 1, sc in joining; work 87 sc evenly spaced around edge: 88 sc; join with sl st in beg sc.

Rnd 2: Ch 1, sc in joining; sc in each sc around, changing to B in last sc; join, cut MC.

Rnd 3: With B, ch 1, sc in joining, sc in next 2 sc; *sc in BLO of next sc, sc in next 3 sc; rep from * around to last sc, sc in BLO of last sc, join.

Rnd 4: Ch 3 (counts as first dc of rnd), dc in each sc around, changing to A in last st: 88 dc; join in 3rd ch of beg ch-3.

Rnd 5: With A, ch 1, sc in joining; sc in BLO of next dc, sc in next dc; * tr in rem FLO of sc 2 rows below, sk next dc (behind tr)**; sc in next dc, sc in BLO of next dc, sc in next dc; rep from * around, ending at **; join in beg sc.

Rnd 6: Ch 3, dc in each st around, joining MC in last st; join in 3rd ch of beg dc; cut A.

Rnd 7: With MC, ch 1, sc in joining; tr in rem FLO of sc 2 rows below; sk next dc (behind tr); *sc in next 3 dc, tr in rem FLO of sc 2 rows below, sk next dc (behind tr); rep from * around, end sc in last 2 dc; join in beg sc, finish off and mark for center back.

EARFLAPS

Count 9 sts on right side from center back and mark for start of right earflap; mark 26th st on left side from center back for start of left earflap.

First Earflap

With right side of work facing and last rnd at top, join MC with sl st in one of the marked earflap sts.

Row 1: Ch 1, sc in joining and in each of next 17 sts: 18 sc; ch 1, turn.

Row 2: Sc2tog over first 2 sts, sc in each st to last 2 sts, sc2tog over last 2 sts: 16 sc; ch 1, turn.

Row 3: Sc in each sc across, ch 1, turn.

Row 4: Rep Row 2: 14 sts; ch 1, turn.

Row 5: Rep Row 3.

Rows 6 through 9: Rep Rows 4 and 5 in sequence; at end of Row 9: 10 sc; ch 1, turn.

Row 10: Rep Row 3.

Rows 11 and 12: Rep Row 2: 6 sc. At end of Row 11, finish off.

Second Earflap

With right side of work facing, join MC with sl st in rem marked earflap st. Complete as for First Earflap.

EDGING

Join MC with sl st in st marked for center back; ch 1, sc in same st; sc around entire outer edge of cap, including side of first earflap to last 4 earflap sts, sc in first 2 earflap sts, ch 60; sc in 2nd ch from hook and in each rem ch , sc in next 2 earflap sts; continue in sc around other edge of earflap and around entire outer edge to next earflap, work next earflap same as first; sc in each rem st around, join in beg sc at center back.

Finish off, weave in all ends.

#65 TERRIFIC TAM

Designed by Susan McCreary

SIZE
Fits up to 20" head

MATERIALS
Bulky weight yarn,
3 oz multi-colored

Note: Photographed model made with Lion Brand Homespun® #360 Mardi Gras

Size K (6.5mm) crochet hook (or size required for gauge)

GAUGE
5 sc = 2"

4 pattern rows
(sc, sc, dc, sc) = 2"

INSTRUCTIONS

Ch 5, join with sl st to form ring.

Rnd 1: 9 sc in ring: 9 sc; join with sl st in first sc.

Rnd 2: Ch 1, 2 sc in same sc as joining, 2 sc in each sc around: 18 sc; join as before.

Rnd 3: Ch 3 (counts as first dc), dc in same sc as joining, 2 dc in each sc around: 36 dc; join with sl st in 3rd ch of beg ch-3.

Rnd 4: Ch 1, sc in same ch as joining, sc in each dc around; join with sl st in first sc.

Rnd 5: Ch 1, 2 sc in same sc as joining, 2 sc in each sc around: 72 sc; join as before.

Rnd 6: Ch 3 (counts as first dc), dc in each sc around; join with sl st in 3rd ch of beg ch-3.

Rnd 7: Rep Rnd 4.

Rnd 8: Ch 1, sc in same sc as joining, sc in each sc around; join with sl st in first sc.

Rnds 9 through 11: Rep Rnds 6 through 8.

Rnds 12 and 13: Rep Rnds 6 and 7.

Rnd 14: Ch 1, sk first sc, sc in next 5 sc, *sk next sc, sc in next 5 sc; rep from * around: 60 sc; join with sl st in first sc.

Rnd 15: Ch 1, sk first sc, sc in next 4 sc, *sk next sc, sc in next 4 sc; rep from * around: 50 sc; join.

Rnds 16 and 17: Rep Rnd 8 twice. At end of Rnd 17, finish off and weave in ends.

#66 ON A ROLL

Designed by Jean Leinhauser

SIZE
Fits up to 23" head

MATERIALS
Bulky weight yarn
5 oz off white

Note: Photographed model made with Lion Brand Wool-Ease® Thick & Quick®, #099 Fisherman

Stitch marker or small safety pin

Size N (10 mm) crochet hook (or size required for gauge)

GAUGE
4 dc = 2"

INSTRUCTIONS

Ch 5, join to form a ring.

Rnd 1: Ch 1, 12 sc in ring, join with sl st in first sc.

Rnd 2: Ch 2 (counts as first dc throughout), dc in base of ch; working in BLO, 2 dc in each sc: 24 dc; join in 2nd ch of beg ch.

Rnd 3: Ch 2, working in BLO, 2 dc in next dc; *dc in next dc, 2 dc in next dc; rep from * around: 36 dc; join.

Rnds 4 through 6: Ch 2, working in BLO, dc in each dc, join.

BRIM

Rnd 1: Working in both lps from here on, ch 1; *sc in next 7 dc, 2 sc in next sc; rep from * three times more, sc to end: 40 sc; do not join, mark beg of rnds.

Rnd 2: Sc in each sc; do not join.

Rep Rnd 2 until Brim measures 3"; sl st in last st, finish off. Weave in ends.

Roll up brim as shown in photo.

#67 FAUX FUR

Designed by Nancy Brown

SIZE

Fits up to 22" head

MATERIALS

Sport weight yarn,
300 yards red

Eyelash yarn,
300 yards red

Note: Photographed model made with Silk City Fibers Wool Crepe #620 Raspberry and Silk City Fibers Ultra Lash #873 Merlot

Stitch marker or small safety pin

Size J (6mm) crochet hook (or size required for gauge)

GAUGE

6 hdc = 2" with 1 strand of each yarn held together

6 rows = 2"

INSTRUCTIONS

With 1 strand of each yarn held tog, ch 2.

Rnd 1: 8 hdc in 2nd ch from hook; do not join, mark end of rnds.

Rnd 2: 2 hdc in each hdc around: 16 hdc.

Rnd 3: 2 hdc in each hdc around: 32 hdc.

Rnd 4: Work around in hdc increasing 5 hdc evenly spaced around.

Rep Rnd 4 until piece measures about 7" in diameter; leave marker in work at end of last row.

Work even in hdc until piece measures about 3¹/₂" from marker.

Next Rnd: Dc in each hdc around.

BRIM

Rnd 1: Hdc in each dc around.

Rnds 2 through 7: Hdc in each hdc around.

Rnd 8: Sl st in each hdc; finish off, weave in ends.

TIE

With 2 strands of each yarn held tog (4 strands in all), make a ch about 30" long. Weave ch through dc rnd just before Brim. Adjust for size and knot. Trim ends to desired length.

#68 LITTLE GIRL'S FLOWER CLOCHE

Designed by Rona Feldman for Judi & Co.

SIZE
Fits up to 18" head

MATERIALS
Raffia yarn,
200 yds multi color

Note: Photographed model made with Judi & Co. raffia, Malibu

Size F (3.75mm) crochet hook for hat (or size required for gauge)

Size E (3.5mm) crochet hook for flower

Stitch marker or small safety pin

GAUGE
7 sc = 2" with larger hook

INSTRUCTIONS

With larger hook, ch 3; join with a sl st to form a ring.

Rnd 1: Ch 1, 8 sc in ring, join with sl st in beg sc.

Rnd 2: Ch 1, 2 sc in each sc around: 16 sc; do not join, mark beg of rnds.

Note: From here on, do not join rnds unless otherwise specified.

Rnd 3: *Sc in next sc, 2 sc in next sc; rep from * around: 24 sc.

Rnd 4: *Sc in next 2 sc, 2 sc in next sc; rep from * around: 32 sc.

Rnd 5: Sc in each sc around.

Rnd 6: *Sc in next 3 sc, 2 sc in next sc; rep from * around: 40 sc.

Rnd 7: Sc in each sc around.

Rnd 8: *Sc in next 4 sc, 2 sc in next sc; rep from * around: 48 sc.

Rnds 9 through 19: Sc in each sc around.

Rnd 20: Sc in each st around, join with sl st in beg sc.

Rnd 21: Ch 3 (counts as first dc of rnd), dc in each sc around, join in 3rd st of beg ch-3.

Rnd 22: Ch 1; *sc in next 2 dc, 2 sc in next dc; rep from * around, do not join.

Rnds 23 through 25: Sc in each sc around, do not join.

Rnd 26: Sc in each sc around, join with sl st in beg sc, turn.

Rnd 27: Ch 1; turn brim up so wrong side is facing (see photo) and work one sl st loosely in each sc around. Finish off, weave in ends.

FLOWER TRIM

With smaller hook, ch 4, join with a sl st to form a ring.

Rnd 1: Ch 3 (counts as a dc), 9 dc in ring: 10 dc; join in 3rd ch of beg ch-3.

Rnd 2: Ch 1, sc in joining; sc in each dc around, join in beg sc: 10 sc.

Rnd 3: *Ch 2, sk next sc, sc in next sc; rep from * around, sc in joining sl st of Rnd 2: 5 ch-5 lps.

Rnd 4: In each ch-5 lp work (sl st, ch 2, 4 dc, ch 2, sl st): 5 petals made.

Rnd 5: Working behind petals, ch 1; *sc in BLO of next skipped sc on Rnd 3, ch 4; rep from * around, join in beg sc: 5 ch-4 lps.

Rnd 6: In each ch-4 lp work (sl st, ch 2, 7 dc, ch 2, sl st): 5 petals made.

Finish off, leaving a long yarn end for sewing. Sew flower to hat as shown in photo.

#69 PRETTY IN PINK

Designed by Nancy Brown for Judi & Co

SIZE
Fits 21" to 23" head

MATERIALS
Raffia yarn,
300 yds pink (main color)
100 yds orange (contrast color)

Note: Photographed model made with Judi & Co Raffia, color Hot Pink(main color) and Orange(contrast color)

Size H (5mm) crochet hook (or size required for gauge)

Size E (3.5mm) crochet hook (for trim)

Stitch marker or small safety pin

GAUGE
8 hdc = 2" with larger hook

INSTRUCTIONS

With main color and larger hook, ch 4, join with a sl st to form a ring.

Rnd 1: Ch 1, 8 hdc in ring; join in top of beg hdc.

Rnd 2: Ch 2 (counts as a hdc), hdc in joining; 2 hdc in each hdc around: 16 hdc; join in beg hdc.

Rnd 3: Rep Rnd 2: 32 hdc.

Rnd 4: Ch 2 (counts as a hdc),hdc in next 2 hdc, 2 hdc in next hdc; *hdc in next 3 hdc, 2 hdc in next hdc; rep from * around: 40 dc; join.

Rnd 5: Ch 2, hdc in next 3 hdc, 2 hdc in next hdc; *hdc in next 4 hdc, 2 hdc in next hdc; rep from * around: 48 hdc; join.

Rnd 6: Ch 2, hdc in next 4 hdc, 2 hdc in next hdc; *hdc in next 5 hdc, 2 hdc in next hdc; rep from * around: 56 hdc, join.

Continue to inc 8 hdc evenly spaced on each rnd until piece measures 7" in diameter. Place a marker or safety pin in this rnd.

BODY

Rnd 1: Working in BLO only, ch 1, hdc in each hdc around, join.

Rnd 2: Working in both lps, ch 1, hdc in each hdc around, join.

Rep Rnd 2 until piece measures 2¼" from marked rnd; change to contrast color in last st. Work even in hdc with contrast color for 3 more rnds.

Next Rnd: Ch 3, dc in each hdc around, join; change to main color in last st, finish off contrast color.

BRIM

Rnd 1: Ch 2, hdc in next 2 sts, 2 hdc in next st; * hdc in next 3 sts, 2 hdc in next st; rep from * around, join.

Rnd 2: Ch 2, hdc in next 8 sts, 2 hdc in next st; *hdc in next 9 sts, 2 hdc in next st; rep from * around.

Rnds 3 and 4: Ch 2, hdc in each st around.

Rnd 5: Rep Rnd 2.

Rnd 6: Rep Rnd 3, change to contrast color in last st; join.

Rnd 7: Ch 1, turn; hdc in each st around, join.

Rnd 8: Sl st in BLO of each st around; finish off, weave in ends.

TIE

With 2 strands of contrast color and larger hook, make a chain about 32" long, finish off, weave in ends. Weave tie through dc rnd and adjust to fit.

BOW

With contrast color and smaller hook, ch 3.

Row 1: 3 sc in 2nd ch from hook, ch 1, turn.

Row 2: 2 sc in first sc, sc in next sc, 2 sc in last sc: 5 sc; ch 1, turn.

Row 3: 2 sc in first sc, sc to last sc, 2 sc in last sc: 7 sc; ch 1, turn.

Row 4: Rep Row 3: 9 sc; ch 1, turn.

Row 5: Sc in each sc, ch 1, turn.

Rep Row 5 until piece measures about 6"

Begin Decreases: to decrease: draw up a lp in each of next 2 sts, YO and draw through all 3 lps on hook: dec made.

Dec Row: Dec over first 2 sts, sc to last 2 sts, dec: 7 sts; ch 1, turn.

Rep Dec Row until 3 sts rem; draw up a lp in each of next 3 sts, YO and draw through all 4 lps on hook. Ch 1, sc in last st; sc evenly in sides of rows around entire piece, join, finish off and weave in ends.

BOW CENTER

With contrast color and smaller hook, ch 6.

Row 1: Sc in 2nd ch from hook and in each rem ch: 5 sc; ch 1, turn.

Row 2: Sc in each sc, ch 1, turn.

Rep Row 2 until piece measures about 1½"; finish off, leaving a long end for sewing.

FINISHING

Fold Bow Center around middle of bow, and sew in back, forming bow shape with long piece. Sew bow to hat as shown in photo.

#70 GLITZY BERET

Designed by Jean Leinhauser

SIZE
Fits up to 20" head

MATERIALS
Worsted weight mohair with metallic yarn,
50 grams (90 yds) black/grey/camel/white

Note: Photographed model made with Trendsetter Dune # 76

Size H crochet hook

GAUGE
7 dc = 2"

INSTRUCTIONS

Ch 5, join with a sl st to form a ring.

Rnd 1: Ch 3 (counts as first dc of rnd), 11 dc in ring: 12 dc; join with a slip st in 3rd ch of beg ch-3.

Rnd 2: Ch 3 (counts as a dc throughout), dc in joining (inc made); 2 dc in each dc around: 24 dc; join as before.

Rnd 3: Ch 3, 2 dc in next dc (inc made); *dc in next dc, inc in next dc; rep from * around: 36 dc; join.

Rnd 4: Ch 3, dc in next dc, inc in next dc; *dc in next 2 dc, inc in next dc; rep from * around: 48 dc; join.

Rnd 5: Ch 3, dc in next 2 dc, inc in next dc; * dc in next 3 dc, inc in next dc, rep from * around: 60 dc; join.

Rnd 6: Ch 3, dc in next 3 dc, inc in next dc; * dc in next 4 dc, inc in next dc; rep from * around: 72 dc; join.

Rnd 7: Ch 3, dc in next 4 dc, inc in next dc; * dc in next 5 dc, inc in next dc; rep from * around: 84 dc; join.

Rnd 8: Dc in each dc, join.

Note: To decrease (dec) on following rows: (insert hook in next st and draw up a lp) twice; YO and draw through all 3 lps on hook: dec made).

Rnd 9: Ch 1; * sc in next 5 dc, dec over next 2 dc; rep from * around: 72 sc; join.

Rnd 10: Ch 1; * sc in next 4 sc, dec over next 2 sc; rep from * around: 60 sc; join.

Rnd 11: Ch 1; * sc in next 3 sc, dec over next 2 sc; rep from * around: 48 sc; join, finish off. Weave in all ends.

#71 CUTIE'S CLOCHE

Designed by Jean Leinhauser

INSTRUCTIONS

HAT

With ombre yarn, ch 4; join with a sl st to form a ring.

Rnd 1: Ch 1, 8 sc in ring; join in beg sc.

Rnd 2: Ch 1, 2 sc in each sc around, join: 16 sc.

Rnd 3: Ch 3 (counts as a dc), 2 dc in next dc; *dc in next dc, 2 dc in next dc; rep from * around, join in 3rd ch of beg ch-3: 24 dc.

Rnd 4: Ch 3, dc in next dc, 2 dc in next dc; * dc in next 2 dc, 2 dc in next dc; rep from * around, join: 32 dc.

Rnd 5: Ch 3, dc in next 2 dc, 2 dc in next dc; *dc in next 3 dc, 2 dc in next dc; rep from * around: 40 dc.

Rnd 6: Ch 3, dc in next 3 dc, 2 dc in next dc; *dc in next 4 dc, 2 dc in next dc; rep from * around: 48 dc.

Rnds 7 through 10: Ch 3, dc in each dc around, join.

Rnd 11: Ch 1, sc in each dc around, join with sc in beg sc.

Rnd 12: *Ch 4, sk next sc, sc in next sc; rep from * around, join with sl st, finish off, weave in ends.

FLOWER

With solid color yarn, ch 4, join with a sl st to form a ring.

Rnd 1: Ch 1, in ring work (sc, hdc, 3 dc, hdc, sc) 4 times; join in beg sc, finish off, leaving a long yarn end for sewing; sew flower to hat as shown in photo.

#72 LOTS OF LOOPS

Designed by Susan McCreary

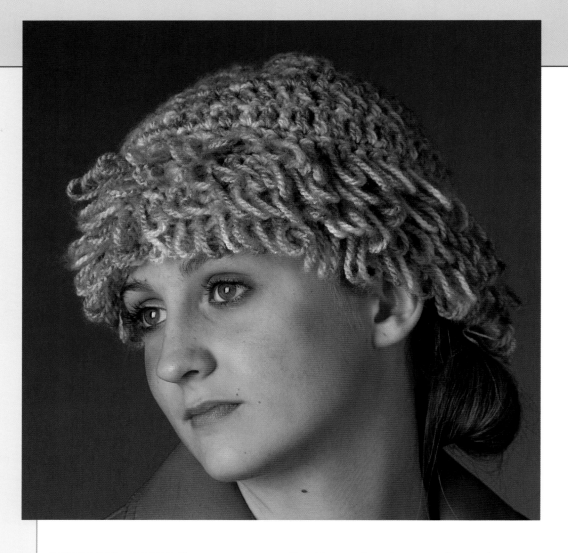

SIZE
Fits up to 24" head

MATERIALS
Chunky weight yarn,
3 oz multi-color

*Note: Photographed
model made with Lion
Brand Jiffy® #330 Salem*

Size K (6.5mm) cro-
chet hook (or size
required for gauge)

GAUGE
5 dc = 2"

4 dc rows = 3$^1/_2$"

STITCH GUIDE

Loop Stitch (Lp st): Insert hook in next sc, lp yarn over left index finger, pull base of left side of yarn through sc until lp measures 1$^1/_4$", drop this lp (2 lps on hook), YO and pull through both lps on hook: Lp st made.

Double crochet decrease (dc dec): (YO, insert hook in next st, YO and pull up a lp, YO and pull through 2 lps on hook) twice, YO and pull through all 3 lps on hook: dc dec made.

INSTRUCTIONS

Starting at bottom of hat, ch 61.

Row 1: Sc in 2nd ch from hook and in each ch across: 60 sc; ch 1, turn.

Row 2: Lp st in each sc across; ch 1, turn.

Row 3: Sc in each sc across; ch 1, turn.

Rows 4 through 7: Rep Rows 2 and 3 two times more.

Row 8: Rep Row 2.

Row 9: Sc in each sc across; ch 3 (counts as first dc on following row), turn.

Row 10: Dc in each sc across; ch 3, turn.

Row 11: (Dc dec in next 2 dc, dc in each of next 4 dc) 9 times, dc dec in next 2 dc, dc in each of next 3 dc; dc in 3rd ch of turning ch-3: 50 dc; ch 3, turn.

Row 12: (Dc dec in next 2 dc, dc in each of next 3 dc) 9 times, dc dec in next 2 dc, dc in each of next 2 dc; dc in 3rd ch of turning ch-3: 40 dc; ch 3, turn.

Rows 13 and 14: Dc in each dc across; ch 3, turn.

Note: On the following row, there will be 40 lps on the hook at the same time; be careful not to let the lps slide off the end of the hook.

Row 15: (YO, insert hook in next dc, YO and draw up a lp, YO and draw through first 2 lps on hook) 39 times: 40 lps rem on hook; YO and draw through all 40 lps, ch 1; finish off, leaving an 18" yarn end for sewing seam. Sew seam closed, weave in ends.

#73 FOR THE APPLE OF YOUR EYE

Designed by Patons Design Staff

SIZE
Fits 17" to 18" head

MATERIALS
DK weight yarn,
1/4 oz variegated (MC)
3/4 oz gold (A)
1/2 oz blue (B)
1/4 oz peach (C)

Note: Photographed model made with Patons® Grace #60901 Tangelo (MC), #60625 Sungold (A), #60733 Peacock (B) and #60451 Mango (C)

Size F (3.75mm) crochet hook (or size required for gauge)

Size E (3.5mm) crochet hook

GAUGE
20 dc = 4" with larger hook

10 dc rows = 4"

INSTRUCTIONS

With larger hook and C, ch 2.

Rnd 1: 6 sc in 2nd ch from hook: 6 sc; join with sl st in first sc.

Rnd 2: Ch 3 (counts as first dc), dc in same sc as joining, (3 dc in next sc, 2 dc in next sc) twice, 3 dc in next sc: 15 dc; join A with sl st in first dc. Finish off C and weave in ends.

Rnd 3: With A, ch 1, sc in same ch as joining, sc in next dc, (2 sc in next dc, sc in each of next 2 dc) 4 times, 2 sc in next dc: 20 sc; join with sl st in first sc.

Rnd 4: Ch 1, sc in same sc as joining, (2 sc in next sc, sc in next sc) 9 times, 2 sc in next sc: 30 sc; join B with sl st in first sc. Finish off A and weave in ends.

Rnd 5: With B, ch 1, working in BLO of each sc, sc in same sc as joining, sc in next sc, (2 sc in next sc, sc in each of next 2 sc) 9 times, 2 sc in next sc: 40 sc; join with sl st in first sc.

Rnd 6: Ch 3 (counts as first dc), dc in each of next 3 sc, (2 dc in next sc, dc in each of next 4 sc) 7 times, 2 dc in next sc: 48 dc; join A with sl st in first dc. Finish off B and weave in ends.

Rnd 7: With A, ch 1, sc in same ch as joining, sc in each of next 4 dc, (2 sc in next dc, sc in each of next 5 dc) 7 times, 2 sc in next dc: 56 sc; join with sl st in first sc.

Rnd 8: Ch 1, sc in same sc as joining, sc in each of next 5 sc, (2 sc in next sc, sc in each of next 6 sc) 7 times, 2 sc in next sc: 64 sc; join MC with sl st in first sc. Finish off A and weave in ends.

Rnd 9: With MC, ch 1, working in BLO of each sc, sc in same sc as joining, sc in each of next 6 sc, (2 sc in next sc, sc in each of next 7 sc) 7 times, 2 sc in next sc: 72 sc; join with sl st in first sc.

Rnd 10: Ch 3 (counts as first dc), dc in each of next 10 sc, (2 dc in next sc, dc in each of next 11 sc) 5 times, 2 dc in next sc: 78 dc; join A with sl st in first dc. Finish off MC and weave in ends.

Rnd 11: With A, ch 1, sc in same ch as joining, sc in each of next 11 dc, (2 dc in next dc, sc in each of next 12 dc) 5 times, 2 sc in next dc: 84 sc; join with sl st in first sc.

Rnd 12: Ch 1, sc in same sc as joining, sc in each sc around; join C with sl st in first sc. Finish off A and weave in ends.

Rnd 13: With C, ch 1, working in back lp only of each sc, sc in same sc as joining, sc in each sc around; join with sl st in first sc.

Rnd 14: Ch 3 (counts as first dc), dc in each sc around; join A with sl st in first dc. Finish off C and weave in ends.

Rnd 15: With A, ch 1, sc in same ch as joining, sc in each sc around; join with sl st in first sc.

Rnd 16: Ch 1, sc in same sc as joining, sc in each sc around; join B with sl st in first sc. Finish off A and weave in ends.

Rnd 17: With B, rep Rnd 13.

Rnd 18: With B, rep Rnd 14.

Rnd 19: With A, rep Rnd 15.

Rnd 20: Ch 1, sc in same sc as joining, sc in each of next 12 sc, (2 sc in next sc, sc in each of next 13 sc) 5 times, 2 sc in next sc: 90 sc; join with sl st in first sc. Finish off and weave in ends.

SCALLOP EDGING

With smaller hook, join MC with sl st in first sc on Rnd 20, ch 1, sc in same sc as joining, *sk next 2 sc, 7 dc in back lp of next sc, sk next 2 sc*; join B with sl st in back lp of next sc. Finish off MC and weave in ends.

With B, rep from * to * once; join C with sl st in back lp of next sc. Finish off B.

Continue working 7-dc scallops around alternating MC, B and C; join with sl st in beg sc. Finish off and weave in ends.

#74 JULIET CAP

Designed by Jean Leinhauser

SIZE
Fits up to 23" head

MATERIALS
Sport weight ribbon yarn, 1 3/4 oz (50 g) black

Sequin run-along yarn, 70 yds

Note: Photographed model made with Patons® Brilliant, #04940 Black Dazzle, and Berroco Lazer FX 6003 gold sequin

Stitch marker

Size F (3.75mm) crochet hook (or size required for gauge)

GAUGE
2 (hdc, ch 3, hdc) sps = 1 1/2"

INSTRUCTIONS

With ribbon yarn, ch 4, join with a sl st to form a ring.

Rnd 1: (Ch 3, hdc in ring) 4 times: 4 ch-3 lps; do not join, place marker to indicate beg of rnds.

Rnd 2: *Ch 3, (hdc, ch 3, hdc: increase made) in next lp; rep from * around: 8 ch-3 lps.

Rnd 3: Rep Rnd 2: 16 ch-3 lps.

Rnd 4: *Ch 3, hdc in next lp) 3 times, (ch 3, hdc) twice in next lp; rep from * around: 20 ch-3 lps.

Rnd 5: *(Ch 3, hdc in next lp) 4 times; (ch 3) twice in next lp; rep from * around: 24 ch-3 lps.

Rnd 6: *(Ch 3, hdc in next lp) 5 times; (ch 3, hdc) twice in next lp; rep from * around: 28 ch-3 lps.

Rnd 7: *Ch 3, hdc in next lp; rep from * around; leave marker in place at end of this rnd.

Work even in pattern as established until piece measures about 3" from marker.

EDGING

Rnd 1: Join sequin yarn, and with both yarns held tog, 2 sc in each ch-3 sp, skipping the hdc sts; do not join.

Rnd 2: Sc in each sc around.

Rep Rnd 2 until edging measures about 1"; join, finish off; weave in all ends.

#75 A HOOD FOR DA HOOD

Designed by Jean Leinhauser

SIZE
Fits up to 24" head

MATERIALS
Worsted weight yarn,
2 oz black

Size I (5.5.mm) crochet hook (or size required for gauge)

GAUGE
6 sc = 2"

INSTRUCTIONS

Ch 4.

Rnd 1 (right side): 13 dc in 4th ch from hook: 14 dc, counting beg ch-4 as a dc; join with a sl st in 4th ch of beg ch-4.

Rnd 2: *Ch 12, hdc in 2nd ch from hook and in each rem ch; skip next dc on Rnd 1, sc in next dc; rep from * 6 times more: 7 spokes made; join in 2nd ch (from base) of beg ch-12, finish off.

Rnd 3: Hold piece with right side facing and join yarn with sc in free end of any spoke, sc again in same end; * ch 8, 2 sc in end of next spoke, being careful not to twist spokes; rep from * around, join.

Rnd 4: Ch 1, sc in joining and in each st around: 70 sc; do not join, work now in continuous rnds.

Work even in sc until piece measures 3" from Rnd 3; finish off, weave in ends.

#76 BODACIOUS BOBBLES

Designed by Nancy Brown

SIZE
Fits up to 21" head

MATERIALS
Worsted weight yarn, 400 yds multi-color

Note: Photographed model made with Interlacements Cheyenne

Size J (6mm) crochet hook (or size required for gauge)

Size H (5mm) crochet hook

Stitch marker or small safety pin

GAUGE
8 hdc = 2" with larger hook

5 rows = 2"

STITCH GUIDE

Bobble (BB): 5 dc in specified st; drop lp from hook, insert hook from front to back in top of first dc and in top of last dc of group; draw top of last dc through top of first dc: BB made.

Single Crochet Decrease (scdec): (Draw up a lp in next st) twice, YO and draw through all 3 lps on hook: scdec made.

INSTRUCTIONS

With larger hook, ch 2.

Rnd 1: 8 dc in 2nd ch from hook; do not join, mark end of rnds.

Rnd 2: 2 hdc in each st around: 16 hdc.

Rnd 3: 2 hdc in each st around: 32 hdc.

Rnd 4: Work around in hdc, increasing 5 hdc evenly spaced on each rnd.

Rep Rnd 4 until piece measures 6 3/4" in diameter, ending with a multiple of 4 sts (a number of sts that can be divided evenly by 4), adjusting the number of increases on last rnd as needed.

Leave marker at end of last rnd. Work even in hdc until piece measures about 1 1/4" from marker.

Bobble Rnd 1: Sl st in next st, ch 3 (counts as first dc). BB in next st, dc in next st, ch 1; * sk next st, dc in next st, BB in next st, dc in next st, ch 1; rep from * around, ending with sl st in top of beg ch-3.

Bobble Rnd 2: Sl st in next BB, sl st in next dc, sl st in next ch-1 sp, ch 3, (2 dc, ch 1) in same sp; * In next ch-1 sp, work (3 dc, ch 1); rep from * around, join.

Bobble Rnd 3: Ch 3, BB in next dc, dc in next dc, ch 1; * dc in next dc, BB in next dc, dc in next dc, ch 1; rep from * around, join.

Rep Bobble Rnds 2 and 3 once. Finish off.

EARFLAPS

Fold piece in half and mark center front and back.

First Earflap

Row 1: With right side facing, with larger hook join yarn in 8th st from one marker. (Note: ch-1 sps will count as a st on this row). Ch 1, working in BLO of this row only, sc in same st and in each of next 15 sts; ch 1, turn.

Row 2: Sc in each st : 16 sc; ch 1, turn.

Row 3: Sc in first st, scdec over next 2 sts, sc to last 3 sts, scdec over next 2 sts, sc in last st: 14 sc; ch 1, turn.

Row 4: Sc in each sc, ch 1, turn.

Rep Rows 3 and 4 until 4 sts rem.

Next Row: Sc in first st, scdec over next 2 sts, sc in last st: 3 sc; ch 1, turn.

Next Row: Sc in each sc, finish off.

Edging

With smaller hook, join yarn in same st as first st of Row 1. Work 1 row of sc evenly spaced around earflap; finish off, weave in ends.

Second Earflap

Rep First Earflap on opposite side.

Edging

Rnd 1: With smaller hook, join yarn at left top of either earflap; ch 1, work one rnd of sc evenly around entire outer edge of hat.

TOP BOBBLES

First Bobble: With larger hook, ch 7, work 6 dc in 4th ch from hook. Drop lp from hook. Insert hook into top of beg ch and into the dropped lp. Pull this lp through the top of the beg ch: BB made. Finish off.

Second Bobble: Make another Bobble but ch 10 instead of ch 7 to start. Sew bobbles to top of hat as show in photograph.

TIES

With larger hook and 3 strands of yarn held tog, join yarn in bottom of one earflap. Ch about 11", finish off. Rep for second earflap.

Weave in all ends.

#77 JUST IN FUN

Designed by Denise Black

SIZE
Fits up to 20" head

MATERIALS
Worsted weight acrylic yarn, 2 1/2 oz blue

Eyelash yarn, 1 1/4 oz variegated

Note: Photographed model made with Red Heart® Kids™ #2845 Blue, and Lion Brand Fun Fur #207 Citrus.

Size I (5.5mm) crochet hook (or size required for gauge)

GAUGE
Rnds 1 and 2 = 2 1/2" diameter

INSTRUCTIONS

CROWN

With blue, ch 4.

Rnd I (right side): 11 dc in 4th ch from hook (3 skipped chs count as dc): 12 dc; join in 3rd ch of 3 skipped chs.

Rnd 2: Ch 1, (sc, dc) in same st as joining, (sc, dc) in each rem st: 24 sts; join in first sc.

Rnd 3: Rep Rnd 2: 48 sts.

Rnd 4: Ch 3 (counts as first dc), sc in next st; *dc in next st, sc in next st; rep from * around; join in first dc.

Rnd 5: Ch 1, sc in same st as joining, (dc in next st, sc in next st) 4 times; (dc, sc) in each of next 2 sts; *(dc in next st, sc in next st) 5 times; (dc, sc) in each of next 2 sts; rep from * to within last st; dc in last st: 56 sts; join as before.

Rnd 6: Ch 3 (counts as first dc), sc in next st; *dc in next st, sc in next st; rep from * around; join in first dc.

Rnd 7: Ch 1, sc in same st as joining, dc in next st; *sc in next st, dc in next st; rep from * around; join in first sc.

Rnds 8 through 23: Rep Rnds 6 and 7 eight times more. At end of Rnd 23, finish off and weave in ends.

BRIM

Hold hat with wrong side facing; join eyelash yarn with sl st in any st on Rnd 23.

Rnd I (wrong side): Ch 3 (counts as first dc), dc in each st around: 56 dc; join in first dc.

Rnds 2 through 4: Ch 3, dc in each dc; join as before. At end of Rnd 4, finish off and weave in ends.

TASSEL

Cut 25 strands of eyelash yarn 22" long. Tie one strand around middle of other 24 strands. Fold 24 strands in half at tied middle and wrap remainder of tied strand around folded strands 1" below tie. Fasten ends. Attach tassel to first rnd of hat.

#78 SMELL THE ROSES

Designed by Jean Leinhauser

SIZE
Fits up to 18" head

MATERIALS
Worsted weight yarn,
2 oz medium rose

Bouclé-type yarn,
1 oz rose

Size I (5.5mm) crochet
hook (or size required for
gauge)

GAUGE
6 dc = 2"

INSTRUCTIONS

With worsted weight yarn, ch 4; join with a sl st to form a ring.

Rnd 1: Ch 3 counts as first dc, 9 dc in ring: 10 dc; join with sl st in 3rd ch of beg ch-3.

Rnd 2: Ch 3, dc in joining; 2 dc in each dc around: 20 dc; join .

Rnd 3: Ch 3, 2 dc in next dc; *dc in next dc, 2 dc in next dc; rep from * around: 30 dc; join.

Rnd 4: Ch 3, dc in next dc, 2 dc in next dc; *dc in next 2 dc, 2 dc in next dc; rep from * around: 40 dc; join.

Rnd 5: Ch 3, dc in next 2 dc, 2 dc in next dc; *dc in next 3 dc, 2 dc in next dc; rep from * around: 50 dc; join.

Rnds 6 through 12: Ch 3, dc in each dc around. At end of Rnd 12, finish off worsted weight yarn.

Rnd 13: Join boucle yarn with sc in any st; sc in each rem st around; do not join, work in continuous rnds until boucle border measures 2". Finish off, weave in ends.

#70 ZIG ZAGS AND CHECKS

Designed by Patons Design Staff

SIZE
Fits up to 18" head

MATERIALS
DK weight yarn,
3/4 oz black (MC)
1/2 oz red (A)
1/4 oz blue (B)
1/2 oz yellow (C)

Note: Photographed model made with Patons® Astra, #2765 Black (MC), #2762 Cardinal (A), #2763 Copen Blue (B), # 2941 School Bus Yellow (C)

Size F (3.75mm) crochet hook (or size required for gauge)

GAUGE
16 dc = 4"

8 dc rows = 4"

STITCH GUIDE

3 single crochet decrease
(3 sc dec): (Insert hook in next st, YO and pull up a lp) 3 times, YO and pull through all 4 lps on hook: 3 sc dec made.

3 triple crochet decrease
(3 tr dec): [YO twice, insert hook in next st, YO and pull up a lp, (YO and pull through 2 lps on hook) twice] 3 times, YO and pull through all 4 lps on hook: 3 tr dec made.

INSTRUCTIONS

With MC, ch 2.

Rnd 1: 6 sc in 2nd ch from hook: 6 sc; join C with sl st in first sc. Finish off MC and weave in ends.

Rnd 2: With C, ch 1, 2 sc in same sc as joining, sc in each of next 2 sc, 2 sc in next sc, sc in each of next 2 sc: 8 sc; join MC with sl st in first sc. Finish off C and weave in ends.

Rnd 3: With MC, ch 1, sc in each sc around; join A with sl st in first sc. Finish off MC and weave in ends.

Rnd 4: With A, ch 1, sc in each sc around; join MC with sl st in first sc. Finish off A and weave in ends.

Rnd 5: With MC, ch 1, 2 sc in same sc as joining, (sc in next sc, 2 sc in next sc) 3 times, sc in next sc: 12 sc; join B with sl st in first sc. Finish off MC and weave in ends.

Rnd 6: With B, ch 1, sc in each sc around; join MC with sl st in first sc. Finish off B and weave in ends.

Rnd 7: With MC, ch 1, sc in each sc around; join C with sl st in first sc. Finish off MC and weave in ends.

Rnd 8: With C, ch 1, sc in each sc around; join MC with sl st in first sc. Finish off C and weave in ends.

Rnd 9: With MC, ch 1, 2 sc in same sc as joining, (sc in next sc, 2 sc in next sc) 5 times, sc in next sc: 18 sc; join A with sl st in first sc. Finish off MC and weave in ends.

Rnd 10: With A, ch 1, 2 sc in same sc as joining, (sc in each of next 2 sc, 2 sc in next sc) 5 times, sc in each of next 2 sc: 24 sc; join MC with sl st in first sc. Finish off A and weave in ends.

Rnd 11: With MC, ch 1, 2 sc in same sc as joining, (sc in each of next 3 sc, 2 sc in next sc) 5 times, sc in each of next 3 sc: 30 sc; join C with sl st in first sc. Finish off MC and weave in ends.

Rnd 12: With C, ch 1, 2 sc in same sc as joining, (sc in each of next 4 sc, 2 sc in next sc) 5 times, sc in each of next 4 sc: 36 sc; join MC with sl st in first sc. Finish off C and weave in ends.

Rnd 13: With MC, ch 1, 2 sc in same sc as joining, (sc in each of next 5 sc, 2 sc in next sc) 5 times, sc in each of next 5 sc: 42 sc; join A with sl st in first sc. Finish off MC and weave in ends.

Rnd 14: With A, ch 3 (counts as first dc), dc in same sc as joining, (dc in each of next 6 sc, 2 dc in next sc) 5 times, dc in each of next 6 sc: 48 dc; join MC with sl st in first dc. Finish off A and weave in ends.

Rnd 15: With MC, ch 1, sc in same ch as joining, working in back lp only of each dc, sc in each of next 4 dc, (2 sc in next dc, sc in each of next 5 dc) 7 times, 2 sc in next dc: 56 sc; join B with sl st in first sc. Finish off MC and weave in ends.

Rnd 16: With B, ch 3 (counts as first dc), dc in same sc as joining, (dc in each of next 6 sc, 2 dc in next sc) 7 times, dc in each of next 6 sc: 64 dc; join MC with sl st in first dc. Finish off B and weave in ends.

Rnd 17: With MC, ch 1, sc in same ch as joining, working in back lp only of each dc, sc in each of next 6 dc, (2 sc in next dc, sc in each of next 7 dc) 7 times, 2 sc in next dc: 72 sc; join C with sl st in first sc. Finish off MC and weave in ends.

Rnd 18: With C, ch 3 (counts as first dc), dc in same sc as joining, (dc in each of next 5 sc, 2 dc in next sc) 11 times, dc in each of next 5 sc: 84 dc; join MC with sl st in first dc. Finish off C and weave in ends.

Rnd 19: With MC, ch 1, sc in same ch as joining, working in back lp only of each dc, sc in each dc around; join A with sl st in first sc. Finish off MC and weave in ends.

Rnd 20: With A, ch 1, sc in same sc as joining, (*hdc in next sc, dc in next sc, 3 tr in next sc, dc in next sc, hdc in next sc*, sc in next sc) 13 times, rep from * to * once; join with sl st in first sc. Finish off and weave in ends.

Rnd 21: With right side facing, join MC with sl st in hdc before joining, ch 1, 3 sc dec in same st as sl st and in next 2 sts, (*sc in each of next 2 sts, 3 sc in next st, sc in each of next 2 sts*, 3 sc dec in next 3 sts) 13 times, rep from * to * once; join with sl st in first 3 sc dec. Finish off and weave in ends.

Rnd 22: With right side facing, join B with sl st in sc before joining, ch 4, [YO twice, insert hook in next st and pull up a lp, (YO and pull through 2 lps on hook) twice] 2 times, YO and pull through all 3 lps on hook: beg tr dec made; *dc in next st, hdc in next st, sc in next st, hdc in next st, dc in next st**, 3 tr dec in next 3 sts, rep from * 13 times, rep from * to ** once; join MC with sl st in beg 3 tr dec. Finish off B and weave in ends.

Rnd 23: With MC, ch 1, sc in same st as joining, sc in each st around: 84 sc; join C with sl st in first sc. Finish off MC and weave in ends.

Rnd 24: With C, rep Rnd 20.

Rnd 25: With MC, rep Rnd 21.

Rnd 26: With A, rep Rnd 22.

Rnd 27: With MC, rep Rnd 23.

Rnd 28: With C, ch 1, sc in same sc as joining, sc in each of next 2 sc, (sc in back lp of next sc, sc in each of next 3 sc) 20 times, sc in back lp of next sc; join with sl st in first sc.

Rnd 29: Ch 1, sc in same sc as joining, sc in each sc around; join MC with sl st in first sc. Finish off C and weave in ends.

Rnd 30: With MC, ch 1, sc in same sc as joining, sc in each of next 2 sc, (dc in front lp of next sc on Rnd 27, sk next sc, sc in each of next 3 sc) 20 times, dc in front lp of next sc on Rnd 27, sk next sc; join with sl st in first sc. Finish off and weave in ends.

#80 HEAD HUGGER

Designed by Nancy Brown

SIZE
Fits up to 21" head

MATERIALS
Fingering weight mohair yarn,
300 yds

Fingering weight bouclé yarn,
300 yds

Note: Photographed model made with Silk City Fibers Kid Mohair , #911 Cotton Candy and Erdal Sassy

Size G (4mm) crochet hook (or size required for gauge)

2 stitch markers or small safety pins

GAUGE
4 hdc = 1" with one strand of each yarn held together

3 rnds = 1"

INSTRUCTIONS

With one strand of each yarn held together, ch 2.

Rnd 1: 8 dc in 2nd ch from hook; do not join, place marker at end of rnd and move up as you work.

Rnd 2: 2 hdc in each st around: 16 hdc.

Rnd 3: 2 hdc in each st around: 32 hdc.

Rnd 4: Work around in hdc, increasing 5 hdc evenly spaced on each rnd.

Rep Rnd 4 until piece measures about 6¼" in diameter; mark end of last rnd.

Work even in hdc until piece measures about 4" from marker.

Next Rnd: Dc in each st around, finish off, weave in ends.

TIES (make 2)

With 4 strands of bouclé, chain about 30", finish off . Thread ties through dc rnd, going under 2 dc and over 2 dc. Tie each into a knot and trim ends to desired length.

FLOWERS

Note: Make one flower with 2 strands of boucle and one flower with one strand of mohair and one strand of boucle.

Ch 4, join with sl st to form a ring.

Rnd 1: (Sc in ring, chain 3) 8 times, join with sl st in beg sc: 8 ch-3 lps.

Rnd 2: In each ch-3 lp work [sc, dc, ch 1, (tr, ch 1) 7 times, dc, sc]: 8 petals made; finish off, leaving a long end for sewing.

Sew flowers to hat as shown in photo, placed above tie ends.

#81 FLOWER CHILD

Designed by Jean Leinhauser

SIZE

Fits 18" to 20" head

MATERIALS

Worsted weight yarn,
2 oz medium rose;
25 yds dark rose,
15 yds light rose

Size I (5.5mm) crochet
hook (or size required
for gauge)

GAUGE

6 dc = 2"

INSTRUCTIONS

HAT

With medium rose, ch 4, join
with a sl st to form a ring.

Rnd 1: Ch 1, 12 sc in ring; join
with a sl st in beg sc.

Rnd 2: Ch 3 (counts as beg dc), dc
in joining; 2 dc in each sc around,
join with sl st in 3rd ch of beg ch-
3: 24 dc.

Rnd 3: Ch 3, 2 dc in next dc; *dc
in next dc, 2 dc in next dc, join:
36 dc.

Rnd 4: Ch 3, dc in next dc, 2 dc in
next dc; *dc in next 2 dc, 2 dc in
next dc; rep from * around, join:
48 dc.

Rnd 5: Ch 3, dc in next 10 dc; 2
dc in next dc; *dc in next 11 dc, 2
dc in next dc; rep from * around,
join: 52 dc.

Rnds 6 through 10: Ch
3, dc in each dc, join.

Rnd 11: Ch 1, sc in
joining and in each dc
around, join in beg sc.

Rnd 12: Ch 3, 2 dc in
joining; *sk next sc, sc
in next sc, sk next sc,
shell of 3 dc in next sc;
rep from * around,
ending sk next sc, sc
in next sc, sk next sc,
join in beg ch-3.

Finish off, weave in ends.

FLOWER

With lt rose, ch 4, join with sl st
to form a ring.

Rnd 1: Ch 1, 10 sc in ring, join
with sc in beg sc; finish off lt rose.

Rnd 2: Join dk rose with sc in any
sc of Rnd 1; ch 5, sc in same sc;
*in next sc work (sc, ch 5, sc);
rep from * around: 10 ch-5 lps;
finish off leaving a long yarn end
for sewing. Sew flower to hat as
shown in photo.

#82 TRADITIONAL WATCH CAP

Designed by Nancy Brown

SIZE
Fits up to 22" head

MATERIALS
DK weight yarn,
4 oz purple

Note: Photographed model made with Cascade Yarns Cascade 220, #8420 Purple

Size J (6mm) crochet hook (or size required for gauge)

Stitch marker or small safety pin

Straight pins

GAUGE
7 hdc = 2"

6 rows hdc = 2"

INSTRUCTIONS

Ch 2.

Rnd 1: 8 hdc in 2nd ch from hook; do not join, mark beg of rnds.

Rnd 2: 2 hdc in each st around: 16 hdc.

Rnd 3: 2 hdc in each st around: 32 sts.

Rnd 4: Work around in hdc, increasing 5 hdc evenly spaced on each rnd.

Rep Rnd 4 until piece measures about 6 1/2" in diameter; leave marker at end of last rnd. Work even in hdc until piece measures about 3 1/2" from marker.

Beading Rnd: Dc in each st around, join with sl st in beg dc, finish off.

BRIM

Ch 19.

Row 1: Sc in 2nd ch from hook and in each ch across: 18 sc; ch 1, turn.

Row 2: Working in back lps only, sc in each sc, ch 1, turn.

Rep Row 2 until piece measures approx 22". Sew last row to first row to form ring.

Pin brim to right side of cap with bottom edges matching, and with right side facing, join yarn and crochet edge of brim to hat as follows: Working through both brim and cap, * sc in end of next row of brim, ch 1; rep from * around, finish off. With wrong side of upper edge of brim facing, join yarn in an end row, sc in joining; * ch 1, sc in end of next row; rep from * around, finish off, weave in ends.

TIE

With 2 strands of yarn held tog, make a chain 30" long, finish off. Thread tie through beading rnd. Try cap on for fit, and knot tie. Fold up brim, then turn half down as pictured in photograph.

#83 GARTER AND CHECKS

Designed by Patons Design Staff

SIZE
Fits 18" head

MATERIALS
DK weight yarn,
3¹/₂ oz navy (MC)
2¹/₂ oz variegated (A)

Note: Photographed model made with Patons® Astra #2849 Navy and #88761 Kool Aid Ombre

14" Size 5 (3.75mm) knitting needles (or size required for gauge)

14" Size 3 (3.25mm) knitting needles

GAUGE
24 sts = 4" with larger needles in stockinette st (knit one row, purl one row)

32 rows = 4"

STITCH GUIDE
M1: Make one st by picking up horizontal lp lying before next st and knitting into back of lp.

INSTRUCTIONS
With A and smaller needles, CO 119 sts .

Rows 1 through 5: Knit. At end of Row 5, cut A and attach MC.

Change to larger needles and work in patt as follows:

PATTERN

Row 1 (right side): With MC, knit.

Row 2: Purl

Row 3: Knit.

Row 4: Purl.

Row 5: Knit.

Row 6: Purl. Cut MC and attach A.

Row 7: With A, knit.

Row 8: Knit. Cut A and attach MC.

These 8 rows form pat.

Rep last 8 rows 3 times more.

SHAPE TOP

Row 1: With MC, K1; *K11, K2tog; rep from * to last st, K1: 110 sts.

Row 2: Purl,

Row 3: Knit.

Row 4: Purl

Row 5: K1; *K10, K2tog; rep from * to last st, K1: 101 sts.

Row 6: Knit. Cut MC and attach A.

Row 7: With A, knit.

Row 8: Purl. Cut A and attach MC.

Row 9: With MC, K2; *K12, K2tog; rep from * to last st, K1: 94 sts.

Row 10: P1; *P2tog, P11; rep from * to last 2 sts, P2: 87 sts.

Row 11: K2; *K10, K2tog; rep from * to last st, K1: 80 sts.

Row 12: P1; *P2tog, P9; rep from * to last 2 sts, P2: 73 sts.

Row 13: K2; *K8, K2 tog; rep from * to last st, K1: 66 sts.

Row 14: P1; *P2 tog, P7; rep from * to last 2 sts, P2: 59 sts. Cut MC and attach A

Row 15: With A, knit.

Row 16: Knit. Cut A, attach MC.

Rows 17 through 24: Rep Rows 1 through 8.

Row 25: With MC, K2; *K6, K2tog; rep from * to last st, K1: 52 sts.

Row 26: P 1; *P2tog, P5; rep from * to last 2 sts, P2: 45 sts.

Row 27: K2; *K4, K2tog; rep from * to last st, K1: 38 sts.

Row 28: P1; *P2tog, P3; rep from * to last 2 sts, P2: 31 sts.

Row 29: *K1, K2tog; rep from * to last st, K1: 21 sts.

Row 30: *P2tog; rep from * to last st, P1: 11 sts. Cut MC, attach A.

Rows 31 and 32: With A, knit. At end of Row 32, cut A and attach MC.

Rows 33 through 40: Rep Rows 1 through 8. At end of Row 40, cut A and attach MC.

Next Row: *K2 tog; rep from * to last st, K1: 6 sts.

Cut yarn, leaving a long end. Thread end into yarn needle and draw through rem sts, pull up tightly and fasten securely. Sew center back seam.

#84 SOMBRERO

SIZE
Fits up to 23" head

MATERIALS
DK weight yarn
1 3/4 oz aqua
1 3/4 oz pink
1 3/4 oz gold
1 3/4 oz white
1 3/4 oz green

Note: Photographed model made with Patons® Grace #60733 Peacock (aqua), #60438 Fuschia (pink), #60625 Sungold , #6005 White and #60712 Lime (green)

Size D (3.25mm) crochet hook (or size required for gauge)

20 gauge wire for brim (found in jewelry departments at craft stores)

Note: Hat is worked tightly to hold its shape; use a hook one or two sizes smaller if needed to get the required gauge

GAUGE
12 sc = 2"

STITCH GUIDE
To increase: Work 2 sts in one st.

To change colors: Work last st with old color until 2 lps rem on hook, YO with new color, do not cut old color; carry colors not in use loosely up work on inside of hat.

COLOR SEQUENCE
Work in this color sequence throughout:

*aqua

white

green

gold

hot pink

Rep from * for color sequence

INSTRUCTIONS
Beginning at top with aqua, ch 5, join with a sl st to form a ring.

Rnd 1: Ch 3 (counts as a dc here and throughout), 15 dc in ring; join with sl st in 3rd ch of beg ch-3: 16 dc; do not turn, work in joined rnds.

Rnd 2: Ch 1 (counts as sc here and throughout), sc in joining; 2 sc in each dc around, changing to next color in sequence in next st: 32 sc; join in beg sc. Note: Do not cut colors not in use; carry them loosely up work.

Rnd 3: Ch 3, 2 dc in next sc; *dc in next sc, 2 dc in next sc; rep from * around, join in beg ch-3: 48 dc.

Rnd 4: Ch 1, sc in same st as joining and in each dc around, changing to next color in last st; join in beg sc: 49 sc, counting beg ch-1.

Rnd 5: Ch 3, 2 dc in each of next 2 sts; *dc in each of next 3 sts, 2 dc in next st; rep from * around, dc in last 2 sts. Join: 62 dc.

Rnd 6: Rep Rnd 4: 63 sc.

Rnd 7: Ch 3, *2 dc in next sc; dc in each of next 3 sts; rep from * around, 2 dc in each of next 2 sts. Join: 80 dc.

Rnd 8: Rep Rnd 4.

Rnd 9: Ch 3, dc in each of next 10 sc, 2 dc in next sc; rep from * around, dc in last 3 sc, join: 88 dc.

Rnd 10: Rep Rnd 4: 89 sc.

Rnd 11: Ch 3, dc in each of next 10 sc, 2 dc in next sc; rep from * around, join: 96 dc.

Rnd 12: Rep Rnd 4: 97 sc.

Rnd 13: Ch 3, dc in each sc, join.

Rnd 14: Rep Rnd 4: 98 sc.

Rnds 15 through 16: Rep Rnds 13 and 14: 99 sc.

BRIM (continue in color sequence)

Rnd 1: Ch 3, dc in next st, 2 dc in next st; *dc in each of next 2 sts, 2 dc in next st; rep from * around, join: 131 dc.

Rnd 2: Ch 1, sc in same st as joining and in each st around, changing to new color in last st; join: 132 sc.

Rnd 3: Ch 3, dc in each st, join.

Rnd 4: Rep Rnd 2: 133 sc.

Rnd 5: Ch 3, dc in next st, 2 dc in next st; * dc in next 3 sts, 2 dc in next st; rep from * around, join: 166 dc.

Rnd 6: Rep Rnd 2: 167 sc.

Rnd 7: Ch 3, dc in next 3 sts, 2 dc in next st; *dc in next 4 sts, 2 dc in next st; rep from * around, join: 200 dc.

Rnd 8: Rep Rnd 2: 201.

Rnd 9: Ch 3, dc in next 3 sts, 2 dc in next st; *dc in next 5 sts, 2 dc in next st; rep from * around, join: 209 dc.

Rnd 10: Rep Rnd 2: 210 sc.

Rnd 11: Ch 3, dc in next 4 sts, 2 dc in next st; *dc in next 6 sts, 2 dc in next st; rep from * around, join: 239 dc.

Rnd 12: Rep Rnd 2: 240 dc.

Rnd 13: Ch 3, dc in next 5 sts, 2 dc in next st; *dc in next 7 sts, 2 dc in next st; rep from * around, join: 264 dc. Do not finish off.

Place hat on a flat surface and measure circumference of brim outer edge, adding 1".

Cut wire to this length. Form wire into a circle and bend each end into a hook; interlock ends.

Rnd 14: Carefully working over wire circle, ch 1, sc in each st of Rnd 13, completely covering wire; join, finish off. Weave in ends.

#85

BREATH OF FRESH AIR

Designed by Joyce Bragg

SIZE

Fits up to 20" head

MATERIALS

Nylon ribbon yarn, 153
yard (50 g) balls,
2 balls green
1 ball orange
1 ball white

*Note: Photographed model
made with Katia "Sevilla"#56
lime green, #55 orange and
#01 white*

Size F (3.75mm)
crochet hook (or size
required for gauge)

Styrofoam® hat form or
round bowl

Stiffy® fabric stiffener by
Plaid

2 stitch markers or small
safety pins

GAUGE

10 sc = 2"

STITCH GUIDE

Reverse sc (rev sc): Ch 1; *Insert
hook in next st to right, YO and
draw up a lp, YO and draw
through 2 lps on hook: rev sc
made; rep from *.

INSTRUCTIONS

CROWN

With green ch 5, join with sl st to
form a ring.

Rnd 1: 8 sc in ring, do not join;
mark ends of rnds.

Rnd 2: 2 sc in each sc: 16 sc.

Rnd 3: (2 sc in next sc, sc in next
sc) 8 times: 24 sc.

Rnd 4: (2 sc in next sc, sc in next
2 sc) 8 times: 32 sc.

Rnds 5 through 7: Sc in each sc.

Rnd 8: Sc in first 2 sc, (2 sc in next
sc, sc in next 2 sc) 10 times: 42
sc.

Rnds 9 and 10: Sc in each sc.

Rnd 11: (2 sc in next sc, sc in next
2 sc) 14 times: 56 sc.

Rnds 12 and 13: Sc in each sc.

Rnd 14: (2 sc in next sc, sc in next
4 sc) 11 times, sc in next sc: 67
sc.

Rnds 15 and 16: Sc in each sc.

Rnd 17: (2 sc in next sc, sc in next
2 sc) 22 times, sc in next sc: 89
sc.

Rnds 18 through 36: Sc in each sc.

BRIM

Rnd 37: (2 sc in next sc, sc in next 4 sc) 17 times, 2 sc in next sc, sc in next 3 sc: 107 sc; place a marker in this rnd.

Rnds 38 through 47: Sc in each sc.

Rnd 48: Ch 1; rev sc in each sc around. Finish off and weave in ends.

FINISHING

To shape hat, place on a Styrofoam® head form or rounded bowl.

Mix Stiffy® with water to make a thin solution. Use a dampened sponge to apply solution to hat. Tip brim front downward and at Rnd 37, fold center back up, remove marker. Allow to dry completely, then tack brim front and center back in place

FLOWERS

Small buds
(make one orange and one white):

Ch 3.

Rnd 1: 8 sc in 3rd ch from hook, do not join.

Rnd 2: (Sk next sc, sl st in next sc) 4 times; finish off leaving a 6" yarn end for sewing to hat.

Small flowers
(make one orange and one white):

Ch 3, join with sl st to form a ring.

Rnd 1: 8 sc in ring, join with sl st in first sc.

Rnd 2: Sc in same sc as joining, (ch 2, sc in next sc) 7 times, ch 2, join with sl st in first sc. Finish off leaving a 6" yarn end for sewing to hat.

Medium flowers
(make 1 orange and 1 white):

Ch 2, join with sl st to form a ring.

Rnd 1: 8 sc in ring, join with sl st in first sc.

Rnd 2: Sc in same sc as joining, (ch 2, sc in next sc) 7 times, join with sl st in first sc.

Rnd 3: *(Sc, hdc, dc, hdc, sc) in next ch-2 sp, rep from * around, join with sl st in first sc. Finish off leaving a 6" yarn end for sewing to hat.

Daisy (make 4):

With orange, ch 4, join with sl st to form a ring.

Rnd 1: 10 sc in ring, changing to white in last sc; cut orange.

Rnd 2: *Sc in next sc, ch 7, sl st in 2nd ch from hook, sc in next ch, hdc in next ch, dc in next ch, trc in next ch, dc in next ch (petal made), sk next sc, rep from * around, join with sl st in first sc: 5 petals. Finish off, leaving a 6" yarn end on white, and weave in orange yarn ends.

Sew one daisy on top of another daisy with petals alternating to make two double-layered flowers.

Three-leaf cluster (make 3):

Rnd 1: Ch 2, 6 sc in 2nd ch from hook; join with sl st in beg sc.

Rnd 2: *Ch 12, sc in 2nd and 3rd chs from hook, hdc in next ch, dc in next ch, tr in next 3 chs, dc in next ch, hdc in next ch, sc in last 2 chs; sk next sc on Rnd 1, sc in next sc on Rnd 1; rep from * twice more; finish off, leaving a 6" yarn end for sewing.

Sew buds, flowers and leaves to hat, arranging in a group as desired and placing flowers over centers of 3-leaf clusters.

#86 NEWSBOY CAP

Designed by Jenny King

SIZE
Fits up to 23" head

MATERIALS
Bedspread-weight (size 10) crochet cotton, 700 yds

Note: Photographed model made with Aunt Lydia's Classic Crochet Thread #484 Myrtle Green

Size 2 (2.5mm) steel crochet hook (or size required for gauge)

Size 4 (2mm) steel crochet hook

8 1/2" x 4 1/2" template plastic or plastic canvas for brim

2 stitch markers or small safety pins

GAUGE
With larger hook, 12 dc = 2"

6 sc rows = 2"

STITCH GUIDE

dc2tog decrease: (YO, insert hook in next st and draw up a lp; YO and draw through first 2 lps on hook) twice; YO and draw through all 3 lps on hook: dc2tog dec made

dc3tog decrease: (YO, insert hook in next st and draw up a lp; YO and draw through first 2 lps on hook) 3 times; YO and draw through all 4 lps on hook: dc3tog dec made.

sc2tog decrease: Draw up a lp in each of next 2 sts, YO and draw through all 3 lps on hook: sc2 tog dec made.

Beg V-st: Ch 4 (counts as a dc and ch-1 sp), dc in joining: beg V-st made.

V-st: (Dc, ch 1, dc) in specified st or sp: V-st made.

V-st in V-st: Work V-st in ch-1 sp of V-st in row below: V-st in V-st made.

INSTRUCTIONS

Note: Hat does not lie flat as it is worked.

With larger hook, ch 7, join with a sl st to form a ring.

Rnd 1 (right side): Ch 4 (equals one dc and one ch-1 sp), 3 dc in ring; * ch 1, 3 dc in ring; rep from * 5 times more, ch 1, 2 dc in ring; join with a sl st in sp between beg ch-4 and first dc: 8-ch-1 sps.

Rnd 2: Beg V-st, dc in next 3 sts; * V-st in next ch-1 sp, dc in next 3 sts; rep from * around, ending last rep with dc in last 2 dc, sl st in 3rd ch of beg ch-4; join as before with sl st between beg ch-4 and first dc.

Rnd 3: Beg V-st, dc in next 5 sts; *V-st in V-st, dc in next 5 sts; rep from * around, ending last rep with dc in last 4 dc, sl st in third ch of beg ch-4; join as before.

Rnd 4: Beg V-st, , dc in next 7 sts; *V-st in V-st, , dc in next 7 sts; rep from * around, ending last rep with dc in last 6 dc, sl st in 3rd ch of beg ch-4; join as before.

Rnds 5 through 9: Continue in this manner, increasing 2 sts between ch-1 sps of each rnd; at end of Rnd 9 there will be 17 dc between each V-st.

Rnds 10 through 23: Beg V-st; dc2tog (decrease made), dc in each st to last st before next V-st, dc2 tog over next st and first dc of V-st; V-st in V-st; dc2tog over next dc of V-st and next dc; *dc in each dc to last st before next V-st, dc2 tog over next st and first dc of V-st; V-st in V-st; dc2tog over next dc of V-st and next dc; rep from * around, ending last rep: dc in each dc to last 2 dc,

(YO, draw up a lp in next st, YO and draw through 2 lps) twice; insert hook in 3rd ch of beg ch-4, hook yarn and draw through ch and rem 3 lps on hook: dec made.

Rnd 24: Beg V-st; * (dc2 tog) twice, dc in next 4 sts, dc 3 tog, dc in next 4 sts, (dc2tog) twice; V-st in V-st; rep from * 3 times more: back of cap completed; (dc2tog) twice, dc in next 11 sts, (dc2tog) twice; V-st in V-st, (dc2tog) twice, dc in next 11 sts, (dc2tog) twice; rep from * 2 times more, join in 3rd ch of beg ch-4: front of cap completed; join, finish off.

BRIM LINING

Hold piece upside down with right side of the 4 Front sections facing you. Place a marker in ch-1 sp of center V-st. Count to right 22 sts (do not count ch-1 sps as sts), and join yarn with a sl st in this st.

Row 1: Ch 1; *sc next 2 sts tog, sc in next 6 sts; rep from * 4 times more, sc 2 tog: 36 sc; ch 1, turn.

Row 2 (wrong side): Working in FLO across row, sc 2 tog, sc in next 15 sc, (2 sc in next sc) twice, sc in next 15 sc, sc 2 tog: 36 sc; ch 1, turn.

Row 3: Working in both lps from here on, sc in first sc, sc 2 tog, sc to last 3 sc, sc 2 tog, sc in last sc: 34 sc; ch 1, turn.

Row 4: Sc in each sc, ch 1, turn.

Rows 5 and 6: Rep Rows 3 and 4: 32 sc.

Rows 7 and 8: Rep Rows 3 and 4: 30 sc.

Rows 9 and 10: Rep Rows 3 and 4: 28 sc.

Rows 11 and 12: Rep Rows 3 and 4: 26 sc.

Rows 13 and 14: Rep Rows 3 and 4: 24 sc.

Row 15: (Sc2tog) twice, sc to last 4 sts, (sc2tog) twice. 20 sc; ch 1, turn.

Row 16: Sc in each sc; finish off.

BRIM FRONT

Hold piece upside down with wrong side facing you; join yarn with a sl st in first unused lp of Brim Lining Row 1.

Rep Rows 2 through 16 of Brim Lining, working Row 2 in unused lps of Row 1; Finish off.

Place front piece of Brim on plastic or plastic canvas, and trace around it. Cut out piece within 1/4" of marked line; set piece aside.

BACK FINISHING

With right side facing you, Place a marker in ch-1 sp at center back. Counting sts and ch-1 sps, count 24 sts to the right; with smaller hook, join yarn with a sl st in next st to right.

Row 1 (right side): Working now with smaller hook, ch 1, sc in same st; sc in each st to marker, sc in marked st, sc in next 25 sts: 51 sc; turn (do not ch-1).

Row 2: Sl st over next 5 sts, sc in next 41 sts, turn.

Row 3: Sl st over next 3 sts, sc in next 35 sts. Do not ch or turn; work now in a rnd.

EDGING

Rnd 1: Sc in next st and in each st to beginning of brim; sc through both Front and Back layers of brim until about 5" remains unjoined; insert plastic shape between the two layers, then continue working sc through both layers and then around outer edge of cap to beg of rnd; join with a sl st, finish off.

Weave in all ends.

#87 HARD HAT

Designed by Susan McCreary

SIZE
Fits up to 22" head

MATERIALS
3-ply Natural Jute Twine
400 feet natural
2 yds white

Note: Photographed model made with Wellington jute twine and Mrs. Fix It white twine

Stitch marker

Size K (6.5mm) crochet hook (or size required for gauge)

I can spray shellac

GAUGE
3 sc = 1"

3 sc rows = 1"

INSTRUCTIONS

With jute twine ch 5, join with a sl st to form a ring.

Rnd 1: Ch 1, 10 sc in ring; do not join, mark beg of rnds.

Rnd 2: 2 sc in each sc: 20 sc.

Rnd 3 and 4: *2 sc in next sc, sc in next sc; rep from * around at end of Row 4: 45 sc.

Rnds 5 through 7: Sc in each sc.

Rnd 8: Sc in BLO of each sc.

Rnds 9 through 14: Sc in both lps of each sc.

Rnd 15: Sc in BLO of each sc.

Rnd 16: *(Hdc, ch 1, hdc) in next sc; rep from * around: .90 hdc.

Rnd 17: *2 sc in next ch-1 sp; rep from * around: 90 sc.

Rnd 18: Sc in each sc.

Rnd 19: *(Hdc, ch 1, hdc) in next sc; rep from * around, ending by working a sl st in top of beg hdc.

Finish off, weave in ends.

TIE

With white twine ch 120, finish off, weave in ends. Tie around hat above brim.

FINISHING

Place hat on a flat protected surface and shape, stuffing crown with plastic bags if necessary and keeping top and brim flat. Spray outside of hat with shellac, and allow to dry completely. When dry turn hat over and spray entire inside of hat with shellac and allow to dry completely. Rep spraying and drying on both sides until hat is stiff.

#88 SHEEPSKIN HAT

Designed by Patons Design Staff

SIZE

Fits 20" to 22" head

MATERIALS

Worsted weight yarn,
2 1/2 ozs off white
3 1/2 ozs shaded grey

Note: Photographed model made with Patons® Classic Merino Wool, #00202 Aran (MC) and #00225 Dark Grey Mix (A)

Size I (5.50 mm) crochet hook (or size required for gauge)

GAUGE

13 sc = 4"; 16 sc rows = 4"

STITCH GUIDE

Picot sc: Insert hook in specified st, YO and pull up a lp, ch 5 (on pulled up lp only), YO and pull through 2 lps on hook: picot sc made.

Sc decrease (sc dec): (Insert hook in next st, YO and pull up a lp) 2 times, YO and pull through all 3 lps on hook: sc dec made.

Front Post dc (FPdc): YO, insert hook from front to back to front around post of specified st, YO and pull up a lp, (YO and pull through 2 lps on hook) 2 times, skip next st on previous row: FPdc made.

Front Post dc decrease (FPdc dec): (YO, insert hook from front to back to front around post of next one of three specified sts, YO and pull up a lp, YO and pull through 2 lps on hook) 3 times, YO and pull through all 4 lps on hook, skip next 3 sts on previous row: FPdc dec made on 3 sts.

INSTRUCTIONS

CUFF

Starting at bottom, with MC, ch 76.

Row 1(wrong side): Sc in 2nd ch from hook and in each ch across: 75 sc; ch 1, turn.

Row 2: Sc in next sc; *picot sc in next sc, sc in next sc; rep from * across: 38 sc and 37 picot sc; ch 1, turn.

Row 3: Sc in next st; *sc in next st, picot sc in next st; rep from * to last 2 sts, sc in each of next 2 sts: 39 sc and 36 picot sc; ch 1, turn. *Note: Push picot sc to the back (right side) of work.*

Rows 4 through 11: Rep Rows 2 and 3 four times more.

Row 12: Rep Row 2.

Row 13: Sc in next 73 sts, sc dec in next 2 sts, changing to A: 74 sc; ch 1, turn. Finish off MC and weave in ends.

CROWN

Row 1 (right side): With A, sc in next 4 sts; *FPdc in next 3 sts 2 rows below, sc in next 6 sts; rep from * 6 times more, FPdc in next 3 sts 2 rows below, sc in next 4 sts: 50 sc and 24 FPdc; ch 1, turn.

Row 2: Sc in each st across: 74 sc; ch 1, turn.

Row 3: Sc in next 4 sc; *FPdc in next 3 FPdc 2 rows below, sc in next 6 sc; rep from * 6 times more, FPdc in next 3 FPdc 2 rows below, sc in next 4 sc: 50 sc and 24 FPdc; ch 1, turn.

Rows 4 through 19: Rep Rows 2 and 3 eight times more.

Row 20: Rep Row 2.

Row 21: Sc in next 4 sc; *FPdc in next 3 FPdc 2 rows below, sc in next 2 sc, sc dec in next 2 sc, sc in next 2 sc; rep from * 6 times more, FPdc in next 3 FPdc 2 rows below, sc in next 4 sc: 43 sc and 24 FPdc; ch 1, turn.

Row 22: Sc in each st across: 67 sc; ch 1, turn.

Row 23: Sc in next sc, sc dec in next 2 sc, sc in next sc; *FPdc in next 3 FPdc 2 rows below, sc dec in next 2 sc, sc in next sc, sc dec in next 2 sc; rep from * 6 times more, FPdc in next 3 FPdc 2 rows below, sc in next sc, sc dec in next 2 sc, sc in next sc: 27 sc and 24 FPdc; ch 1, turn.

Row 24: Sc in each st across: 51 sc; ch 1, turn.

Row 25: Sc in next sc, sc dec in next 2 sc; *FPdc in next 3 FPdc 2 rows below, sc in next sc, sc dec in next 2 sc; rep from * 6 times more, FPdc in next 3 FPdc 2 rows below, sc in next sc, sc dec in next 2 sc: 18 sc and 24 FPdc; ch 1, turn.

Row 26: Sc in each st across: 42 sc; ch 1, turn.

Row 27: Sc in next 2 sc; *FPdc in next 3 FPdc 2 rows below, sc dec in next 2 sc; rep from * 6 times more, FPdc in next 3 FPdc 2 rows below, sc in next 2 sc: 11 sc and 24 FPdc; ch 1, turn.

Row 28: Sc in each st across: 35 sc; ch 1, turn.

Row 29: Sc dec in next 2 sc; *FPdc dec in next 3 FPdc 2 rows below, sc in next sc; rep from * 6 times more, FPdc dec in next 3 sts, sc dec in next 2 sc: 9 sc and 8 FPdc. Finish off, leaving a long end. Thread yarn end into a tapestry needle and draw end through rem sts and fasten securely. Sew center back seam. Fold lower edge to right side and tack in place at seam.

EARFLAPS (make 2)

With A, ch 15.

Row 1 (right side): Sc in 2nd ch from hook and in each ch across: 14 sc; ch 1, turn.

Row 2: Sc in each sc, ch 1, turn.

Row 3: Sc in next sc, FPdc in next 3 sc 2 rows below, sc in next 6 sc, FPdc in next 3 sc 2 rows below, sc in next sc: 8 sc and 6 FPdc; ch, turn.

Row 4: Sc across: 14 sc; ch 1, turn.

Row 5: Sc in next st, FPdc in next 3 FPdc 2 rows below, sc dec in next 2 sts, sc in next 2 sts, sc dec in next 2 sts, FPdc in next 3 FPdc 2 rows below, sc in next st: 6 sc and 6 FPdc; ch 1, turn.

Row 6: Sc in each st across: 12 sc; ch 1, turn.

Row 7: Sc in next st, FPdc in next 3 FPdc 2 rows below, (sc dec in next 2 sts) 2 times, FPdc in next 3 FPdc 2 rows below, sc in next st: 4 sc and 6 FPdc; ch 1, turn.

Row 8: Sc: 10 sc; ch 1, turn.

Row 9: Sc in next st, FPdc in next 3 FPdc 2 rows below, sc dec in next 2 sts, FPdc in next 3 FPdc 2 rows below, sc in next st: 3 sc and 6 FPdc; ch 1, turn.

Row 10: Sc in each st across: 9 sc; ch 1, turn.

Row 11: Sc in next st, FPdc dec in next 3 FPdc 2 rows below, skip next st, FPdc dec in next 3 FPdc 2 rows below, sc in next st: 2 sc and 2 FPdc; ch 1, turn.

Row 12: Sc in each st across: 4 sc; ch 1, turn.

Row 13: (Insert hook in next st, YO and pull up a lp) 4 times, YO and pull through all 5 lps on hook. Finish off and weave in ends.

Sew Row 1 of earflaps to Row 1 of Crown at sides of hat.

TWISTED CORD (make 2)

Cut 2 strands of A 23" long. Hold both strands together at one end with someone holding other end, twist strands to the right until they begin to curl. Bring the 2 ends together and tie in a knot so they will not unravel. The strands will now twist themselves together. Adjust length if desired. Sew one twisted cord to point of each Earflap.

#80 TIBETAN HAT

Designed by Patons Design Staff

SIZE

Small fits child 12-18 months

Large fits child 2-4 years

Note: Instructions are written for small size; changes for large size are in parentheses.

MATERIALS

DK weight yarn,
2 oz blue (MC)
2 1/2 oz green (A)
2 oz red (B)
2 1/2 oz yellow (C)

Note: Photographed model made with Patons® Astra #2733 Electric Blue (MC), #2939 Kelly Green (A), #2762 Cardinal (B), #2941 School Bus Yellow (C)

14" Size 5 (3.75mm) knitting needles (or size required for gauge)

14" Size 3 (3.25mm) knitting needles

2 stitch markers or small safety pins

GAUGE

24 sts = 4" with larger needles in stockinette st (knit one row, purl one row)

32 rows = 4"

INSTRUCTIONS

Starting at bottom of hat, with A and smaller needles, CO 96 (108) sts.

Row 1 (right side): Knit.

Row 2: Purl.

Row 3: Rep Row 1.

Row 4: Rep Row 2.

Row 5 (Picot row): K1; *K2tog, YO; rep from * to last st, K1.

Row 6: Purl.

Row 7: Knit.

Row 8: Purl.

For small size only:

Row 9: *K5, inc in next st; rep from * to end of row: 112 sts.

For large size only:

Row 9: K6, *K5, inc in next st; rep from * to last 6 sts, K6: 124 sts.

For both sizes:

Row 10: Purl. Cut A and attach MC and C.

Change to larger needles and work Chart in stockinette st to end of chart reading knit rows from right to left and purl rows from left to right, noting 4 st rep will be worked 28 (31) times. Carry color not in use loosely across back. Continue working chart until work measures 3¼" (4¼") from CO row, ending by working a purl row. Cut MC and C and attach B.

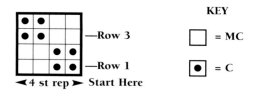

KEY

□ = MC

▣ = C

—Row 3

—Row 1

◄ 4 st rep ► Start Here

With B and smaller needles

For small size only:

Row 1: *K5, K2tog; rep to end of row: 96 sts. Place marker at end of row.

For large size only:

Row 1: K6, *K5, K2tog; rep to last 6 sts, K6 108 sts. Place marker at end of row.

For both sizes:

Row 2: Purl.

Row 3: Knit.

Row 4: Purl

Row 5 (Picot row): K1; *K2tog, YO; rep from * to last st, K1.

Row 6: Purl.

Row 7: *K15 (17), inc in next st; rep to end of row: 102 (114) sts.

Row 8: Purl. Place marker at end of row. Cut C and join MC.

SHAPE TOP

With MC and larger needles:

Row 1: *K2, sl 1, K1, PSSO, K19 (22), K2tog; rep from * to last 2 sts, K2: 94 (106) sts.

Row 2 and all even rows: Purl.

Row 3: *K2, sl 1, K1, PSSO, K17 (20), K2tog; rep from * to last 2 sts, K2: 86 (98) sts.

Row 5: *K2, sl 1, K1, PSSO, K15 (18), K2tog; rep from * to last 2 sts, K2: 78 (90) sts.

Row 7: *K2, sl 1, K1, PSSO, K13 (16), K2tog; rep from * to last 2 sts, K2: 70 (82) sts.

Row 9: *K2, sl 1, K1, PSSO, K11 (14), K2tog; rep from * to last 2 sts, K2: 62 (74) sts.

Row 11: *K2, sl 1, K1, PSSO, K9 (12), K2tog; rep from * to last 2 sts, K2: 54 (66) sts.

Row 13: *K2, sl 1, K1, PSSO, K7 (10), K2tog; rep from * to last 2 sts, K2: 46 (58) sts.

Row 15: *K2, sl 1, K1, PSSO, K5 (8), K2tog; rep from * to last 2 sts, K2: 38 (50 sts).

Row 17: *K2, sl 1, K1, PSSO, K3 (6), K2tog; rep from * to last 2 sts, K2: 30 (42) sts.

Row 19: *K2, sl 1, K1, PSSO, K1 (4), K2tog; rep from * to last 2 sts, K2: 22 (34) sts.

Row 21: *K2, sl 1, K1, PSSO, K0 (2), K2tog; rep from * to last 2 sts, K2: 14 (26) sts

For large size only

Row 23: *K2, sl 1, K1, PSSO, K2tog; rep from * to last 2 sts, K2: 18 sts.

For both sizes:

Work 7 rows of stockinette st. Cut MC and attach A.

With A:

Rows 1 and 3: Knit.

Rows 2 and 4: Purl

Row 5: *K2tog; rep from * to end of row: 7 (9) sts.

Row 6: Purl.

Row 7: K1; *K2tog; rep from * to end of row: 3 (5) sts. Cut yarn, leaving a long end. Thread end into yarn needle and draw through rem sts and fasten securely.

EARFLAPS (make 2)

Starting at top of earflap, and with MC and larger needles, cast on 17 sts.

Row 1 (wrong side): Knit.

Row 2: Knit.

Rep Rows 1 and 2 until work measures 1" from cast-on row.

Next Row: K2 tog, Knit to last 2 sts, K2 tog.

Next Row: Knit.

Rep these 2 rows until 3 sts rem. BO.

TWISTED CORD (make 2)

With MC, cut 2 strands of yarn 20" long. With both strands tog hold one end and with someone holding other end, twist strands to the right until they begin to curl. Fold the 2 ends tog and tie in a knot so they will not unravel. The strands will now twist themselves tog. Adjust length if desired. Sew a twisted cord to each earflap.

FINISHING

Fold bottom edge to inside along picot row and sew in position. Fold edge of B to inside along picot row and sew tog rows with markers.

Sew center back seam of hat. Sew earflaps to hat as shown in photo.

Corner Tassels (make 4)

With A, cut 8 strands of yarn 3 1/2" long. Draw 8 strands halfway through picot edge at each corner of hat as shown in photo. Wind MC tightly around strands 1/2" above fold. Fasten securely. Trim ends evenly.

Top Tassel

With B, cut 12 strands of yam 3 1/2" long. Draw 12 strands through cast-off edge at top of hat as shown in photo. Wind MC tightly around strands 1/2" above fold. Fasten securely. Trim ends evenly.

#90 LADY VICTORIA'S FELTED HAT

Designed by Sheila Jones

SIZE

Fits 21 ½" to 23" head

(Actual size is determined in the felting process.)

MATERIALS

Worsted weight 100% wool yarn,
190 yards black
130 yards red

Note: Use a yarn that felts easily. Do not use a Superwash wool.

Note: Photographed model made with Brown Sheep Lamb's Pride Worsted, #M-05 Onyx and #M-81 Red Baron

24" Size 11 (8mm) circular knitting needles (or size required for gauge)

8" Size 11 (8mm) four double-pointed needles

Stitch marker or small safety pin

Hat blocker or bowl (to use for shaping)

GAUGE

12 sts = 4" in circular stockinette st (knit each row on circular needles) with two strands of yarn held tog.

STITCH GUIDE

Slip, slip, knit (SSK): Sl 2 sts as if to knit, one at a time, to right-hand needle. Insert tip of left-hand needle into fronts of these 2 sts and knit them tog: SSK made.

INSTRUCTIONS

Note: Hat is worked with two strands of yarn held tog.

Starting at lower edge with double strands of black, CO 70 sts. Place marker, join to knit in the round.

Rnd 1: Knit.

Rnd 2: Knit.

Work even in circular stockinette st until hat measures 6" from CO edge.

ROLLED EDGE

Rnds 1 through 3: Purl.

Rnd 4: *With the right side facing, pick up the back loop of the last knit rnd (directly below the next st on needle) and sl this st onto the left needle. Knit the lifted st tog with the next st; rep from * around: 70 sts. At end of rnd, cut black yarn, join red.

CROWN

Note: Change to double-pointed needles when necessary.

Rnds 1 through 3: Knit.

Rnd 4: *K5, K2tog; rep from * around: 60 sts.

Rnds 5 and 6: Knit.

Rnd 7: *K4, SSK: rep from * around: 50 sts.

Rnd 8: Knit.

Rnd 9: *K3, K2tog; rep from * around: 40 sts.

Rnd 10: Knit.

Rnd 11: *K2, SSK; rep from * around: 30 sts.

Rnd 12: Knit.

Rnd 13: *K1, K2tog; rep from * around: 20 sts.

Rnd 14: *SSK; rep from * around: 10 sts.

Rnd 15: *K2tog; rep from * around: 5 sts.

FINISHING

Cut yarn, leaving a 6" end. Thread end into a yarn needle and draw through rem 5 sts; tighten and secure end. Weave in all ends.

FELTING

Using the lowest water level setting and hottest water on washing machine, felt to desired size. After the first 10 minutes, check felting process every five minutes for size. You may have to reset your washer to the wash cycle to complete felting process. Do not let it go through spin and rinse cycles. When the felting process is complete, rinse the hat by hand with cold water. Mold to desired shape using hat blocker or bowl, and roll up the edge to form the brim. Let dry.

FLOWER EMBELLISHMENT

Flower Petals

Starting at outside edge of flower with a single strand of red, CO 54 sts . Do not join, work back and forth in rows.

Rows 1 through 3: *P1, P2tog; rep from * across. At end of Row 3: 16 sts.

Row 4: *K3tog; rep from * across to last st, K1: 6 sts

Row 5: P3tog twice: 2 sts.

Draw yarn through rem 2 sts and fasten off. Sew short edges of flower tog. Sew flower securely to side of hat when hat is completely dry.

Flower Center

With black and double-pointed needles, cast on 3 sts.

*K3, do not turn. Slide sts to the other end of the double-pointed needle, bringing yarn around back of work; rep from * until piece measures 2$\frac{1}{2}$".

Cut yarn, leaving a 6" end.

Thread end into a yarn needle and draw through rem sts; tighten and secure end. Weave in all ends. Sew to center of flower on hat making a circle button.

#91 CIRCLES AND FUR

Designed by Rita Weiss

INSTRUCTIONS

Starting at cuff with eyelash and white worsted weight yarn held tog, CO 78 sts, place marker to mark beg of row, join.

Rnds 1 through 8: With eyelash and white worsted weight held tog, knit. At end of Rnd 8, cut eyelash.

Rnds 9 through 14: With white worsted weight only, knit. At end of Rnd 14, cut white and attach black.

Rnds 15 through 20: Knit. At end of Rnd 20, cut black and attach white.

Rnds 21 through 26: Knit. At end of Rnd 26, cut white and attach black.

Rnds 27 through 32: Knit. At end of Rnd 32, cut black and attach white.

Rnds 33 through 38: Knit. At end of Rnd 38, cut white and attach black.

Rnds 39 through 44: Knit. At end of Rnd 44, cut black and attach white.

Rnds 45 through 50: Knit. At end of Rnd 50, cut white and attach black.

Rnds 51 through 56: Knit. At end of Rnd 56, cut black and attach white.

Rnd 57 (eyelet rnd): K4; * K3, K2tog, YO; rep from * around to last 4 sts, K4.

Rnd 58: Knit, working each YO as a st.

Rnd 59: Knit. At end of Rnd 59, join eyelash. Do not cut white worsted weight.

Rnds 60 through 65: With white worsted and eyelash yarns held tog, knit. At end of Rnd 65, BO. Cut yarns and weave in ends.

CORD

With double-pointed needles, CO 4 sts, leaving a 6" yarn tail; K4, do not turn. *Slide stitches to other end of double-pointed needle, bringing yarn around the back of sts, K4; rep from * until cord measures about 10" long; BO, leaving a 6" yarn tail.

FINISHING

Weave cord through eyelets at top of hat. Draw up cord and tie. Attach beads to tails and secure with loop knot.

#92 CROWNING GLORY

Designed by Patons Design Staff

SIZE

Fits 16" head (2 to 4 yrs old)

MATERIALS

DK weight yarn,
1 ³/₄ oz red
1 oz blue

Note: Photographed model made with Patons® Astra, #2762 Cardinal (MC) and #2733 Electric Blue (A)

Size F (3.75mm) crochet hook (or size needed for gauge)

¹/₂" Button

GAUGE

19 sts = 4"

13 pattern rows (sc, dc, sc, dc, etc) = 4"

STITCH GUIDE

Sc decrease (sc dec): (Insert hook in next st, YO and pull up a lp) 2 times, YO and pull through all 3 lps on hook: sc dec made.

Dc decrease (dc dec): (YO, insert hook in next st, YO and pull up a lp, YO and pull through 2 lps on hook) 2 times, YO and pull through all 3 lps on hook: dc dec made.

INSTRUCTIONS

CROWN

Starting at top with A, ch 2.

Rnd 1 (right side): 6 sc in 2nd ch from hook: 6 sc; join with sl st in first sc.

Rnd 2: Ch 3 (counts as first dc), dc in same sc as joining; (3 dc in next sc, 2 dc in next sc) twice, 3 dc in next sc: 15 dc; join with sl st in first dc.

Rnd 3: Ch 1, sc in same ch as joining, sc in next dc; *2 sc in next dc, sc in each of next 2 sc; rep from * 3 times more, 2 sc in next dc: 20 sc; join with sl st in first sc.

Rnd 4: Ch 3 (counts as first dc), dc in same sc as joining; *dc in next sc, 2 dc in next sc; rep from * 8 times more, dc in next sc: 30 dc; join with sl st in first dc.

Rnd 5: Ch 1, sc in same ch as joining, sc in next dc; *2 sc in next dc, sc in each of next 2 dc; rep from * 8 times more, 2 sc in next dc: 40 sc; join with sl st in first sc.

Rnd 6: Ch 3 (counts as first dc), dc in same sc as joining, dc in each of next 4 sc; *2 dc in next sc, dc in each of next 4 sc; rep from * 6 times more: 48 dc; join with sl st in first dc.

Rnd 7: Ch 1, sc in same ch as joining, sc in each of next 2 dc; *2 sc in next dc, sc in each of next 3 dc; rep from * 10 times more, 2 sc in next dc: 60 sc; join with sl st in first sc.

Rnd 8: Ch 3 (counts as first dc), dc in same sc as joining, dc in each of next 4 sc; *2 dc in next sc, dc in each of next 4 sc; rep from * 10 times more: 72 dc; join with sl st in first dc.

Rnd 9: Ch 1, sc in same ch as joining, sc in each of next 7 dc; *2 sc in next dc, sc in each of next 8 dc; rep from * 6 times more, 2 sc in next dc: 80 sc; join with sl st in first sc. Do not finish off.

FIRST SET OF POINTS

Point One

Row 1: Working in FLO of each sc, ch 1, sc in same sc as joining, sc in each of next 9 sc: 10 sc; ch 1, turn.

Row 2: Sc dec in next 2 sc, sc in each of next 6 sc, sc dec in next 2 sc: 8 sc; ch 1, turn.

Row 3: Sc in each sc, ch 1, turn.

Row 4: Sc dec in next 2 sc, sc in each of next 4 sc, sc dec in next 2 sc: 6 sc; ch 1, turn.

Row 5: Rep Row 3.

Row 6: Sc dec in next 2 sc, sc in each of next 2 sc, sc dec in next 2 sc: 4 sc; ch 1, turn.

Row 7: Rep Row 3.

Row 8: (Sc dec in next 2 sc) twice: 2 sc; ch 1, turn.

Row 9: Sc dec in next 2 sc: 1 sc. Finish off and weave in ends.

Points Two through Eight

Row 1: Working in FLO of each sc, join A with sl st in next sc on Rnd 9 of Crown, ch 1, sc in same sc as joining, sc in each of next 9 sc: 10 sc; ch 1, turn.

Rows 2 through 9: Work same as Rows 2 through 9 of Point one.

Transition Rnd: With right side facing, join MC with sl st in unused back lp of first sc on Rnd 9 of Crown, ch 1, sc in back lp of same sc as joining, sc unused back lp of each sc around: 80 sc; join with sl st in first sc. Do not finish off.

SECOND SET OF POINTS (all sizes)

Point one

Row 1: Working in FLO of each sc on Transition Rnd, ch 1, sc in same sc as joining, sc in each of next 9 sc: 10 sc; ch 1, turn.

Rows 2 through 9: Work same as Rows 2 through 9 of Point One in First Set of Points.

Points Two through Eight

Row 1: Working in FLO of each sc, join MC with sl st in next sc on Transition Rnd, ch 1, sc in same sc as joining, sc in each of next 9 sc: 10 sc; ch 1, turn.

Rows 2 through 9: Work same as Rows 2 through 9 of Point One in First Set of Points.

JOINING POINTS

With right side of Crown facing, join MC with sl st in edge of first sc on Row 1 of Point 1 in First Set of Points, ch 1, working through first and second set of points at the same time, sc in edge of Rows 1 through 8 of same point; *3 sc in sc on Row 9, sc in other edge of Rows 8 through 1 of same point; ** sc in edge of Rows 1 through 8 of next point; rep from * 6 times more; rep from * to ** once: 152 sc; join with sl st in first sc. Finish off and weave in ends.

BODY

Rnd 1: With right side facing, join MC with sl st in unused back lp of first sc on Transition Rnd, ch 1, sc in back lp of same sc as joining, sc in unused back loop of each sc around: 80 sc; join with sl st in first sc (center back).

Rnd 2: Ch 3 (counts as first dc), dc in each of next 8 sc; *2 dc in next sc, dc in each of next 9 sc; rep from * 6 times more, 2 dc in next sc: 88 dc; join with sl st in first dc.

Rnd 3: Ch 1, sc in same ch as joining, sc in each dc around: 88 sc; join with sl st in first sc.

Rnd 4: Ch 3 (counts as first dc), dc in next sc and in each sc around: 88 dc; join with sl st in first dc.

Rnds 5 through 8: Rep Rnds 3 and 4 two times more. At end of Rnd 8, finish off and weave in ends.

FACE OPENING

Row 1: Mark 30th dc on each side of center back (28 dc on center front will be left unworked). With right side facing, join MC with sl st in first marked dc, ch 1, sc in same dc, sc in each of next 59 dc: 60 sc; ch 3 (counts as first dc on next row), turn.

Row 2: Dc in each of next 22 sc; *dc dec in next 2 sc, dc in next sc; rep from * 4 times more, sc in each of next 22 sc: 55 dc; ch 1, turn.

Row 3: Sc in each dc; ch 3 (counts as first dc on next row), turn.

Row 4: Dc in each of next 20 sc; *dc dec in next 2 sc, dc in next sc; rep from * 4 times more, dc in each of next 19 sc: 50 dc; ch 1, turn.

Row 5: Rep Row 3.

Row 6: Dc in next sc and in each sc; ch 1, turn.

Row 7: Rep Row 3.

Row 8: Rep Row 6.

FIRST CHIN STRAP

Row 1: Sc in each of next 13 dc: 13 sc; ch 3 (counts as first dc on next row), turn. Leave rem 37 dc unworked.

Row 2: Dc dec in next 2 sc, dc in each of next 10 sc: 12 dc; ch 1, turn.

Row 3: Sc in first dc and in each dc across; ch 3 (counts as first dc on next row), turn.

Row 4: Dc dec in next 2 sc, dc in each of next 9 sc: 11 dc; ch 1, turn.

Row 5: Rep Row 3.

Row 6: Dc dec in next 2 sc, dc in each of next 8 sc: 10 dc; ch 1, turn.

Row 7: Rep Row 3.

Row 8: Dc dec in next 2 sc, dc in each of next 7 sc: 9 dc; ch 1, turn.

Row 9: Rep Row 3.

Row 10: Dc in next sc and in each sc across: 9 dc; ch 1, turn.

Row 11: Rep Row 3.

Row 12: Dc dec in next 2 sc, dc in each of next 3 sc, dc dec in next 2 sc, dc in next sc: 7 dc. Finish off and weave in ends.

SECOND CHIN STRAP

Row 1: Skip next 28 dc on Row 8 of Face Opening. With right side facing, join MC with sl st in next dc, ch 1, sc in same dc as joining, sc in each of next 12 dc: 13 sc; ch 3 (counts as first dc on next row), turn.

Row 2: Dc in next 10 sc, dc dec in next 2 sc: 12 dc; ch 1, turn.

Row 3: Sc in each dc across; ch 3 (counts as first dc on next row), turn.

Row 4: Dc in next 9 sc; dc dec in next 2 sc: 11 dc; ch 1, turn.

Row 5: Rep Row 3.

Row 6: Dc in next 8 sc; dc dec in next 2 sc: 10 dc; ch 1, turn.

Row 7: Rep Row 3.

Row 8: Dc in next 7 sc, dc dec in next 2 sc: 9 dc; ch 1, turn.

Row 9: Rep Row 3.

Row 10: Dc in next sc and in each sc across: 9 dc; ch 1, turn.

Row 11: Rep Row 3.

Row 12: Dc dec in next 2 sc, dc in each of next 3 sc, dc dec in next 2 sc, dc in next sc: 7 dc. Finish off and weave in ends.

OUTER EDGING

With right side facing, join A with sl st in any dc on Row 8 of Face Opening, ch 1, sc in same dc, sc in each st around outer edge of Face Opening, Chin Straps and Body of Hat; join with sl st in first sc. Finish off and weave in ends.

Sew button to left Chin Strap (Note: Center of last dc row on right Chin Strap forms buttonhole).

#93 CAROUSEL HAT

Designed by Patons Design Staff

SIZE

Small fits child 12-18 months

Large fits child 2-4 years

Note: Instructions are written for small size; changes for large size are in parentheses.

MATERIALS

DK weight yarn,
2 ½ oz bright blue (MC)
2 ½ oz variegated (A)
2 oz red (B)
2 ½ oz yellow (C)

Note: Photographed model made with Patons® Astra #2733 Electric Blue (MC), #88761 Kool Aid Ombre(A), #2762 Cardinal (B) and #2941 Yellow (C)

14" Size 5 (3.75mm) knitting needles (or size required for gauge)

14" Size 3 (3.25mm) knitting needles

GAUGE

24 sts = 4" with larger needles in stockinette st (knit one row, purl one row)

32 rows = 4"

STITCH GUIDE

Make Five Stitches (M5): (K1, YO, K1, YO, K1) all in next st: M5 made

Make Bobble (MB): K5, turn, K5, turn, K5: MB made

Slip 4 (Sl 4): Sl next 4 sts as if to knit: sl 4 made

INSTRUCTIONS

Note: When working from chart, wind small balls of the colors to be used one for each separate area of color in the design. Start new colors as indicated on chart. To change colors, twist the two colors around each other where they meet, on wrong side, to avoid a hole.

Starting at bottom of hat, with A and smaller needles, CO 100 (116) sts.

Rows 1 through 9: Knit. At end of Row 9, cut A and join MC.

Row 10: Knit.

Row 11: Purl.

Row 12 (right side): With MC, K2; then work first row of chart, reading row from right to left, noting 8 st rep will be worked 12 (14) times; end with MC, K2.

Row 13: With MC, P2; purl 2nd row of chart reading row from left to right; end with MC, P2.

Rows 14 through 23: Continue working chart in stockinette st (knit one row, purl one row).

Rows 24 and 25: With MC, work 2 rows in stockinete st. At end of Row 25, cut MC and attach B.

Row 26: With B, knit.

Row 27: Purl.

Row 28: With B, P9. Attach C and *with C, M5, with B, P7; rep from * to last 3 sts; with C, M5, with B, P2.

Row 29: With B, K2, with C, MB; *with B, K7, with C, MB; rep from * to last 9 sts; with B, K9. Cut C.

Row 30: With B, P9; *Sl 4, K1, PSSO, P7; rep from * to last 7 sts, Sl 4, K1, PSSO, P2.

For small size only:

Row 31: With B, K1, inc in next st, knit to last 2 sts, inc in next st, K1: 102 sts. At end of row, cut B and join A.

For large size only:

Row 31: With B, K1, K2tog, knit to last 3 sts, K2 tog, K1: 114 sts. At end of row, cut B and attach A.

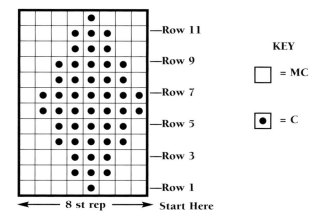

KEY

☐ = MC

▣ = C

—Row 11
—Row 9
—Row 7
—Row 5
—Row 3
—Row 1

← 8 st rep → Start Here

SHAPE TOP

Row 1: With A, *K2, sl 1, K1, PSSO, K19 (22), K2tog; rep from * to last 2 sts, K2: 94 (106) sts.

Row 2 and all even rows: Purl.

Row 3: *K2, sl 1, K1, PSSO, K17 (20), K2tog; rep from * to last 2 sts, K2: 86 (98) sts.

Row 5: *K2, sl 1, K1, PSSO, K15 (18), K2tog; rep from * to last 2 sts, K2: 78 (90) sts.

Row 7: *K2, sl 1, K1, PSSO, K13 (16), K2tog; rep from * to last 2 sts, K2: 70 (82) sts.

Row 9: *K2, sl 1, K1, PSSO, K11 (14), K2tog; rep from * to last 2 sts, K2: 62 (74) sts.

Row 11: *K2, sl 1, K1, PSSO, K9 (12), K2tog; rep from * to last 2 sts, K2: 54 (66) sts.

Row 13: *K2, sl 1, K1, PSSO, K7 (10), K2tog; rep from * to last 2 sts, K2: 46 (58) sts.

Row 15: *K2, sl 1, K1, PSSO, K5 (8), K2tog; rep from * to last 2 sts, K2: 38 (50) sts.

Row 17: *K2, sl 1, K1, PSSO, K3 (6), K2tog; rep from * to last 2 sts, K2: 30 (42) sts.

Row 19: *K2, sl 1, K1, PSSO, K1 (4), K2tog; rep from * to last 2 sts, K2: 22 (34) sts.

For large size only

Row 21: *K2, sl 1, K1, PSSO, K2, K2tog; rep from * to last 2 sts, K2: 26 sts.

Row 23: K5; *K2tog; rep from * to last 5 sts, K5: 18 sts.

For small size only:

Row 21: K3; *K2tog; rep from * to last 3 sts, K3: 14 sts.

For both sizes:

Next Row: Purl.

Next Row: K1, *K2tog; rep from * to last st, K1: 8 (10) sts.

Next Row: Purl

Work 10 more rows even in stockinette st. Cut yarn leaving a long end. Thread yarn into yarn needle and draw through rem sts. Fasten securely.

EARFLAPS (make 2)

Starting at top of earflap with MC and larger needles, CO 17 sts.

Row 1 (wrong side): Knit.

Row 2: Knit.

Rep Rows 1 and 2 until work measures 1" from CO edge.

SHAPING EARFLAPS

Row 1: K1, K2tog, K to last 3 sts, K2tog, K1: 15 sts.

Rows 2 through 7: Rep Row 1. At end of row 7: 3 sts. BO.

TWISTED CORD (make 2)

With A, cut 2 strands of yarn 20" long. With both strands tog hold one end and with someone holding other end, twist strands to the right until they begin to curl. Fold the 2 ends tog and tie in a knot so they will not unravel. The strands will now twist themselves tog. Adjust length if desired.

FINISHING

Sew center back seam of hat. Sew earflaps to hat 2¼" from either side of back seam. Sew twisted cords to earflaps.

#04 RIBBON TRIMMED HAT

Designed by Susan McCreary

SIZE
Fits up to 22" head

MATERIALS
Bulky weight yarn,
4 oz brown

Note: Photographed model made with Lion Brand® Wool-Ease® Thick & Quick® #426, Cabin Brown

Size L (8mm) crochet hook (or size required for gauge)

1 1/2" wide ribbon, 32"

stitch marker

GAUGE
3 sc = 1 1/2"

3 sc rows = 1 1/2"

INSTRUCTIONS

Ch 4, join with a sl st to form a ring.

Rnd 1: Ch 1, 5 sc in ring; do not join, place marker to indicate beg of rnds..

Rnd 2: 2 sc in each sc: 10 sc.

Rnd 3: Sc in each sc.

Rnds 4 through 7: Rep Rnds 2 and 3 at end of Row 7: 40 sc.

Rnd 8: *2 sc in next sc, sc in each of next 7 sc; rep from * around: 45 sc.

Rnd 9: Sc in BLO of each sc.

Rnds 10 through 13: Sc in both lps of each sc.

Rnd 14: Sc in FLO of each sc.

Rnd 15: Working in both lps of each sc, * 2 sc in next sc, sc in each of next 8 sc; rep from * around: 50 sc.

Rnd 16: Sc in each sc.

Rnd 17: *2 sc next sc, sc in each of next 4 sc; rep from * around: 60 sc.

Rnd 18: Sc in each sc.

Finish off, weave in ends.

Place ribbon around hat. Knot at back or front, as desired. Spot tack in place.

#95 VERY RETRO

Designed by Rita Weiss

SIZE
Fits up to 23" head

MATERIALS
Bulky weight yarn,
5 oz black and white
mix

*Note: Photographed
model made with Red
Heart® Casual Cot'N™
#3550 Zebra*

14" Size 10 knitting
needles (or size
required for gauge)

GAUGE
6 sts = 2" in garter st
(knit every row)

INSTRUCTIONS

SIDE CROWN (make 2)

CO 28 sts.

Rows 1 through 8: Knit.

Row 9: K2tog; knit to last two sts; K2tog: 26 sts.

Rows 10 through 14: Knit.

Row 15: K2tog; knit to last 2 sts; K2tog: 24 sts,

Row 16: Knit.

Rows 17 through 27: Rep Rows 15 and 16. At the end of Row 27: 12 sts.

Row 28: Knit.

BO.

CENTER CROWN

CO 8 sts.

Rows 1 through 22: Knit.

Row 23: K1, inc (knit in front and back of next st), knit to last 2 sts, inc in next st, K1:10 sts.

Rows 24 through 28: Knit.

Row 29: K1, inc in next st, knit to last 2 sts, inc in next st, K1: 12 sts.

Rows 30 through 34: Knit,

Row 35: K1, inc in next st, knit to last 2 sts, inc in next st, K1: 14 sts.

Rows 36 through 42: Knit.

Row 43: Sl 1, K1, PSSO, knit to last 2 sts, K2tog: 12 sts.

Rows 44 through 48: Knit.

Row 49: Sl 1, K1, PSSO, knit to last 2 sts, K2tog: 10 sts.

Rows 50 through 54: Knit.

Row 55: Sl 1, K1, PSSO, knit to last 2 sts, K2tog: 8 sts.

Rows 56 through 74: Knit.

BO.

BRIM

CO 67 sts.

Row 1: *K2, inc in next st; rep from * to last st, K1: 89 sts.

Rows 2 through 8: Knit.

Row 9: K5; *inc in next st, K7; rep from * to last 4 sts, inc in next st, K3: 100 sts.

Rows 10 through 16: Knit.

Row 17: K8, inc in next st; rep from* to last st, K1: 111 sts.

Row 18: Knit.

BO loosely.

BAND

CO 6 sts.

Row 1 (right side): Knit.

Row 2: Purl.

Rep Rows 1 and 2 until band measures about 22 1/2". BO.

FINISHING:

With right sides tog, sew Side Crown sections to Center Crown. With right sides tog, sew Band to Crown. Sew center back seam. Join center back seam of Brim. With right sides tog, sew Brim to lower edge of Band.

#96 PANAMA HAT

Designed by Joyce Bragg

Fits up to 22" head

Size 3 cotton crochet thread, 200 yds ecru

Note: Photographed model made with J & P Coats Speed-Cro-Sheen #61 New Ecru

Size C (2.75mm) crochet hook (or size required for gauge)

Stitch marker or small safety pin

Stiffy® fabric stiffener

Small sponge

Styrofoam® head form

14 sc = 2"

14 sc rows = 2"

INSTRUCTIONS

CROWN

Ch 5, join with sl st to form a ring.

Rnd 1: 8 sc in ring; do not join; mark beg of rnds.

Rnd 2: 2 sc in each sc: 16 sc.

Rnd 3: *2 sc in next sc, sc in next sc; rep from * around: 24 sc.

Rnd 4: Sc in each sc.

Rnd 5: 2 sc in each sc: 48 sc.

Rnds 6 and 7: Sc in each sc.

Rnd 8: *Sc in next sc, ch 1, sk next sc; rep from * around: 24 sc and 24 ch-1 sps.

Rnd 9: *Sc in next sc, 2 sc in next ch-1 sp; rep from * around: 72 sc.

Rnds 10 and 11: Sc in each sc.

Rnd 12: *Sc in next sc, ch 1, sk next sc; rep from * around: 36 sc and 36 ch-1 sps.

Rnd 13: *Sc in next sc, 2 sc in next ch-1 sp; rep from * around: 108 sc.

Rnds 14 through 22: Sc in each sc.

Rnd 23: Working in BLO, sc in each sc.

Rnds 24 through 29: Working in both lps of each st, sc in each sc.

Rnd 30: *Sc in next sc, ch 2, sk 2 sc; rep from * around.

Rnd 31: *Sc in next sc, 2 sc in next ch-2 sp; rep from * around.

Rnds 32 through 35: Sc in each sc.

Rnd 36: Rep Rnd 30.

Rnd 37: Rep Rnd 31.

Rnds 38 through 40: Sc in each sc.

Rnd 41: Rep Rnd 30.

Rnd 42: Rep Rnd 31.

Rnds 43 through 45: Sc in each sc.

BRIM

Rnd 1: *2 sc in BLO of next sc, sc in BLO of next 2 sc); rep from * around: 162 sts.

Rnds 2 through 10: Sc in each sc; at end of last rnd, join with a sl st in beg sc, finish off and weave in ends.

FINISHING

Dampen sponge; dip in fabric stiffener and coat hat. Let dry completely on a head form to shape, turning brim up slightly.

#97 COZY HAT

Designed by Patons Design Staff

SIZE

Small fits child 12-18 months

Large fits child 2-4 years

Note: Instructions are written for small size; changes for large size are in parentheses.

MATERIALS

DK weight yarn,
2 oz navy (MC)
2 1/2 oz red (A)
2 1/2 oz purple (B)
3 oz yellow (C)

Note: Photographed model made with Patons®Astra#2849 Navy (MC), #2762 Cardinal (A), #2740 Purple (B) and #2941 School Bus Yellow (C)

14" Size 5 (3.75mm) knitting needles (or size required for gauge)

2 stitch markers or small safety pins

GAUGE

24 sts = 4" in stockinette st (knit one row, purl one row)

40 rows = 4"

STITCH GUIDE

M1: make one st by picking up horizontal lp lying before next st and knitting into back of lp.

Increase (inc): knit in front and in back of st

INSTRUCTIONS

RIBBING

Starting at bottom of hat, with MC, CO 106 (112) sts.

Row 1 (wrong side): Knit.

Rows 2 through 5: Knit. At end of Row 5, cut MC and attach A.

Row 6 (right side): With A, K1; *K12 (10), inc in next st; rep from *to last st, K1: 114 (122) sts.

Row 7: P2; *K2, P2; rep from * to end of row.

Row 8: K2; *P2, K2; rep from * to end of row.

Rep Rows 7 and 8 until piece measures 3" from CO row, ending by working a right-side row. Place a marker, at end of last row. At end of last row, cut A and attach C. Pattern will now reverse for cuff turnback.

HAT

Row 1 (right side): With C, knit.

Row 2: Purl.

Rep these 2 rows until work measures 5" (5½") from marker, ending by working a wrong-side row. BO.

Sew center back seam, reversing seam at marker for cuff turnback. Turn hat inside out and following diagram, sew top seam of hat.

Turn Hat inside out.
Fold top of Hat as illustrated.
Sew through 4 thicknesses indicated with arrows.

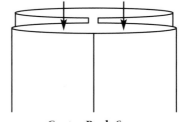

Center Back Seam

EARFLAPS (make 2)

Starting at bottom of earflap, with B, CO 5 sts.

Row 1 (wrong side): Knit.

Row 2: K1, M1, knit to last st, M1, K1: 7sts.

Rep last 2 rows 7 (8) times more: 21 (23 sts).

Next Row: Knit.

Knit even until work measures 3" from CO row, BO.

Place markers on last row of ribbing 2¼" from each side of back seam. Sew bound-off edge of earflaps to last row of ribbing inside hat, beg at markers.

TWISTED CORD (make 2)

Cut 3 strands of MC, 28" long. With all strands tog hold one end and with someone holding other end, twist strands to the right until they begin to curl. Fold the 2 ends tog and tie in a knot so they will not unravel. The strands will now twist themselves tog. Adjust length if desired. Sew one to end of each earflap.

#98 SHIRRED BERET

Designed by Zelda K

SIZE
Fits up to 22" head

MATERIALS
Worsted weight yarn,
6 oz dark green

Note: Photographed model made with Lion Brand Wool-Ease® #180 Forest Green Heather

Sizes G (4.5mm) and K (6.5mm) crochet hooks (or sizes required for gauge)

Stitch marker

GAUGE
20 sc = 4" with smaller hook

24 sc rows = 4" with smaller hook

15 sc = 4" with larger hook

20 sc rows = 4" with larger hook

STITCH GUIDE

Sc2tog (decrease): (Insert hook in next st and pull up lp) twice; YO and pull through all 3 lps on hook: sc2tog made.

Reverse sc: Ch 1;* insert hook in next st to right and pull up a lp; YO and pull through both lps on hook; rep from *, continuing to work from right to left.

double triple crochet (dtr): YO hook 3 times, insert hook in specified st and draw up a lp, (YO and draw through first 2 lps on hook) 4 times: dtr made.

triple triple crochet (trtr): YO hook 4 times, insert hook in specified st and draw up a lp, (YO and draw through first 2 lps on hook) 5 times: trtr made.

INSTRUCTIONS

Note: Work is started at top of crown. Oversized crown is worked in spiral sections which are later join to make a circle.

SECTION 1

With smaller size hook, ch 23.

Row 1 (right side): Sl st in 8th ch from hook (ring formed); sc in next ch, hdc in each of next 2 chs; dc in next ch, 2 dc in next ch, dc in next ch; tr in next ch, 2 tr in next ch, tr in next ch; dtr in next ch, 2 dtr in next ch, dtr in next ch; trtr in next ch, 2 trtr in next ch, trtr in next ch; ch 1, do not turn.

Row 2: Using FLO, work rev sc in each of 19 sts, sl st in ring, do not turn.

SECTION 2

Row 1: Working in BLO of Row 1 of Section 1, sc in sc, hdc in each of next 2 sts; dc in next st, 2 dc in next st, dc in next st; tr in next st, 2 tr in next st, tr in next st; dtr in next st, 2 dtr in next st, dtr in next st; trtr in next st, 2 trtr in next st, trtr in next st; leaving rem sts unworked, ch 1, do not turn.

Row 2: Work rev sc in FLO in each of 19 sts, sl st in ring, do not turn.

SECTIONS 3 THROUGH 16

Row 1: Working in BLO of Row 1 of section just completed, sc in sc, hdc in next 2 sts; dc in next st, 2 dc in next st, dc in next st; tr in next st, 2 tr in next st, tr in next st; dtr in next st, 2 dtr in next st, dtr in next st; trtr in next st, 2 trtr in next st, trtr in next st; ch 1, do not turn.

Row 2: Work rev sc in FLO in each of 19 sts, sl st in ring, do not turn.

At end of Section 16, finish off, leaving a long yarn end for sewing. With right sides tog, sew Section 16 to Section 1.

SIDES

With size larger hook, join yarn in tip of any section (tip is top of last trtr in a Row 1 of a section).

Rnd 1: *5 sc in tip of section, 5 sc along trtr at end of section, sc in each of 3 BLs of next section; rep from 15 times: 208 sc; do not join, mark beg of rnds.

Rnd 2: Sc in each of first 2 sc; *5 sc in tip sc (center sc of 5-sc group), sc in each of next 6 sc, sk 2 sc, sc in each of next 4 sc; rep from * around, end with 2 sc instead of 4 at end of final rep: 240 sc.

Rnd 3: Sc in each of first 4 sc; *5 sc in tip, sc in each of next 7 sc, sk 2 sc, sc in each of next 5 sc, rep from * around, end with 1 sc instead of 5 sc at end of final rep: 272 sc.

Rnd 4: *Sc in each of next 6 sc, 5 sc in tip, sc in each of next 8 sc, sk 2 sc, rep from * around: 304 sc.

Rnds 5 through 9: Sk first sc; *sc in each of next 7 sc, 3 sc in tip, sc in each of next 9 sc, sk 2 sc, rep from * around; end with 1 sc at end of final rep: 304 sc.

Rnd 10: Sk first sc; *sc in each of next 7 sc, 3 sc in tip (center sc of 3-sc group), sc in each of next 9 sc, hdc in next sc, sk next sc, rep from * around: 320 sts.

Rnd 11: Sk first sc; *sc 2tog, sc in each of next 5 sc, 3 sc in tip, sc in each of next 9 sts, hdc in next st, dc in next st, sk next st, rep from * around, end with dc: 320 sts.

Rnd 12: Sk 2 sc; *sc 2tog, sc in each of next 4 sc, 3 sc in tip, sc in each of next 9 sts, hdc in each of next 2 sts, dc in next st, sk next st, rep from * around: 320 sts.

Rnd 13: *Sk 1 sc; sc, sc, 2 tog, sc in each of next 3 sc, 2 sc in tip, sc in each of next 8 sts, hdc in each of next 3 sts, dc in each of next 2 sts, rep from * around: 304 sts.

Rnd 14: *Sk 2 sts, sc in each of next 11 sts, hdc in each of next 3 sts, dc in each of next 2 sts, tr in next st, rep from * around: 272 sts.

Rnd 15: *Sk 1 st, sc in each of next 16 sc, rep from * around: 256 sc.

Rnd 16: *Sc 2 tog, rep from * around: 128 sc.

Rnd 17: *Sc 2 tog, rep from * around: 64 sc.

Rnd 18: Sc in each sc, join with sl st in beg sc.

Rnds 19 through 22: Sc in each sc; do not join.

Rnd 23: Rep Rnd 18.

Rnd 24: Reverse sc in each sc around, join in beg sc. Finish off.

#99 ENTRELAC BRIM HAT

Designed by Joyce Renee Wyatt
(for the advanced crocheter)

SIZE
Fits 18" to 20" head

MATERIALS
Worsted weight yarn,
1 1/2 oz multi-colored
1 oz blue

Note: Photographed model made with Red Heart Super Saver, #984 Shaded Dusk (A) and #382 Country Blue (B)

Size J (6mm) crochet hook, or size required for gauge.

Size L (8mm) crochet hook

GAUGE
With J hook:
10 sc = 3"
12 sc rows = 3"

STITCH GUIDE

Sc decrease (sc dec): (Insert hook in next specified st, YO and pull up a lp) twice, YO and pull through all 3 lps on hook: sc dec made.

3 Sc decrease (3 sc dec): (Insert hook in next specified st, YO and pull up a lp) 3 times, YO and pull through all 4 lps on hook: 3 sc dec made.

INSTRUCTIONS

HEADBAND (starting at bottom of hat)

With smaller hook and A, ch 54 loosely; join with sl st to form a ring; ch 1, turn.

Rnd 1 (right side): Sc in back lp of first ch and in back lp of each ch: 54 sc; sl st in first sc.

Rnds 2 and 3: Ch 1, sc in same sc as joining, sc in each sc; sl st in first sc.

Rnd 4: With larger hook, ch 1, sc in same sc as joining, sc in each sc around: 54 sc; sl st in first sc; ch 1, turn.

Triangle #1

Row 1: With wrong side facing and larger hook, sc loosely in first sc; turn.

Row 2: 2 sc in sc: 2 sc; ch 1, turn.

Row 3: 2 sc in first sc, sc in next sc: 3 sc; skip next sc on Rnd 4 of Headband, sl st in following sc on Rnd 4 of Headband; turn.

Row 4: 2 sc in first sc, sc in next 2 sc: 4 sc; ch 1, turn.

Row 5: 2 sc in first sc, sc in following 3 sc: 5 sc; skip next sc on Rnd 4 of Headband, sl st in following sc on Rnd 4 of Headband; turn.

Row 6: 2 sc in first sc, sc in next 4 sc: 6 sc; ch 1, turn.

Row 7: 2 sc in first sc, sc in following 5 sc: 7 sc; skip next sc on Rnd 4 of Headband, sl st in following sc on Rnd 4 of Headband; turn.

Row 8: Sc in each sc; ch 1, turn.

Row 9: Sc in each sc: 7 sc; skip next sc on Rnd 4 of Headband, sl st in following sc on Rnd 4 of Headband. Do not turn.

Triangles #2 through #6

Row 1: Sc loosely in next sc on Rnd 4 of Headband; turn.

Rows 2 through 9: Rep Rows 2 through 9 of Triangle #1. At end of Row 9 on Triangle #6, sl st in first sc on Triangle #1. Finish off and weave in ends.

Square #1

Row 1: With right side facing and working along edge of triangle, join B with sl st in first sc on Row 9 of Triangle #1 (at top of triangle), ch 1, sc in same sc, working down left side of triangle, sc in edge of next 6 rows: 7 sc; sl st in last sc on Row 9 of Triangle #6; turn.

Row 2: Sc in each sc; ch 1, turn.

Row 3: Sc in each sc, sl st in next 2 sc on Row 9 of same triangle as last sl st; turn.

Rows 4 through 7: Rep Rows 2 and 3 two times more.

Row 8: Rep Row 2.

Row 9: Sc in each sc . Do not turn.

Squares #2 through #6

Row 1: Sc in edge of last sc on Row 8 of same triangle as last sl st, sc in edge of next 6 rows: 7 sc; sl st in last sc on Row 9 of next triangle; turn.

Rows 2 through 9: Rep Rows 2 through 9 of Square #1. At end of Row 9 on Square #6, sl st in edge of first sc on Row 1 of Square #1. Finish off and weave in ends.

Square #7

Row 1: With wrong side facing and working across edge of square, join A with sl st in edge of last sc on Row 8 of Square #1 (at top corner), ch 1, sc in edge of same sc as joining, sc in edge of next 6 rows: 7 sc; sl st in last sc on Row 9 of Square #6; turn.

Row 2: Sc in each sc; ch 1, turn.

Row 3: Sc in each sc , sl st in next 2 sc on Row 9 of same square as last sl st; turn.

Rows 4 through 7: Rep Row 2 and 3 two times more.

Row 8: Rep Row 2.

Row 9: Sc in each. Do not turn.

Squares #8 through #12

Row 1: Sc in edge of last sc on Row 8 of same square as last sl st, sc in edge of next 6 rows: 7 sc; sl st in last sc on Row 9 of next square; turn.

Rows 2 through 9: Rep Rows 2 through 9 of Square #7. At end of Row 9 on Square #12, sl st in edge of first sc on Row 1 of Square #7. Finish off and weave in ends.

Decrease Square #1

Row 1: With right side facing and working across edge of square, join B with sl st in edge of last sc on Row 8 of Square #12 (at top corner), ch 1, sc in edge of same sc as joining, sc in edge of next 6 rows; 7 sc; sl st in last sc on Row 9 of next square; turn.

Row 2: Sc in each sc; ch 1, turn.

Row 3: Sc in next 2 sc, sc dec in next 2 sc, sc in next 3 sc: 6 sc; 3 sc dec in next 3 sc on Row 9 of same square as last sl st; turn.

Row 4: Skip 3 sc dec, sc in each sc; ch 1, turn.

Row 5: Sc in next 2 sc, sc dec in next 2 sc, sc in next 2 sc: 5 sc; 3 sc dec in next 3 sc on Row 9 of same square as last 3 sc dec; turn.

Row 6: Rep Row 4.

Row 7: Sc in each sc: 5 sc. Do not turn.

Decrease Squares #2 through #6

Row 1: Sc in edge of last sc on Row 8 of same square as last 3 sc dec, sc in edge of next 6 rows: 7 sc; sl st in last sc on Row 9 of next square; turn.

Rows 2 through 7: Rep Rows 2 through 7 of Decrease Square #1. At end of Row 7 of Decrease Square #6, sl st in edge of first sc of Decrease Square #1. Finish off and weave in ends.

Decrease Triangle #1

Row 1: With wrong side facing and working across edge of decrease square, join A with sl st in edge of last sc on Row 6 of Decrease Square #1 (at top corner), ch 1, sc in edge of same sc as joining, sc in edge of next 4 rows: 5 sc; sc dec in last 2 sc on Row 7 of next Decrease Square; turn.

Row 2: Skip sc dec, sc in each sc across; ch 1, turn.

Row 3: Sc in next 2 sc, sc dec in next 2 sc, sc in next sc: 4 sc; 3 sc dec in next 3 sc on Row 7 of same Decrease Square as last sc dec; turn.

Row 4: Skip 3 sc dec, sc in each sc; ch 1, turn.

Row 5: Sc in next sc, sc dec in next 2 sc, sc in next sc: 3 sc. Do not turn.

Decrease Triangles #2 through #6

Row 1: Sc in edge of last sc on Row 6 of same Decrease Square as last 3 sc dec, sc in edge of next 4 rows: 5 sc; sc dec in last 2 sc on Row 7 of next Decrease Square; turn.

Rows 2 through 5: Rep Rows 2 through 5 of Decrease Triangle #1. At end of Row 5 on Decrease Triangle #6, sl st in edge of first sc on Decrease Triangle #1. Finish off and weave in ends.

Closing Rnds

Rnd 1: With right side facing, join B with sl st in last sc on Row 4 of Decrease Triangle #1, ch 1, sc in same sc as joining, sc in next 2 sc on same Decrease Triangle, (*sc in edge of last sc on Row 4 of same Decrease Triangle, sc in edge of next 2 rows of same Decrease Triangle*, sc in next 3 sc on next Decrease Triangle) 5 times, rep from * to * once: 36 sc; sl st in first sc. Do not turn.

Rnd 2: Ch 1, sc dec in same sc as joining and in next sc, (sc dec in next 2 sc) 17 times: 18 sc; sl st in first sc. Do not turn.

Rnd 3: Ch 1, sc dec in same sc as joining and in next sc, (sc dec in next 2 sc) 8 times: 9 sc; sl st in first sc. Finish off, leaving a long end.

FINISHING

Draw end through rem sc on Rnd 3 and fasten securely. Weave in ends.

#100 RED GRANADA HAT

Designed by Joyce Bragg

SIZE
Fits 21" head

MATERIALS
Sport weight yarn, 350 yds red

Fingering weight yarn, 15 yds red

Note: Photographed model made with Katia Granada #11 and Twilleys Gold Fingering #58

Size G (4mm) crochet hook (or size required for gauge)

Size F (3.75mm) crochet hook

Size C (2.75mm) crochet hook

Stitch marker or small safety pin

Fabric stiffener

Styrofoam® head form

4 red faceted beads, optional

Matching sewing thread

Sewing needle

GAUGE
16 sc = 3" with G hook

18 sc rows = 3" with G hook

STITCH GUIDE

Beginning Block Stitch (Beg Blk St): Ch 3, skip first sc, dc in next sc; (YO, insert hook from front to back to front around post of dc just made, YO and pull up a loose lp) 4 times; YO, insert hook in next sc, YO and pull up a loose lp, YO and pull through all 11 lps on hook, ch 1: Beg Blk St made.

Block Stitch (Blk St): Skip next sc, dc in next sc; (YO, insert hook from front to back to front around post of dc just made, YO and pull up a loose lp) 4 times; YO, insert hook in next sc, YO and pull up a loose lp, YO and pull through all 11 lps on hook, ch 1: Blk St made.

Edging Block Stitch (Edg Blk St): Ch 2, skip next sc, dc in next sc; (YO, insert hook from front to back to front around post of dc just made, YO and pull up a loose lp) 4 times; YO, insert hook in next sc, YO and pull up a loose lp, YO and pull through all 11 lps on hook, sl st in same sc where last lp was pulled up: Edg Blk St made.

Medallion Block Stitch (Med Blk St): (YO, insert hook from front to back to front around post of dc just made, YO and pull up a loose lp) 4 times; YO, insert hook in next dc, YO and pull up a loose lp, YO and pull through all 11 lps on hook: Med Blk St made.

INSTRUCTIONS

CROWN

With G hook and sport yarn, ch 2.

Rnd 1: 8 sc in 2nd ch from hook: 8 sc; do not join, mark ends of rnds.

Rnd 2: 2 sc in each sc: 16 sc.

Rnd 3: 2 sc in each sc : 32 sc.

Rnd 4: (2 sc in next sc, sc in next sc) 16 times: 48 sc.

Rnds 5 through 11: Sc in each sc.

Rnd 12: (2 sc in next sc, sc in next 2 sc) 16 times: 64 sc.

Rnd 13: Sc in each sc.

Rnd 14: (2 sc in next sc, sc in next 3 sc) 16 times: 80 sc.

Rnds 15 through 21: Sc in each sc.

Rnd 22: (2 sc in next sc, sc in next 7 sc) 10 times: 90 sc.

Rnd 23: (2 sc in next sc, sc in next 9 sc) 9 times: 99 sc.

Rnd 24: (2 sc in next sc, sc in next 11 sc) 8 times, sc in next 3 sc: 107 sc.

Rnd 25: (2 sc in next sc, sc in next 14 sc) 7 times, sc in next 2 sc: 114 sc.

Rnds 26 and 27: Sc in each sc.

Rnd 28: Work Beg Blk St in first 3 sc, work 37 Blk Sts in next 111 sc: 38 Blk Sts; join with sl st in 3rd ch of beg ch-3.

Rnds 29: Work 3 sc across top of each block st (working 1 sc in dc, st around post and ch-1): 114 sc.

RED GRANADA HAT

Rows 30 through 34: Sc in each sc.

Rnd 35: Rep Rnd 28.

BRIM

Rnds 36 and 37: Sc in each st: 114 sc.

Rnd 38: Sc in next 3 sc, (2 sc in next sc, sc in next sc) 54 times, sc in next 3 sc: 168 sc.

Rnds 39 through 41: Sc in each sc.

Rnd 42: Work Beg Blk St in first 3 sc, work 55 Blk Sts in next 165 sc: 56 Blk Sts; join with sl st in 3rd ch of beg ch-3.

Rnd 43: Work 3 sc at top of each block st: 168 sc.

Rnds 44 through 46: Sc in each st : 168 sc.

EDGING

Work Edg Blk St in first 3 sc, work 55 Edg Blk Sts in next 165 sc: 56 Edg Blk Sts. Finish off and weave in ends.

LARGE MEDALLION (make 1)

With F hook and sport yarn, ch 3; join to form a ring.

Rnd 1: Ch 3 (counts as dc), 13 dc in ring: 14 dc; join with sl st in 3rd ch of beg ch-3.

Rnd 2: Ch 3, dc in same ch as joining, dc in next dc, work Med Blk St, (2 dc in next dc, dc in next dc, work Med Blk St) 6 times: 7 Med Blk Sts; join with sl st in 3rd ch of beg ch-3. Finish off and weave in ends.

SMALL MEDALLION (make 3)

With C hook and fingering yarn, ch 3; join to form a ring.

Rnd 1: Ch 3 (counts as dc), 11 dc in ring: 12 dc; join with sl st in 3rd ch of beg ch-3.

Rnd 2: Ch 3, dc in same ch as joining, dc in next dc, work Med Blk St, (2 dc in next dc, dc in next dc, work Med Blk St) 5 times: 6 Med Blk Sts; join with sl st in 3rd ch of beg ch-3. Finish off and weave in ends.

FINISHING

Lightly stiffen hat and place on form to dry. With matching thread, sew medallions to hat at bottom of Crown. **Optional:** Sew bead in center of each medallion.

GENERAL DIRECTIONS

ABBREVIATIONS AND SYMBOLS

Knit and crochet patterns are written in a special shorthand, which is used so that instructions don't take up too much space. They sometimes seem confusing, but once you learn them, you'll have no trouble following them.

These are Standard Abbreviations

BB . . . . bobble
Beg . . . . beginning
Blk st . . . . block stitch
BLO . . . . back loop only
BO . . . . bind off
BPdc . . . . Back post double crochet
BPsc . . . . Back post single crochet
BPscdec . . . . . Back post single crochet decrease
CL(s) . . . . cluster(s)
CO . . . . cast on
Cont . . . . continue
Ch(s) . . . . chain(s)
Dc . . . . double crochet
Dc2tog . . . . Double crochet 2 sts together decrease
Dc3tog . . . . Double crochet 3 sts together decrease
Dc4tog . . . . Double crochet 4 sts together decrease
Dec . . . . decrease
Dtr . . . . double triple crochet
Fig . . . . figure
FPdc . . . . front post double crochet
FPdc dec . . . front post double crochet decrease
FPPS . . . . front post puff stitch
FPsc . . . . front post single crochet
FPtr . . . . front post triple crochet
G . . . . gram(s)

Hdc . . . . half double crochet
Inc . . . . increase(ing)
K . . . . knit
K2tog . . . . knit 2 together
Lp(s) . . . . loop(s)
Lpcl . . . . loop cluster
Lpst . . . . loop stitch
M1 . . . . Increase one stitch
Mm . . . . millimeter(s)
Oz . . . . ounces
P . . . . purl
P2tog . . . . purl 2 together
Patt . . . . pattern
Prev . . . . previous
PSSO . . . . pass the slipped stitch over
Rem . . . . remain(ing)
Rep . . . . repeat(ing)
Rev Sc . . . . reverse single crochet
Rnd(s) . . . . round(s)
Sc . . . . single crochet
Sc dec . . . . single crochet decrease
Sc2tog . . . . single crochet 2 stitches together decrease
Sc3tog . . . . single crochet 3 stitches together decrease
Sk . . . . skip
Sl . . . . slip
Sp(s) . . . . space(s)
SSK . . . . slip, slip, knit
St(s) . . . . stitch(es)
Stock st . . . . stockinette stitch
Tbl . . . . through back loop
Tog . . . . together
Tr . . . . triple crochet
Trtr . . . . triple triple crochet
YB . . . . yarn in back of needle or hook
YF . . . . yarn in front of needle or hook
YO . . . . Yarn over the needle or hook
YRN . . . . Yarn around needle

These are Standard Symbols

*An asterisk (or double asterisks**) in a pattern row, indicates a portion of instructions to be used more than once. For instance, "rep from * three times" means that after working the instructions once, you must work them again three times for a total of 4 times in all.

: The number after a colon tells you the number of stitches you will have when you have completed the row or round.

( ) Parentheses enclose instructions which are to be worked the number of times following the parentheses. For instance, "(ch1, sc, ch1) 3 times" means that you will chain one, work one sc, and then chain again three times for a total of six chains and 3sc, or "(K1, P2) 3 times" means that you knit one stitch and then purl two stitches, three times.

Parentheses often set off or clarify a group of stitches to be worked into the same space or stitch. For instance, "(dc, ch2, dc) in corner sp."

[ ] Brackets and ( ) parentheses are also used to give you additional information.

TERMS

Front Loop—This is the loop toward you at the top of the crochet stitch.

Back Loop—This is the loop away from you at the top of the crochet stitch.

Post—This is the vertical part of the crochet stitch

Join—This means to join with a sl st unless another stitch is specified.

Finish off—This means to end your piece by pulling the cut yarn end through the last loop remaining on the hook or needle. This will prevent the work from unraveling.

Continue in Pattern as Established—This means to follow the pattern stitch as it has been set up, working any increases or decreases in such a way that the pattern remains the same as it was established.

Work even—This means that the work is continued in the pattern as established without increasing or decreasing.

Right Side—This means the side of the hat that will be seen.

Wrong Side—This means the side of the hat that is inside when the hat is worn.

Knitting Needles Conversion Chart

U.S.	0	1	2	3	4	5	6	7	8	9	10	10½	11	13	15	17
Metric	2	2.25	2.75	3.25	3.5	3.75	4	4.5	5	5.5	6	6.5	8	9	10	12.75

Crochet Hooks Conversion Chart

U.S.	B-1	C-2	D-3	E-4	F-5	G-6	H-8	I-9	J-10	K-10 12	N	P	Q
Metric	2.25	2.75	3.25	3.5	3.75	4	5	5.5	6	6.5	0	10	15

Steel Crochet Hooks Conversion Chart

U.S.	00	0	1	2	3	4	5	6	7	8	9	10	11	12	13	14
Metric	3.5	3.25	2.75	2.25	2.1	2	1.9	1.8	1.65	1.5	1.4	1.3	1.1	1.0	0.85	0.75

GAUGE

This is probably the most important aspect of knitting and crocheting!

GAUGE simply means the number of stitches per inch, and the numbers of rows per inch that result from a specified yarn worked with hooks or needles in a specified size. But since everyone knits or crochets differently—some loosely, some tightly, some in-between—the measurements of individual work can vary greatly, even when the crocheters or knitters use the same pattern and the same size yarn and hook or needle.

If you don't work to the gauge specified in the pattern, your hat will never be the correct size, and you may not have enough yarn to finish your project. Hook and needle sizes given in instructions are merely guides, and should never be used without a gauge swatch.

To make a gauge swatch, crochet or knit a swatch that is about 4" square, using the suggested hook or needle and the number of stitches given in the pattern. Measure your swatch. If the number of stitches is fewer than those listed in the pattern, try making another swatch with a smaller hook or needle. If the number of stitches is more than is called for in the pattern, try making another swatch with a larger hook or needle. It is your responsibility to make sure you achieve the gauge specified in the pattern.

The patterns in this book have been written using the knitting and crochet terminology that is used in the United States. Terms which may have different equivalents in other parts of the world are listed below.

United States	International
Double crochet (dc)	treble crochet (tr)
Gauge	tension
Half double crochet (hdc)	half treble crochet (htr)
Single crochet	double crochet
Skip	miss
Slip stitch	single crochet
Triple crochet (tr)	double treble crochet (dtr)
Yarn over (YO)	yarn forward (yfwd)
Yarn around needle (yrn)	yarn over hook (yoh)

FRINGE

Basic Instructions

Cut a piece of cardboard about 6" wide and half as long as specified in the instructions for strands, plus 1/2" for trimming allowance. Wind the yarn loosely and evenly lengthwise around the cardboard. When the card is filled, cut the yarn across one end. Do this several times; then begin fringing. You can wind additional strands as you need them.

Single Knot Fringe

Hold the specified number of strands for one knot of fringe together, then fold in half.

Hold the project with the right side facing you. Using a crochet hook, draw the folded ends through the space or stitch from right to wrong side.

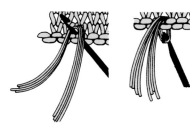

Pull the loose ends through the folded section.

Draw the knot up firmly.

Space the knots evenly and trim the ends of the fringe.

POMPONS

From cardboard cut two circles 1/2" larger in diameter than desired size of pompon. In center of each circle cut or punch a 1/2" hole. Hold the two circles together and thread two long strands of yarn into a yarn needle. Going from outer edge to center of circles, wrap yarn around circles until they are full, adding new yarn as needed. With sharp scissors, cut yarn around outer edge of circles. Cut a piece of yarn 6" long and insert between circles, draw up tightly and knot. Remove cardboard circles, rub pompon in your palms to fluff, trim to desired size.

Senior Technical Editor: Susan Lowman

Technical Editors: Donna Druchunas, Jodi Lewanda, and Linda Taylor

Photography: James Jaeger

Photo Coordinator: Carrie Cristiano

Book Design: Graphic Solutions, inc-chgo

Produced by: Creative Partners,™ LLC.

The authors extend their thanks and appreciation to these contributing designers:

Denise Black, Oceanside, California

Joyce Bragg, Wilmington, North Carolina

JC Briar, Corvallis, Oregon

Nancy Brown, Belfair, Washington

Doris Chan, Boothwyn, Pennsylvania

Rona Feldman, Malibu, California

Sheila Jones, Port Orchard, Washington

Zelda K, Mount Vernon, Ohio

Jenny King, Bli Bli, Australia

Ruthie Marks, Ojai, California

Susan McCreary, Erie, Pennsylvania

Marty Miller, Greensboro, North Carolina

Laura Polley, Indianapolis, Indiana

Sandy Scoville, San Marcos, California

Joyce Renée Wyatt, Los Angeles, California

A special note of thanks to Catherine Blythe and the design department at Patons Yarns, for sharing many of their most creative designs and to Judi Alweil of Judi & Co for sharing her hats with us.

Most of the hats in this book were tested to ensure accuracy and clarity of the instructions. We are grateful to the following pattern testers:

Denise Black, Oceanside California

Kim Britt, Gurnee, Illlinois

Carrie Cristiano, Escondido, California

Wendy Meier, Escondido, California

Whenever we have used a specialty yarn, we have given the brand name. If you are unable to find these yarns locally, write to the following manufacturers who will be able to tell you where to purchase their products, or consult their internet sites. We also wish to thank these companies for supplying yarn for this book.

Bernat Yarns
320 Livingston Avenue South
Listowel, Ontario
Canada N4W 3H3
www.bernat.com

Berroco, Inc.
P. O. Box 367
14 Elmdale Rd.
Uxbridge, Massachusetts 01569
www.berroco.com

Brown Sheep
10062 County Road 16
Mitchell, Nebraska 69357
www.brownsheep.com

Caron International
Customer Service
P. O. Box 222
Washington, North Carolina 27889
www.Caron.com

Cascade Yarns
1224 Andover Park E
Tukwila, Washington 98188-3905
www.cascadeyarns.com

Interlacements
P. O. Box 3089
Colorado Springs, Colorado 80934-3082
www.interlacementsyarns.com

J&P Coats
Coats and Clark
Consumer Services
P. O. Box 12229
Greenville, South Carolina 29612-0229
www.coatsandclark.com

Judi & Co
18 Gallatin Drive
Dix Hills, New York 11746
www.judiandco.com

Lion Brand Yarn
34 West 15th Street
New York, New York 10011
www.LionBrand.com

Patons Yarns
2700 Dufferin St.
Toronto, Ontario
Canada M6B 4J3
www.patonsyarns.com

Red Heart Yarns
Coats and Clark
Consumer Services
P. O. Box 12229
Greenville, South Carolina 29612-0229
www.coatsandclark.com

Skacel Collection, Inc.
P. O. Box 881 10
Seattle, Washington 98138
www.skacelknitting.com

TLC Yarns
Coats and Clark
Consumer Services
P. O. Box 12229
Greenville, South Carolina 29612-0229
www.coatsandclark.com

Trendsetter Yarns
16745 Saticoy Street #101
Van Nuys, California 91406-2710
www.trendsetteryarns.com

INDEX